Ideology
and
National
Competitiveness

Ideology and National Competitiveness

An Analysis of Nine Countries

Edited by George C. Lodge

and Ezra F. Vogel

 HBS **Harvard Business School Press**

Boston, Massachusetts

PRESS

Harvard Business School Press, Boston 02163

90 89 88   5 4 3

Library of Congress Cataloging-in-Publication Data

Ideology and national competitiveness.

    includes index.
    1. Competition, International.   2. Ideology.
3. Individualism.   4. Community.   I. Lodge, George C.
II. Vogel, Ezra F.
HF1414.I34   1987   338.6'048   86-19569
ISBN 0-87584-147-3

Contents

PREFACE

This book describes an approach to the analysis of nations which we believe is useful to policymakers, especially corporate managers. It suggests that ideology, as defined in chapter 1, is a particularly effective tool for understanding national communities: how and why they have evolved, what the tensions within them are, and how they differ from one another. Furthermore, an awareness of ideology helps one inspect assumptions about such matters as the role of government, the purpose of business, the relationships between the two, the relations between managers and managed, and sources of management authority.

For analytical purposes we start by outlining two ideological types: individualism and communitarianism. In chapters 2–10 we trace the evolution of various forms and combinations of these two in nine countries. Each chapter ends with some speculation about how the future may unfold.

The final chapter sets forth three propositions which seem to follow from our studies:

The first is that countries can be analyzed according to their ideological strength—in a sense, their comparative advantage—as measured by the degree to which their ideology is both coherent and adaptable to the changing environment. Using this approach we found that the countries studied fell into four general categories: (1) Japan, Korea,* and Taiwan; (2) Germany; (3) France and Brazil; and (4) the United States, the United Kingdom, and Mexico. This ranking correlates closely with the degree of competitiveness of these nations in the world economy *(see table 11–1).*

The second proposition is that developments in the coming decades are likely to reinforce this ranking. These developments include, for example: increasing scale and interdepend-

---

*The South Korean situation is somewhat complicated. We rank Korean ideology as strong on the basis of its coherence and adaptability insofar as business and commerce and government-business relations are concerned. There are, nevertheless, intense ideological divisions and serious tensions and conflict about ideology reflecting underlying value differences between different groups in Korea, as Vincent Brandt points out in chapter 8.

ence among major public and private institutions, increasing transnational connections, growing efficiency in manufacturing, the impact of these developments on human beings, and the heightening of global competition.

Finally, if East Asian nations continue to be more competitive than other industrial nations, the members of the world trading system generally will, of necessity, become more communitarian, with increased integration among business firms around the world and more global management of competition.

Our decision to organize this project followed our participation in a research project conducted in 1981–1984 on United States competitiveness in the world economy with Professor Bruce Scott and others at the Harvard Business School. That project revealed that ideology was a significant factor in the erosion of United States competitiveness: traditional conceptions about the proper role and relationships of government, business, and labor constituted a barrier to change toward a more competitive system. In picking the nine countries, we sought a fair representation of the non-communist industrial world. If this method of country analysis proves useful, it can, of course, be applied to all countries.

As editors we would like to express our gratitude to the other authors. Since beginning this project in the spring of 1984 we have spent some sixty hours meeting together and many more in separate research in the nine countries. This has been very much a team effort. Without all of us helping one another, this book could not have been written.

In January 1986 a three-day colloquium at the Harvard Business School brought together leaders of business, government, and academia from the nine countries for discussion of the papers which comprise this book. We are most grateful for the many insights and suggestions of those who were present:

Akira Arai, *Japan Economic Journal;* Rudolf Beger, Esso Chemie GmbH, Germany; Hans A. L. Behnke, Siemens AG, Germany; Pat Choate, TRW, U.S.; Jan Dauman, InterMatrix Inc., U.S.; David M. Davis, Tate & Lyle, PLC, U.K.; Henry Ergas, OECD, France; Nobuo Fujiwara, Mitsui & Company (USA) Inc.; Dionisio Garza-Medina, Grupo Industrial ALFA,

S.A., Mexico; David Gompert, AT&T International, U.S.; Dr. Charles Hampden-Turner, London Business School, U.K.; Prof. Paul S. P. Hsu, The College of Law, National Taiwan University, Taiwan; Prof. Peter Katzenstein, Cornell University, U.S.; Prof. Kim Duk-Choong, Sogang University, Korea; Jae Hak Kim, Korean Heavy Industries and Construction Co., Korea; Li Ki Seung, Samsung Electronics Corporation, Korea; Prof. Lee Hahn Been, Kyung Hee University, Korea; Pat Maddox, Fairbank Center for East Asian Research, Harvard University; Prof. Alistair Mant, South Bank Polytechnic, U.K.; Charles McKittrick, Jr., IBM, U.S.; Karl Moskowitz, Korea Strategy Associates, Inc., U.S.; Masumi Nishikata, AMF KK, Japan; Dr. Carlos F. Obregón, Economist, Mexico; Francois Perrin-Pelletier, Peugeot, S.A., France; Pedro Pick, Arthur D. Little, U.S.; Timotheus Pohl, Daimler-Benz of North America; Clyde Prestowitz, U.S. Department of Commerce; Prof. Roger Quant, INCAE, Costa Rica; Prof. Raimar Richers, Getulio Vargas Foundation School of Business, Brazil; Edward R. Roberts, Eli Lilly International Corp., U.S.; Paul J. Roessel, E. I. du Pont de Nemours, Inc., U.S.; Daniel A. Sharp, Xerox, U.S.; Sir John Thomson, Ambassador to the United Nations, U.K.; Prof. Michael Useem, Boston University, U.S.; Christopher Wilkinson, Commission of the European Communities, Belgium; Erik Willenz, Carnegie Endowment for International Peace, U.S.; Diane Y. P. Ying, *Commonwealth Magazine*, Taiwan.

We also have been greatly helped by our colleagues at Harvard, many of whom have read various drafts of the book's chapters. In particular, we would like to mention Professors Alice Amsden, Christopher Bartlett, Norman A. Berg, Joseph L. Bower, Alfred D. Chandler, Jr., Dennis J. Encarnation, Thomas K. McCraw, Bruce R. Scott, Barbara L. Toffler, Richard E. Walton, Richard H. K. Vietor and Philip A. Wellons as well as Post-Doctoral Fellow Benzion Chanowitz and Researchers Anita McGahan, Jane Marsden and Elise Walton. We are especially grateful to Professor Michael G. Rukstad of the Harvard Business School for his preparation of the table in chapter 11 which correlates ideological strength and national competitiveness.

Our thanks go also to the Dean of the Harvard Business School, Professor John H. McArthur, to the Director of Research, Professor E. Raymond Corey and to Kathryn Neeld May of the Division of Research. Their generous support and enthusiastic encouragement have been essential. Our efforts were made possible by the Bertrand Fox Publication Fund and the Shell Companies Foundation.

Finally, we owe a profound debt to Dr. Marten Liander, who has been research associate as well as administrative director of the project from its inception.

George C. Lodge
Ezra F. Vogel

September 1986
Boston, Massachusetts

Ideology
and
National
Competitiveness

1

INTRODUCTION

Ideology and Country Analysis

George C. Lodge

Politics, social forces, culture, economic developments, psychological attitudes, and historical habits shape the ever-changing surroundings within which the corporation and its managers live and act. The relevant environment for many organizations is not merely a nation but many nations, indeed the world, especially its industrializing portions. The purpose of this book is to help managers understand and cope more effectively with the environment surrounding them.

In the mid-1980s the most striking feature of that environment was the intensification of global economic competition. The United States had a $150 billion trade deficit, of which $50 billion was with Japan. The European countries faced similar competitive pressures from Asia. Brazil and Mexico owed close to $100 billion each to foreign lenders and faced serious competitive obstacles as they sought to increase their exports to earn the foreign exchange necessary to pay their debts. In brief, external pressures have been forcing internal changes upon government, business, and labor, changes that are often

1

at variance with the dominant set of beliefs about how these institutions should function. Adaptation eventually occurs but at the cost of serious strains that have intricate and far-reaching implications for managers in the private as well as the public sector.

To provide a framework for understanding these strains we offer a hypothesis: each nation has an ideology, perhaps several. These are a set of beliefs and assumptions about values that the nation holds to justify and make legitimate the actions and purpose of its institutions. A nation is successful when its ideology is coherent and adaptable, enabling it to define and attain its goals, and when there is the least distance between the prevailing ideology and the actual practice of the country's institutions.

The eight authors of this book have converted that hypothesis into an analytical tool that enables us to use a more or less common set of variables to examine nine different countries, and to identify significant questions, the answers to which are important for decision makers in corporations as well as in government and labor. The nations we study here constitute a reasonable sample of the industrial world and are taken in the roughly historical order of their industrial development: the United Kingdom, France, Germany, the United States, Japan, Taiwan, South Korea, Brazil, and Mexico.

The claim we make for the concept of ideology as an investigative tool is that it enables us to perceive and analyze systematically the evolution of communities through time while we simultaneously inspect familiar assumptions about how the institutions belonging to those communities behave and relate to each other. Making visible the inertia of the past should thereby provide a guide to future possibilities for managers of corporations as well as for others in government and labor who face critical choices.

What is ideology? How can its analysis broaden the understanding of decision makers?

THE CONCEPT OF IDEOLOGY

Ideology is the collection of ideas that a community uses to make values explicit in some relevant context. The term "values" in this definition refers to timeless, universal, noncontroversial notions that virtually every community everywhere has always cherished: survival, for example, or justice, economy, self-fulfillment or self-respect. As we shall use the term, values are held by communities rather than by individual persons. The phrase "relevant context" is the collection of phenomena, facts, events, insights, institutions, and forces that affect the community from within and from without: the surrounding reality, the actual environment.

Ideology connects the two: values and relevant context. Ideology gives values institutional vitality; it makes them live in a particular place at a particular time.

This definition of "ideology" elaborates on, but nevertheless follows, that of Antoine Destutt de Tracy, who invented the word in 1801 to describe the study of those ideas that have a formative effect on society. Our definition is quite different from that of Karl Marx and others for whom ideology was a set of beliefs used by the ruling class to obscure reality with the sole purpose of perpetuating domination by that class. By our definition, the concept of ideology may be a weapon of propaganda, but it is also an analytic tool for the study of societies in the tradition of Max Weber, who used the concept to trace the effects of religion on the rise of individualism, and of Karl Mannheim, who developed it as a method of social research.[1]

Here are some examples of how ideology works to link values and context. In ancient Egypt, the values "justice" and "self-fulfillment" involved most inhabitants in lugging stones to glorify the god-king, motivation coming importantly from a whip across the laborer's back. Ideologically the community was organized around the ideas of a theocratic hierarchy, an imposed consensus kept in place by force, and an extensive set of duties with few rights of membership. A variety of contextual phenomena, including strong policemen and the need to keep the gods happy to obtain rain, sustained the ideology for thousands of years.

In the United States of the early nineteenth century, slavery was justified, at least in the eyes of Southerners, since slaves were deemed to be property, and property rights were sacred according to the dominant ideology. Furthermore, slavery was

consistent with community need as that need was seen by
some states, a view justified in turn by the idea of states' rights.
When the North denied that slaves were property and asserted
the dominance of the federal government over the states in
support of this belief, a civil war ensued. That war changed
two components of American ideology concerning property
and the power of the states. A new way of defining the value
"justice" was thus ushered in; an ideological change had
occurred.

"Economy" is a value in that everyone wants more benefits
than costs, but what counts as a benefit and what counts as a
cost changes in response to contextual changes. The value
"economy" remains, but ideology varies. For example, the
insights of ecologists forced an extensive clarification of community needs regarding air and water. At first, business resisted
the increased costs associated with environmental regulation
by government, arguing by its implicit if not explicit ideology
that the marketplace was the appropriate mechanism for fixing
costs. As time passed, however, ecological insights became
increasingly accepted or "real," and business managers were
consequently required to accept—and to manage accordingly—an irreversible ideological change in the way the value
"economy" would henceforth relate to the new context.

Ideology is thus a dynamic structure, a bridge by which
timeless values are connected to the surrounding reality in
various cultures at different points in space and time. It is the
hymns a community sings to justify and make legitimate what
it is doing, or, perhaps, what it would like to do. In some
communities the hymns have little to do with reality, and yet
the ideology remains in force; it becomes dogma. Such communities waste considerable time, money, and blood trying to
adapt practices to an outdated and rigid ideology; eventually
their efforts fail. One might say that a community is successful—that is, effective in clarifying and implementing its goals—
when it can manage ideological change while maintaining
institutional efficiency and legitimacy in the face of contextual
change.

In the 1980s Japan was relatively more successful than the
USSR and the United States because its ideology conformed
better to reality and thus supported the actions of government,

HARVARD BUSINESS SCHOOL PRESS, BOSTON, MA 02163

THANK YOU FOR YOUR INTEREST IN THIS BOOK

We would like to know more about our readers. Please complete and return this card:

Book Title/Author _____
Purchased at _____
Comments _____
_____

Your Job Title/Industry _____

🙞 🙞 🙞 🙞 🙞 🙞

☐ **Please send me a complete catalog of Harvard Business School Press books.**

☐ **Please send me information on forthcoming books in the following areas:**

☐ Finance
☐ Manufacturing/Operations Mgmt.
☐ Marketing
☐ Human Resource Management

☐ General Management/Business Policy
☐ International Business
☐ Business & The Public Sector
☐ Industry Studies—please specify:

_____

YOUR NAME _____
ADDRESS _____

CITY _____ STATE _____ ZIP _____

Special discounts are available for bulk purchases of HBS Press books.
For further information, call (617) 495-6700.

RRC1

HBS
PRESS

Harvard Business School Press
Boston, Massachusetts 02163

BUSINESS REPLY MAIL
FIRST CLASS   PERMIT NO. 2725   BOSTON, MA

POSTAGE WILL BE PAID BY ADDRESSEE:

Harvard Business School Press
Gallatin E-118
Harvard Business School
Boston, Massachusetts 02163

business, and labor as they competed in the world. Japan's ideology arose, as did ours and the USSR's, from its efforts to connect certain values to its surrounding reality. A collection of small infertile islands with a population of 120 million people, Japan is almost totally dependent on an often hostile world for the vital natural resources upon which its survival depends. Naturally the ideology of Japan—the framework of ideas it uses to make values explicit and to justify its institutions—is different from that which took root in nineteenth-century America, where a sparse population was trying to tame a wilderness and develop abundant resources. Thus, in Japan attitudes about the role of government, the role of business, the relationship between the two, the role of trade unions, the means to self-fulfillment and self-respect for the individual in the family, in the village, in the firm, and in the nation are all different from corresponding attitudes in the United States.

Most people, perhaps especially Americans, do not acknowledge that they have an ideology. They believe that their traditions and practices are obviously good and proper, compatible with the laws of God and nature; it is "the others" who have an ideology, the foreigners whose ways are so frequently misguided. "We" are pragmatic and sensible. "They" are hobbled by ideology. The fact is that every community has an ideology, perhaps two or three. If the community is to function effectively, its ideology requires scrutiny from time to time so that beliefs and practice can be made more coherent with one another.

A wide variety of contextual factors shapes ideology and is in some cases affected by it. They are both internal to the community and external. Internal factors include economic performance (recession, growth, levels of income and income distribution, productivity, trade balances, employment rates, and inflation); religions (Confucianism, Christianity); geography and demography; and political parties and movements. External factors include colonialism or its threat, wars and foreign occupations, missionaries, resource dependencies, foreign sources of capital, immigration, multinational corporations, and international competition.

Among the more important elements of the relevant context are geography and demography. Resources are scarce or plentiful, populations sparse or dense. Then there is economic performance: the economy may be growing or receding; labor may be plentiful or scarce; prices high or low. The community may be competitive in the world economy or not—a winner or a loser. Changes in resources and economic performance force changes in institutional practice, which in turn may force change in the underlying ideology.

Not only are physical and economic elements part of the context: accepted notions about the nature of matter, of spirit, and of feeling are also important. While this realm once belonged to poets and priests, in the last three hundred years scientists have taken over the field. Reality came to be regarded as a collection of elements, ordered according to natural laws that could be confirmed by scientific experimentation. The trouble was that scientific discovery continually modified what we originally thought to be irrefutable laws of nature. For Sir Isaac Newton, physical reality was to be understood in terms of the particles of nature and the laws of motion that governed the particles. Einstein found, however, that only by perceiving the relationship among the particles in time and space could one grasp reality. Today ecologists, microbiologists, geneticists, and others are telling us that reality is profoundly different from what we used to think, and they by no means agree about what it is. As some scientists continue to peer down the dark tunnels of specialization, others are aware that an understanding of reality requires a conception of wholes, not merely of pieces. These changing insights are forcing technological and institutional changes that have profound implications for prevailing ideology.

The example of Adam Smith helps us to distinguish between what we mean by "ideology" and "relevant context." Smith, writing *The Wealth of Nations* in the 1770s, was part of the relevant context of Europe and America. Subsequently, his ideas of marketplace competition and the "invisible hand" were to become important components of Western ideology, serving as a basis of legitimacy for both government and business.

At any given time, the relevant context is dominated by a certain set of institutions and institutional arrangements. Then new ones appear, challenging the old and forcing them to adapt or perish. In the 1970s OPEC was such an institution, and the government-business partnership of Japan has been such an institutional arrangement. These two have forced and may continue to force change in the structure and behavior of every institution in their path: in industries such as oil, autos, steel, semiconductors, and banking; in governments, whether of the oil-producing or -consuming countries, in the rich as well as in the poor world; in trade unions, especially those related to the most affected industries; and in the more specialized departments of universities jarred by the necessity to think holistically. Institutional adjustment to these challenges strains traditional ideological assumptions and evokes different ones.

The relationship between ideology and practice generally follows a fairly standard pattern over a period of time. During a certain interval, institutional practice conforms to the prevailing ideology. Then changes in the real world induce or compel the institutions to behave differently. At that point, practice begins to depart from ideology. After another interval, institutional practice differs markedly from what ideology declares: the old hymns may be sung but they are not practiced. Ideological schizophrenia sets in: the new practice may evoke a new ideology to justify it, but loyalty to the old ideology discourages its being articulated. There is a gap between institutional practice and ideology—a legitimacy gap. As it widens, two forms of pressure are increasingly brought to bear on leaders. Some in the community seek to haul the institutions back into line with the traditional ideology. Others argue for a new ideology to justify the institutions' actual practice. The feature of ideology that both excites and exasperates those who study it is that frequently an old ideology tends to linger on, uninspected, while institutions depart from it in many pragmatic ways. People do not practice what they preach, and they find it difficult to preach what they practice—at least immediately.

Ideology is particularly important to managers because it justifies their power, role, and behavior. It is the set of beliefs and assumptions that constitutes the source of their authority. For a time they may act consistently with a prevailing ideology, but when circumstances change, managers naturally respond to take advantage of, or merely cope with, the change. In so doing they may depart from the traditional ideology and thus be found illegitimate by those who continue to adhere to it. Their authority erodes and they are pressed to return to the old ideology or to articulate a new one that justifies what they are doing. Alternatively, managers may be reluctant to adapt to change in the real world because of the pull of the old ideology. In so doing they may become progressively irrelevant, inefficient, and ineffective, again losing authority but for a different reason: their old solutions fail in the new context that they are unable to perceive. Managers who adhere psychologically to the traditional ideology face an additional problem when the exigencies of the surrounding environment require them to depart from it: they are regularly required to do things they do not think are right.

During the middle decades of the twentieth century, changes in the global environment of business have been considerable. Western institutions have responded to these changes in one of two ways:

1. Some have responded relatively quickly by moving pragmatically, adapting practices, and evolving a new set of justifications for their actions.
2. Others have found the transition difficult to manage, constrained by traditional ideological assumptions and the perceptions and decision-making patterns that flow from them.

Institutions that have followed the second path have experienced uncertainty, waste, and crisis. In the United States and Western Europe, the result has often been bankruptcies, loss of managerial influence, and inefficiency. The community as a whole has suffered.

The analysis of ideology provides a way of understanding institutional change, inspecting assumptions about it, and managing it more effectively.

COMPONENTS OF IDEOLOGIES

An ideology can be conveniently divided into five components concerning:

1. The relationship between the human being and the community, the individual and the group; and the means to individual fulfillment and self-respect;
2. The institutional guarantees and manifestations of that relationship, such as property rights;
3. The most appropriate means of controlling the production of goods and services;
4. The role of the state; and
5. The prevailing perception of reality and conception of nature, concerning, for example, the role of science and the functions of education.

Ideology has to do with how communities think about those five things. If the relevant context is composed of what actually exists in and around the community, ideology affects how members of the community see it and why what they see looks the way it does. Joined together, these components become a framework of ideas for legitimizing institutions that distinguishes one community from another. Using them we can obtain a more or less objective perspective on each country's evolution, illuminating why and how government, business, and labor in that country have dealt with a variety of issues.

TWO IDEAL-TYPE IDEOLOGIES*

Ideologies existing in the contemporary world can be seen as mixtures and variations of two ideal types. We shall call them "individualism" and "communitarianism," using their first component as a name for the ideology as a whole. Individualism suggests an atomistic conception of society, one in which the individual is the ultimate source of value and meaning. The interests of the community are defined and achieved by self-

---

*An *ideal type* is a concept borrowed from Max Weber. He defines it as a " . . . mental construct derived from observable reality although not conforming to it in detail because of deliberate simplification and exaggeration. It is not ideal in the sense that it is excellent, nor is it an average; it is, rather, a logical ideal used to order reality by selecting and accentuating certain elements." (*Micropaedia,* 15th ed., s.v. "ideal type.")

interested competition among many, preferably small, proprietors. Communitarianism, however, takes a more organic view, regarding the community as more than the sum of its individuals and requiring explicit definition of its needs and priorities. *Figure 1-1* outlines the five components of each. In their extreme versions these two formulations may be viewed as end points on an ideological spectrum, but in reality they are various blends in the middle. In each of the nine countries discussed in this book, the dominant ideology will be a variant of these ideal types. In some cases, one ideology will be clearly dominant; in others there will be two or three conflicting and competing with one another. In some, institutional practice— the behavior of government and business, for example—will be consistent with the prevailing ideology; in others it will be at variance with it. From an analysis of these points of harmony or tension we can gain an understanding of choices confronting the different national systems and their managers.

The traditional ideology of the United States exemplifies individualism. Its ideas first came to America in the eighteenth century, having been set down in seventeenth-century England as natural laws by John Locke, among others. These ideas found fertile soil in the vast, underpopulated wilderness of America and served the country well for a hundred years or so. Although throughout U.S. history the ideas have been buffeted and eroded by communitarian practices, particularly in times of crisis, they continue to be remarkably resilient. "They are," says Samuel Huntington, "at the very core of (our) national identity. Americans cannot abandon them without ceasing to be Americans in the most meaningful sense of the word—without, in short, becoming un-American."[2]

INDIVIDUALISM

A review of the five components of this ideology provides a starting point for understanding changes under way in our nine countries and for comparing them with each other.

1. *Individualism.* As mentioned above, this is the atomistic notion that the community is no more than the sum of the

Figure 1–1   Ideology: A Bridge between Values and the Relevant Context

Values	Individualism	Communitarianism	Relevant Context
Survival	1) Individualism Equality (Opportunity)	1) Communitarianism Equality (Result) or Hierarchy Consensus	Geography
Justice	Contract		Demography
Economy			Economic Performance
Fulfillment	2) Property Rights	2) Rights and Duties of Membership	Technology
Self-respect	3) Competition to Satisfy Consumer Desires	3) Community Need	Scientific Insights: Newton Einstein Ecologists, et al.
Etc.	4) Limited State	4) Active, Planning State	Traditional Institutions vs. New: e.g., OPEC, Japan
	5) Scientific Specialization	5) Holism	Traditional Behavior Patterns

Interest Groups

individuals in it. Fulfillment lies in an essentially lonely struggle in what amounts to a wilderness where the fit survive—and where, if you do not survive, you are somehow unfit. Alexis de Tocqueville stressed another aspect of the word: " 'Individualism' is a word recently coined," he wrote in *Democracy in America*, "to express a new idea . . . (It) is a calm and considered feeling which disposes each citizen to isolate himself from the mass of his fellows and withdraw into the circle of family and friends; with this little society formed to his taste, he gladly leaves the greater society to look after itself."[3] Ralph Waldo Emerson added a certain militance: "Society is everywhere in conspiracy against the manhood of every one of its members."[4] Closely tied to individualism is the idea of *equality*, in the sense implied in the phrase "equal opportunity," and the idea of *contract*, the inviolate device by which individuals are tied together as buyers and sellers, employers and employees. In the political order, individualism evolved into *interest group pluralism*, which became the preferred means of directing society and setting priorities.

2. *Property Rights.* According to this ideology, the best guarantee of individual rights lies in the sanctity of property rights. By virtue of this concept, the individual is assured freedom from the predatory powers of the state; and from this notion the corporate manager derives the authority to manage.

3. *Competition to Meet Consumer Desire.* Adam Smith most eloquently articulated the idea that the uses of property are best controlled by each individual proprietor competing in an open market to satisfy individual consumer desires. It is explicit in traditional U.S. antitrust law and practice. According to this idea, what counts as a good community, including achieving it, flows automatically from marketplace competition: the more competition the better.

4. *Limited State.* This is the conviction that the least government is best. Exponents of individualism are concerned about the size of government but, more importantly, about its role: they are reluctant to allow it to focus its authority. In the United States, for example, the parts of government are to be kept

separate from each other, checked and balanced. And whatever happens in the real world, the cry is, do not let government plan—particularly in Washington. Says Huntington: "Because of the inherently antigovernment character of the American Creed, government that is strong is illegitimate, government that is legitimate is weak."[5]

5. *Scientific Specialization and Fragmentation.* This is the corruption of Newtonian mechanics, which says that if we attend to the parts, as experts and specialists, the whole will take care of itself. As a result of this idea, the tasks of scientific inquiry were divided into an increasing number of "disciplines," separated from one another by language, concepts, and modes of abstraction. The pursuit of these disciplines became the justification for schools and universities with academics seeking ever-narrower distinctions and finer lines of difference, ignoring the relationships among their separate areas of study.

Implicit in individualism is the assumption that human beings have the desire to acquire power, that is, to control external events, property, nature, the economy, politics, or whatever. Under the concept of the limited state, the presence of this desire means the guarantee of progress through competition, notably when combined with the Darwinian notion that the inexorable processes of evolution are constantly working to improve on nature. Scientific specialization has been part of this "progress," fragmenting knowledge while straining society's adaptability.

Considering the range of human history, one is struck by the extent to which this atomistic, individualist ideology constitutes a fundamental—and in many ways noble—aberration from the communitarian norm. It justified radical changes in practice—the industrial revolution, for example—and it achieved its most extreme manifestation in nineteenth-century America. In the twentieth century, it has been steadily deteriorating in the face of various challenges—wars, depressions, new economic and political systems, the concentration and growth of both population and corporations, environmental degeneration, and a recognition of the scarcity of natural resources.

Even so, the five components of the individualist ideology

retain great resilience throughout the West. They are the assumed source of legitimacy and authority for many of the West's great institutions. The resulting difficulty is twofold:

1. The old ideas perform less and less well as definers of values in today's reality.
2. Many important institutions—notably large, publicly held corporations and national governments—have either radically departed from the old ideology or are in the process of doing so in response to needs for efficiency, economies of scale, productivity, and global competitiveness.

Although the practices of small enterprise may remain acceptably consistent with the terms of individualist ideology, the managers of large institutions in both the private and public sectors are forced not to practice what they preach. The notion of "the free enterprise system" is clearly a corollary of individualist ideology. If that system is, therefore, regarded as the only legitimate way to conduct the affairs of government, business, and labor, we can see why so much of institutional America, for example, lacks legitimacy and authority. Changes in the real world—the relevant context—oblige institutions to adopt new ways even though public opinion clings affectionately to the old ideology. In practice, institutions depart from it—partly as a result of public demand—but no new ideology explicitly replaces the old one, either in the minds of managers or the public generally, so illegitimacy abounds. It is this gap between the behavior of institutions and what they claim to be appropriate or legitimate behavior that causes trauma. If we were to ask, what is the ideology that would legitimize the actual behavior of many Western institutions, we would come up with five counterparts to individualism.

COMMUNITARIANISM

Briefly put, the five counterparts to individualism are:

1. Communitarianism, characterized by equality of result *or* hierarchy, and consensus, which may be coerced or arrived at more or less voluntarily;

2. Rights and duties of membership;
3. Community need;
4. The active, planning state; and
5. Holism.

Although this ideology might appear new to some, it is not. If we were to use the notion of *hierarchy* in place of equality of result in #1, this ideology resembles the dominant ideologies of Europe before the eighteenth century. These came to the United States in different ways at different times with successive waves of European immigrants, and, laced with a dose of egalitarianism, were made manifest in such institutions as the New England town meeting and the farmers' cooperative movements of Wisconsin and Minnesota. But at least since the late nineteenth century, individualism has been dominant in America and, as we shall see, has vied with communitarianism for dominance in France and the United Kingdom. Today, however, in the United States as well as in the others of our nine countries, the increasing need for, and introduction of, communitarian practices makes explicit recognition of the ideological implications of those practices useful and necessary. Since a form of communitarian ideology is, and always has been, dominant in Korea, Taiwan, and Japan, an understanding of that ideology also helps us to perceive the nature of Western competition with those countries. It is, for example, difficult to translate the word "individualism" into Japanese with any other meaning than selfishness and egocentricity. Ideology pervades even our languages.

1. *Communitarianism.* The community is more than the sum of the individuals in it; it is organic, not atomistic. The community as a whole has special and urgent needs that go beyond the needs of its individual members. The values of survival, justice, self-respect, and so forth, depend on the recognition of those needs.

Individual fulfillment, therefore, depends on a place in a community, an identity with a whole, participation in an organic social process. If the community—the factory, the neighborhood, or the country—is well designed, its members will have a strong sense of identity with it. They will be able to make maximum use of their capacities. If the community or its components are poorly designed, people will be correspondingly alienated and frustrated.

Both corporations and unions have played leading roles in eroding the old idea of individualism in the West, thus creating the need for something new. But invariably they have been ideologically unmindful of what they have done. Therefore, they have tended to linger with the old forms and assumptions even after those have been critically altered.

Communitarianism may be relatively autocratic and statist as in Brazil and South Korea or nonstatist as in Germany. Its form is shaped by history, whether it be traditions of feudalism or the vestiges of colonialism and precolonial Indian life as in Mexico.

(a) *Equality of Result or Hierarchy.* In the West there has also been a shift away from the old notion of equality before the law. It used to be equality of opportunity, an individualistic conception under which blacks, whites, men, and women presumably had an equal place at the starting line, and each could supposedly go as far as he or she was able without discriminatory obstruction.

In both the United States and Europe there has been increasing concern in recent years that the old idea was not insuring adequate or acceptable results. Too many were being left behind. Thus, in a variety of ways, governments have intervened to impose guarantees and safeguards. Under this idea, the good corporation or community is one that adapts itself to inequalities in the surrounding environment so as to produce equality of result.

As managers of government and business contemplate the implementation of the idea of equality of result, a variety of issues comes to the fore. How does one avoid mediocrity, placing lead belts on the speedy, as it were? How does one handle the appeals of countless groups for representation?

We are reminded by the examples of medieval Europe and modern Japan that this slot in communitarian ideology has generally been filled not at all by equality but by the notion of hierarchy. That is, individual fulfillment and self-respect result from knowing and accepting one's place in a social structure.

One's place may be fixed in a variety of ways, by God, by the king, or, as in modern Japan, meritocratically by a sequence of rigorous examinations from which an elite emerges—the *summa cum laudes* of the University of Tokyo. The vestiges of medieval hierarchy are still plainly evident in the United Kingdom where class consciousness has a dogged resilience, the working class, for example, regarding itself as pitted in an inexorable struggle against the owning class. The fact that the "owning class" has to a great extent dissolved into government, an anonymous stock market, and the banks has not yet removed the ideological strain between the old hierarchy and the new equality.*

(b) *Consensus.* In a communitarian society, the relationships between individuals are governed not so much by *contract* as by *consensus*, which may be imposed autocratically by fiat or arrived at through democratic and participative means. In Europe the new arrangements are called industrial democracy, codetermination, workers' councils, and the like. They tend to replace the adversarial contractual relationship between managers and managed with a consensual one, which may proceed from the top down or from the bottom up. Japan's manager-managed relationships have generally been consensual, at first feudal in nature with a good deal of coercion, and adapting over time to changing needs and expectations. In the United States more consensual practices fall under several headings: organization development, employee involvement, workers' participation in management, and quality-of-worklife programs. Whatever the form, the result for managers tends to be the same: the right to manage is coming from the managed in democratic systems or from government in autocratic ones.

In many countries the transition from individualist to

---

*Under the ideology of individualism hierarchy does, of course, exist; it is rooted in the ideas of property and contract. For example, the owner contracts for the labor of those who are bound thus to obey him. But the idea of equality dispels any notion of hierarchical permanence or importance, theoretically at least, in favor of mobility in the tradition of Horatio Alger. "Elitism" is an inherently bad word to individualists; it may be a perfectly acceptable one to communitarians.

communitarian practices is impeded by the hegemony of individualist ideology. Trade unions are naturally loath to give up the power and legitimacy that once was theirs under the old notion of the adversarial, bargained contract. Managers, too, are nervous about moving away from the old bases of authority implicit in property rights and the contract. If improved productivity depends upon the transition, the issue is clear: how much crisis, how much recession before countries like the United Kingdom and the United States catch up with the Japanese and others who are more able to achieve consensus? The problem in the United Kingdom is complicated by the presence of the ideas of class. In Germany, however, the idea of worker participation in managerial decisions is deeply rooted in that country's communitarian traditions and may thus be a boon to German competitiveness.

There are signs that this transition from contract to consensus is contributing to, if not causing, the weakening of trade unions in those Western countries where the adversarial mission of a union is taken for granted. Union membership has been declining. The influence of unions has been eroding; their confidence about their role and mission is less sure. Artful managers are increasingly seeking means of "union avoidance," employing the techniques of consensualism. The question then arises: is a strong trade-union movement good for the community and its corporations? If the answer is yes, then it is important to redefine the union's mission. Pragmatic innovation without ideological renovation is not sufficient.

In South Korea and Japan, as well as in Brazil and Mexico, we shall see that consensus in the community as a whole is usually imposed by a ruling elite, with government playing a leading role in its design and enforcement. Where dissidents are not suppressed, they are co-opted by a process that Asian communities condone through the religious conviction that consensus is a moral virtue. In the West, religious beliefs have tended to assign at least as much virtue to adversarial and contractual notions such as due process and the right to strike.

2. *Rights and Duties of Membership.* For some years in the West a set of social rights has been superseding property rights in political and social importance. These are rights to survival,

income, pensions, health, and other entitlements associated with membership in the community or in some component of that community, such as a corporation. These rights are not legitimized through reference to individualist ideology. Rather, they are best understood in the context of communitarianism, as rights that public opinion holds to be consistent with a good community.

The problem in the West—one that European socialism and U.S. liberalism tend to ignore—is that emphasis on rights has not been accompanied by as clear a concern about duties. Duties are just as integral a part of communitarian ideology as rights: if the community assures rights, it must—and eventually will—require duties. In those countries where communitarianism has been relatively undiluted by individualism, such as Japan, we shall see that duties are regarded as equally if not more important than rights. Western ambivalence on this point is proving increasingly costly as government and business strain to pay the escalating costs of rights while duties remain elusive. It is one of a number of causes of the West's competitive deterioration in the world economy.

As rights and duties of membership have become more important, the notion of property rights has diminished as a source of authority for managers. This is due to a number of actual developments in the context, including the dispersion of ownership among many thousands of shareholders who have little motivation or ability to actually own "their property," and the escalating demands of government that business conform to community needs in such matters as employment, environmental protection, and safety. Thus, in practice, the source of management authority in the West has moved away from shareholders and toward debtholders, the managed, and the community acting through government. In this area the West and the East appear to be converging.

3. *Community Need.* The needs of the community (we are focusing on the nation) for clean air and water, safety, energy, jobs, competitive exports, and so forth are becoming increasingly distinct from, and more important than, what individual consumers may desire. As a consequence, the means of determining community need (the national interest) require explicit

attention, especially when it is impossible for the community to meet all its needs at once.

This concept is radically different from the individualist idea that the public interest emerges *naturally* from the pulling and hauling of interest groups and from free and vigorous competition among numerous aggressive, individualistic, and preferably small companies attempting to satisfy consumer desires.

Business purpose, according to communitarian ideology, is fixed by community need as defined by the community, generally through government or with its participation. Once community need has been determined, business activity can be harmonized with it in four ways: prescribed or ordered marketplace competition; regulation of business by government; partnership between government and business; and the corporate charter through which government gives business its license to exist. A wise choice among the four requires a clear definition of community need in the first place, a reliable delineation of the relevant community, and an understanding of what makes a business function efficiently and effectively in different social settings.

In the production and sale of shoes, for example, competition to satisfy consumer desires may be the most efficient way to assure that the community is properly shod. Other products—food and drugs, for example—would equally obviously require regulation. And either the partnership or charter route might be the best way to harmonize community need with the energy industry, communications satellites, or banking.

It is important to note that although communitarians are not prepared to leave the *definition* of community need to the vagaries of the marketplace, they may well allow the use of competition in the marketplace as a means of controlling and directing the activities of business toward the *implementation* of that need.

4. *Active, Planning State.* The role of the state in a communitarian society is to define community needs and to insure that they are implemented. Inevitably, the state takes on important tasks of coordination, priority setting, and planning. It needs to be efficient and authoritative, capable of making the difficult and subtle trade-offs among, for example, environmental purity,

energy supply, economic stability and growth, rights of membership, and global competition.

As we observe this and the other communitarian ideas unfold in the chapters that follow, it will be apparent that there are wide and significant variations among the forms that the general notion of the active, planning state may take. In some countries whose dominant ideology is clearly communitarian, government may be democratic and tolerant, while in others it is autocratic and brutal. Some may be relatively centralized (Japan and Korea), and others comparatively federal (Brazil). Another critical variable among communitarian governments is their ability to produce a consensus to support and implement their "plan"; some use naked force, others more sophisticated devices. It is important to delineate as precisely as possible the particular institutional forms that have evolved within the general context of communitarian ideology in the several countries.

Once these matters concerning the planning state are clear, it then becomes possible to describe and analyze the tensions between that particular form and current institutional practice, and to consider how those tensions are likely to develop in the future. For example, what would happen if the government of Japan moved to a more autocratic form of communitarianism, or if Brazil sought radical centralization? Ideological analysis helps us to answer those questions, as it would have in the 1960s if we had been trying to predict the failure of the French government to generate the consensus necessary to implement "Le Plan."

5. *Holism—Interdependence.* Finally, the idea of scientific specialization is replaced in a communitarian ideology by a consciousness of the interrelatedness of all things. Spaceship earth, the limits of growth, the fragility of our life-supporting biosphere, have dramatized the ecological and philosophical truth that everything is related to everything else. Harmony between the works of man and the demands of nature is no longer the romantic plea of conservationists. It is an absolute rule of survival, and thus it is of profound significance; its practical ramifications subvert individualist ideology in many ways.

One variety of holism is exemplified by the presumption of

this book. To understand any particular aspect of a community, for example, its economic performance, it is necessary to view the community as a system, perceiving the critical roles and relationships of institutions, such as government, business, labor union, and school. For the holist there is no separation between what the economists refer to as "macro" and "micro." The motivation of workers on the shop floor is inseparably tied to overall policies and incentives having to do with savings, investment, and work.

On the international level, understanding the problems of Third-World debt requires simultaneously analyzing the nature of the world trading system, and what impedes debtor countries from competing in that system to earn the foreign exchange with which to pay their debts.

These examples of holism demonstrate the problem for specialists and specialized education. If understanding the real world depends upon holistic analysis, the traditional expert may well be at best tangential and at worst downright wrong.

Lest the reader conclude that communitarianism is just another word for socialism, big government, the welfare state, and an antibusiness bias in society, it is important to point out that Japan will be revealed to be unquestionably more coherently communitarian than Britain and yet suffers from none of these maladies. President Mitterrand may have been less socialist when in the early 1980s he redefined rights and duties in France to make business more competitive, but he was no less communitarian. Japan's preference for little government involvement in enterprise ownership does not spring from an ideological reverence for property rights; it is a communitarian concern with efficiency. Perhaps ironically, the Asian communitarians seem to be substantially more probusiness than the more individualistic West, but, of course, their conception of the purpose of business is different: it is closely tied to community need. And whereas, in periods of economic decline, communitarian impulses cause Western countries to emphasize rights more than duties, the reverse seems to be true in Japan and perhaps in Taiwan and Korea. It is important, therefore, to clear the head of old ideological shibboleths if one is going to be precise, and indeed one of the major purposes of ideological analysis is to allow more precision than is generally associated with words like capitalism, socialism, communism, left, right, liberal, and conservative.

GLOBAL COMPETITION AND NATIONAL TENSIONS

The two ideal-type ideologies described above, the variants of which will be discussed in the following chapters, constitute assumptions and premises that have become increasingly important to the competitiveness of nations in world trade.

Individualism, for example, assumed a world economy in which numerous private firms competed with one another, producing in one country and exporting their goods and services to the open markets of another. These firms and the nations in which they are located benefited—or suffered—from certain God-given "comparative advantages," such as natural resources and climate, with which the nation was endowed. The role of government was to keep the marketplace free and open so that Adam Smith's "invisible hand" might assure the good of all. Communitarianism, on the other hand, especially as practiced in Japan, other East Asian societies, and more recently Brazil, has held quite different premises. Competition in world trade is among nations as well as firms, and national governments compete to make their jurisdictions the most hospitable locations for global production systems. Governments may play an active role in those systems. Far from merely being a referee they become coach, manager, even a key player. And comparative advantage is by no means God given; it is created by the nation through collective action following the dictates of a national strategy laid down by government in close collaboration with business and labor.[6] "This newer concept," notes Chalmers Johnson, "helps explain why 18 million Taiwanese export about the same amount as 130 million Brazilians and about four times as much as 75 million Mexicans, even though Mexico is located next door to the world's largest market and Taiwan is 6,000 miles away."[7]

We shall see that the Asian countries in this study have clearly defined their community need as maintaining competitiveness in the world economy. This has been and is top priority. As Ezra Vogel has written about the Japanese system, "The basic skill from which all else stems is thinking through the implications of global competition for all aspects of national policy."[8] They have what Bruce Scott has termed a "developmental national strategy," focused on baking the economic pie before distributing it. The West is more ambivalent. A profusion of needs—high levels of consumption; national defense; welfare; environmental purity; subsidies for housing, real estate, and other industries insulated from foreign competition—have contributed to eroding the capacity of the Western countries to compete with the Asians.[9]

Individualism in the West has produced an adversarial society characterized by interest-group pluralism in the political system, and contractual, often adversarial, bargaining of labor and management in the economic system, in each case the name of the game being a larger share of the pie, not necessarily a larger pie. The East's competitive superiority is causing many to question the desirability of such behavior. Can the West learn from the Asians as for so long they learned from us? Peter Berger reminds us that it is not so easy. There are no free lunches, economically or ideologically. "Every societal strategy exacts a price. The East Asian societies . . . deemphasize individual autonomy as against collective solidarity and discipline. Are the much more individualistic people of the (West) willing to pay this price for economic success?"[10] We hope that the analysis in the chapters that follow will at least enable readers to deal with this question more precisely and effectively.

We begin with Britain, the first of our nine countries to industrialize. Joel Krieger describes the erosion of the tenuous communitarian consensus among government, business, and labor that dominated British ideology after World War II, and Prime Minister Thatcher's attempt to impose the practices of individualism. He describes the choices for Britain: continued fragmentation and deterioration, or a renewal of the traditional communitarian symbiosis.

Janice McCormick analyzes the historic tensions in France

between individualism and communitarianism. She sees the possibility of a new communitarian rule emerging.

Christopher Allen reveals that Germany is and always has been dominated by both communitarian practice and ideology. It has, however, been torn by competing forms of communitarianism: statist versus nonstatist, centralized versus decentralized, authoritarian versus democratic.

George Lodge finds the United States, like Britain, haunted by ambivalence. He sees government, business, and labor hesitantly moving in practice away from individualism and in a communitarian direction, but without a new ideology to justify or clarify what is happening.

Ezra Vogel describes the long history of Japanese communitarianism, adapting over time to external pressures. He sees the old form of communitarianism, authoritarian and hierarchical, giving way to a more individualistic variety. Japanese ideology and institutional practice are thus in line with one another, mutually supporting, vital and strong.

Edwin Winckler points out that Taiwan's business community is divided and strained by two ideologies that also mark the relations of business and government: familism and statism. But the context, both external and internal, is putting increasing pressure on Taiwan, up to now an economic miracle.

Vincent Brandt writes of "the desperate longing for individualism" in South Korea, a society that has been and continues today to be dominated by authoritarian statist communitarianism. Tension mounts as business's freedom to innovate and grow becomes increasingly essential to the country's ability to service its mounting foreign debt.

In Brazil, Jorge Domínguez sees a powerful and deeply rooted "macroideology" competing with and threatened by a number of varied "microideologies." Overall, there is a relatively authoritarian variety of state-centered communitarianism, an ideology widely shared by the elites who run the country.

In another chapter, Domínguez analyzes the far deeper ideological cleavages that torment Mexico. There the old formal revolutionary ideology has eroded, but a new one is not yet formed.

Finally, Vogel summarizes our conclusions and suggests some directions for the future.

METHOD OF STUDY AND ITS USE TO MANAGERS

In this study we take ideology as it exists and as it changes, asking what were the ideas at a certain point in time and in a particular place that sustained and justified institutional roles and relationships. At the same time we seek to reveal the ideas that reflect what those institutions were actually doing in spite of the expressed ideology. We thus highlight controversy inherent in a community's policies and institutions, forcing into the open assumptions and preconceptions that are frequently hidden or glossed over.

There are two parts to our analysis of each country. The first is historic, the second looks to the future. We shall explore what have been the dominant ideologies in the nine countries and how and why the various ideologies have changed. We shall focus on several sets of issues: the management of rising and declining economic sectors; the role of government and its policies toward business; and the purpose of business, including the authority of managers and their relationships to the managed. We believe that our method is designed to avoid three deficiencies in conventional analyses: excessive specialization so that systemic change is not perceived; reliance on outdated paradigms that sustain unrealistic assumptions; and a static rather than a dynamic approach—a snapshot in time instead of a historical movie.

We shall pay particular attention to legitimacy gaps, the lags or distance between the prevailing ideology in each country and institutional practices; to the adaptability of the prevailing ideology to competitive pressures in the international economy; and to friction among competing ideologies. In this way we will identify points of tension in each country, speculate about the impact of likely events on the ideological fabric, and consider what that impact will mean for institutional choices and behavior. We believe that this will be useful to managers because it will allow them to perceive the shape of crisis relatively soon and to change their practices accordingly. For many the issue is how to make maximum use of minimum crisis for maximum change.

Ideological analysis helps managers ask and answer such questions as: What assumptions have I left uninspected? How are the sources of my authority changing? Will what I am doing today be acceptable tomorrow? Old assumptions about competition, for example, might delay fruitful cooperation among competitors. Conceptions of property rights and the limited state could discourage or prevent a more effective relationship with government. Adversarial conceptions of labor-management relations could hamper more effective and humane cooperation among the members of a business organization. Mergers or partnerships among firms from different national settings obviously depend upon a full appreciation of one another's ideological assumptions and the ability to manage the gap between them.

If you are managing a foreign subsidiary of a multinational corporation, it is important to know what your ideological assumptions and behavior are and how they fit with the prevailing ideological mix. For example, if you rely on contractual relationships between employers and employees and the prevailing norm is consensual, you will be in trouble, as you will be if you assume managerial rights from the idea of property while the prevailing ideology ascribes authority to government. And if your ideological practice is at variance with that of headquarters another set of conflicts will arise.

If you are managing in an environment that is ideologically divided and conflict is prevalent, there may be ways of insulating yourself so that you can become an island of coherence. Foreigners in Britain, for example, often have a special advantage when it comes to designing and implementing effective human resource management strategies, because they are not part of the conflicted establishment. Of course, where the prevailing ideology is strong, coherent, and stable, you have little choice but to conform. It is thus important to know what the ideological situation is.

Similarly, it is helpful to know what the ideological role of government is and which way it is drifting. If it is communitarian, then your relationships will more than likely be with bureaucrats; if it is individualistic, then lobbying with many interest groups is more in order. This reflects the fact that the communitarian government's task is to define community need and assure its fulfillment, whereas the individualistic government's preoccupation is with the representation of the desires of individuals and interest groups.

Since ideologies are *systems* of ideas, a movement in one component has certain implications for other components: the idea of individualism goes with that of the limited state, it is threatened by the active, planning state; rights imply duties; reliance on community need implies a state capable of defining it; a hierarchy is always governed by criteria, acceptable to some but often not to others, and those criteria are rooted in other components of the ideology. History seems to show that communities have an exceptionally difficult time dealing with ideological change because of the resilience of tradition. Change comes slowly, often with considerable crisis, and only when forced by contextual pressures. The manager who understands the system and how it works, will be better prepared for crisis.

* * *

None of the countries we examine here are entirely free of ideological tension and ambivalence, although some, like Japan, are freer than others.[11] Individualism and communitarianism are ideal types; in fact, a variety of forms of each exists, sometimes blended harmoniously and sometimes in bitter conflict.

Are we utopians? Definitely not. We have no particular bias toward or affection for any ideology. We are not interested in describing an "ideal" society. We are suggesting, however, that successful communities are those that are effective at managing ideological change and contradictions by being able to clarify goals in a changing context and to achieve them. We further suggest that effective managers must understand the ideological implications of their actions. Finally, we suggest that Western economies in particular confront problems that derive in large part from the differing ideological assumptions and premises of the various participants in the global economic game.

2

THE UNITED KINGDOM

Symbiosis or Division

Joel Krieger

Many have noted the institutional continuities of British political life that make "the English government . . . one of the most remarkable in the world,"[1] a symbol of durability and constancy of modern representative government. Indeed, observers have long sought in British political culture the secrets of stable democracy: a successful balance between deference for authority and respect for the rights of individuals; constitutional flexibility; the encouragement of political opposition; and, except for Northern Ireland, the strong preference for negotiation over violence as a means of conflict resolution.[2] From the eighteenth century, historically constituted symbiosis between individualism and communitarianism represented a crucial aspect of Britain's enviable stability. This resonant ideological mix—which operated above party and helped politically integrate a diverse set of interests—served well to motivate the successful conduct of economic affairs and political choice for two hundred years or more.

By the 1970s, however, international pressures and growing

divisions within domestic political alliances (notably between the Labour Party and the trade union movement) reduced cohesion and heightened ideological ambivalence. The decline of its international competitiveness and a radical loss of geopolitical influence throughout the postwar era have left Britain economically exposed and politically divided. As John Dearlove and Peter Saunders note:

> British politics have been undergoing some quite dramatic and fundamental changes and upheavals over the last few years. As the country's economy has lurched into recession, and as different sections of the population have posed different and often irreconcilable demands across a variety of issues ranging from the deployment of nuclear weapons to the future of the welfare state, so long-established political arrangements have begun to crack under the strain.[3]

The erosion of the two-party system with the formation of the Social Democratic Party in 1981, the riots in a host of English cities in 1981 (and again in 1985), and the violence and unusual longevity of the miners' strike of 1984–85, all illustrate a new and unexpected fragility in British political culture. Today, the breakdown of civil and industrial peace, and the destabilization of the party-electoral system may indicate a serious weakening in the communitarian-individualist symbiosis.

It will be an aim of this chapter to consider the consequences—for economic management, for the determination of social policy, for labor-management relations—of a repoliticization of ideology and an expansion of individualism at the cost of communitarian values. How have new "images and sentiments that function as operative ideals"[4] in the British political community helped motivate the conduct of economic affairs and the expressions of political choice? Have elements in the contemporary ideological mix contributed to the growing rigidities of Britain's political-economic structures? Have they reduced the prerogatives or misdirected the energies of Britain's corporate executives, public sector industrial managers, and political elites?

First, I discuss the historical evolution of British ideological traditions, from organic communitarianism to the Conservative-Labour consensus that oriented Britain's classic postwar synthesis. Second, I indicate the decline of ideological symbiosis in the 1970s. Third, I illustrate some areas of conflict that have emerged as characteristic expressions of the dominant ideological mix of the 1980s: industrial relations; the role of the state in economic management; and rights and duties of community membership. I conclude with a set of speculative proposals about useful ideological and policy directions.

THE HISTORICAL CONTEXT

Organic Corporatism

The historical evolution of British ideologies can usefully be charted by reference to *corporatism*, the social allocation of rights and duties in accordance with a dominant vision of community need. In corporatism, observed J. T. Winkler, "[s]ociety is seen as consisting of diverse elements unified into one body, forming one *corpus*, hence the word corporatism."[5] This organic communitarianism has oriented a powerful value scheme in British society from the time of the medieval estates.

Corporatism began from the premise that harmony among economic interests and organic unity were essential to society. These ends could be secured if the various producer groups, notably capital and labor, were "imbued with a conception of natural rights and obligations somewhat similar to that presumed to have unified the medieval estates."[6] This principle of organic unity—the sovereign as the "head" of the "body politic," the "members" of parliament as the active parts (the "limbs")—lies at the traditional core of British political culture. The organic "body politic" metaphor, as Samuel Beer demonstrates with an illustration from the sixteenth-century rule of Elizabeth I, was intended quite seriously as the justification for the sovereign acts of state:

Elizabeth herself had used the head and body analogy to clinch her claim that the monarch has controlling responsibility for the great matters of public policy. At the close of the Parliament of 1566, she warned the House of Commons not to meddle further with the question of the succession and asked rhetorically: "Who is so simple that doubts whether a prince that is head of all the body may not command the feet not to stray when they would slip?"[7]

The Emergence of a Communitarian-Individualist Symbiosis

But even in the seventeenth century Thomas Hobbes and John Locke were beginning to raise crucial doubts about an exclusively communitarian ideal of political right linked to premises of the natural sovereignty of a monarch. Insisting that sovereignty should derive from contract, they each in quite different ways argued that the legitimacy of the state should be limited, that it must rest on its ability to represent, rightfully and effectively, the individual needs of persons in a competitive society.[8] By asserting individualist ideology, Hobbes and Locke encouraged an individualist-communitarian symbiosis that would help unify Britain's political community and orient its economic behavior from the eighteenth until well past the mid-point of the current century.

It is safe to say, therefore, with Beer, that despite "lip service to Locke, eighteenth-century England was far from being an individualist society and, on the plane of operative ideals, the image of social reality had a strong corporatist tinge."[9] It is equally true, however, that by the nineteenth century, a pronounced expansion of individualism, linked to the processes of industrialization, was influencing the ideological mix in significant ways.

Thus, an environment for successful entrepreneurship was secured by encouraging unambiguously individualist principles. Partly because of Britain's industrial priority, economic policy in Britain developed from below as a consequence of market competition and interest-group pluralism, both associated with individualism, not as the planned consequence of community-based and state-enforced design. As Barry Supple observes:

[T]he British economy, which had initiated the Industrial Revolution, without the direct intervention of the state, prolonged and heightened its supremacy on the basis of market forces. Indeed, the main trend of British legislation after the [Napoleonic] Wars . . . was precisely in the direction of a continued dismantling of the structural, fiscal, and economic barriers to the mobility of men and resources.[10]

Perhaps most characteristically, the reduction of tariffs in the 1820s and the 1846 repeal of the Corn Laws dramatized the hold of free trade and laissez-faire precepts, symbolizing the passive but ultimate approval by the government of competition and of interest-group pluralism, both associated with individualist ideology. English manufacturers were divided but nonetheless substantially opposed to the foreign competition of free trade. The repeal of the Corn Laws likewise— "in the teeth of bitter opposition from farmers and the squirearchy"[11]—subjected British agriculture to its first overseas challenges. Indeed, the legislative history of free trade involves classically powerful interests as intermediaries: greater London commercial interests prevailing over manufacturing in the removal of protective tariffs; cotton exporters, the Manchester Chamber of Commerce, and the Anti-Corn Law League defeating agricultural interests in the repeal of the Corn Law.[12]

Limited state, laissez-faire competition, interest-group pluralism: these elements of individualism dominated economic policy in Britain with little interruption until the beginning of the twentieth century and up to the start of the First World War. But this is only half the story of Britain's ideological formation.

Individualism in economic affairs was, from an early period, counterbalanced by communitarianism in the evolution of political rights. Throughout the nineteenth century, citizenship rights were expanded in Britain. Civil rights, the first rights of citizenship, are those necessary to individual freedom—free speech, liberty of person, the "right to own property and conclude valid contracts." They were already secure, as T. H. Marshall puts it, "[b]y 1832 when political rights made their . . . infantile attempt to walk." By 1918, when political rights of franchise and participation were universalized as explicit second rights of citizenship, the third element of citizenship—social rights—was acquiring ideological and programmatic significance. By the late 1930s, citizenship came to include the right to economic welfare and "to share to the full in the social heritage and to live the life of a civilized being according to the standards prevailing in the society."[13] The individualism of laissez-faire was accompanied by the communitarianism of a welfare state ethos.

The mix between economic ideals of individualism and the political/social pull of communitarianism was not altogether harmonious. In the early nineteenth century, the utilitarianism of James Mill and Jeremy Bentham led to the more determinedly democratic stance of John Stuart Mill, who linked individual political participation to moral development and who insisted that the right to vote be extended to men without property and to women equally. At the same time, popular movements to extend the franchise beyond the limits of the 1832 reform assumed a radicalizing trajectory that recast the logic of struggles for political representation from individualist to class-communitarian terms. Dorothy Thompson notes the inexorable transformation of the ideal of representation from its Lockean origins to its socialist implications.

> The great Reform Act of 1832 had defined more clearly than at any time before or since in British history, and more clearly than had been done in any other country, a qualification for the inclusion in the political institutions of the country based entirely on the possession of property and the possession of a regular income. The line drawn for the exercise of the franchise was precisely made to include all members of the middle and upper classes, and to exclude all wage-laborers. Voters had to be men, but no other qualification, whether of race, religion, or educational achievement, was considered apart from property. A movement to extend the franchise was bound to divide the country on class lines.[14]

Thus, communitarian pressures from below—for fuller participation in the life of the community, for the political rights that antedate full social rights—were resisted as economic and market-based distinctions took precedence.

Nor does the current century demonstrate any unambiguous reconciliation between the individualism of the marketplace and the universalism of citizenship rights. "[I]n the twentieth century, citizenship and the capitalist class system have been at war," observed T. H. Marshall. "Perhaps the phrase is rather too strong, but it is quite clear that the former has imposed modifications on the latter. . . . Social rights in their modern form imply an invasion of contract by status, the subordination of market price to social justice, the replacement of the free bargain by the declaration of rights."[15]

Thus, from the organic Old Tory cosmology that justified the hierarchies of Elizabethan England,[16] to the Lockean arguments for popular sovereignty, to the twentieth-century tensions between the sanctity of contract and the social rights of citizenship, British ideology has reflected a balance between individualism and communitarianism: the individualist ethos of capitalist industrialism mixed with the communitarian impulses that motivated political reform.

Contemporary Corporatism

Corporatism justifies communitarian theories about the way society should be organized and political choice exercised. *Pluralism*, which involves a very different set of claims, has been introduced to help legitimize a political system sustained by individualist ideologies. The distinctions are significant:

> Whereas pluralism assumes a competition among divided interests with the struggle for factional advantage resulting in a political equilibrium which defines the policy options of a weak state, corporatism presupposes "a shared interest in collective existence" and cooperation expressed through the strategic exercise of power by a strong central state.[17]

It is perhaps not too much to say that the resurgence of "corporatist theory" in academic circles in the 1970s and the efforts to apply the theory, in defiance of its fundamental logic, to a set of institutional practices in Britain and elsewhere, represent an important battle for ideological direction in these societies. However, the resurgence of corporatism can also be construed as a serious effort to defend communitarian tradi- tions against the clear indication of their demise in the United Kingdom.

Until the twentieth century, "corporatism" has referred exclusively to state corporatism—corporatism from above. The fascist states of Italy and Germany in the 1930s were "exem- plary" instances of modern European corporatism. But in these countries corporatism was no more than a "decorative facade"[18] for an organic unity attained by consistent repres- sion. However, a new variant of the concept of corporatism— corporatism from below or societal corporatism—has emerged with growing academic support as an explanation of contem- porary Britain and other capitalist democracies. Philippe Schmitter characterizes societal corporatism as the system of representing interests that typically accompanies the "post- liberal, advanced capitalist, organized democratic welfare state."[19] In what has become the standard reference point for subsequent debates, Schmitter defines contemporary corporat- ism in ideal-type terms as:

> A system of interest representation in that the constituent units are organized into a limited number of singular, compulsory, hierarchically ordered and functionally dif- ferentiated categories, recognized or licensed (if not cre- ated) by the state and granted a deliberate representational monopoly within their respective categories in exchange for observing certain controls on their selection of leaders and articulation of demands and supports.[20]

In this version of corporatism, the directive capacities of the state increase, and "interest intermediation" becomes system- atized along less plural and less voluntary lines of power: membership is compulsory in the few powerful peak associa- tions (trade unions or business confederations); a single orga- nization negotiates binding settlements that are recognized as legitimate by the state; and in return for this "representational monopoly," the representatives of corporate interests deliver support for agreed policies and discipline their members.

The traditional corporatist premise of organic unity is preserved in this new theoretical amalgam. For example, an incomes policy—the product of tripartite negotiations through which government secures the support of business and labor—becomes the modern equivalent of the medieval cathedral, whose painstaking construction represents the solidity, organic unity, and ostensible harmony of the society. The state manipulates claims so as to achieve a compromise that freezes the balance of class power in the interests of economic stability and well-being. When this is successful, ideological symbiosis is enhanced: the representation of interests that is fundamental to individualism may be harmonized with community needs.

In the end, however, corporatist forms of interest intermediation are transitory and contradictory for a number of reasons. First, the process of elite political bargaining over economic issues tends to erode the broad membership support needed for the successful implementation of policy accommodations. Second, the focus on the "crisis management" in these corporatist agreements neglects structural problems, for example, processes of "de-industrialization" or the general decline in national competitiveness. Third, because capitalist and state interests can keep critical issues off the bargaining table—sectoral investment strategies, restrictions on the flow of capital abroad, corporate tax and profit rates—neither the trade unions nor allied parties feel obligated to accept and enforce agreed policies.[21]

When the Keynesian welfare state (KWS) was dominant, economic growth encouraged political and economic elites to harmonize interests in ways that obscured the self-defeating character and contradictory forms of corporatist institutions. These same institutions were also converting conflict into communitarian motifs that rendered individualist claims less legitimate. Duties to the common good of economic growth should induce unions and managers to voluntarily forego their rights to hard collective bargaining. The KWS consensus encouraged a view that wages drift was antithetical to the common need for enhanced performance. Both sides of industry should make efforts to reduce custom and practice agreements and to restrict work-group efforts at defending outmoded prerogatives. Planning and investment initiatives should reduce regional and sectional imbalances, even at the cost of profitability if necessary.

Nowadays it is increasingly obvious that corporatist institutions cannot fully contain the tension between individualist and communitarian goals, particularly in their asymmetrical and limited exercise in Britain. Accordingly, the decline in Keynesianism is more than a decline in an approach to economics. It represents decline in support for a kind of society, the eclipse of communitarian ideals. George Ross observed that when growth slackened and employment fell precipitously, "[p]ainfully-institutionalized positions of 'corporatist' power which social groups had negotiated in the postwar boom to maintain their situations are threatened."[22] Growth reduced distributional conflicts but now economic distress has removed the central basis for consensus among business, labor, and government elites. Interests are divided and there is no longer a "postwar settlement"—a compromise involving "full" employment through governmental management of demand, and increased social and welfare expenditures in return for relative social harmony and labor peace. Keynesianism meant that conflict would be mediated through nonmarket political institutions, as "[p]olitics turned into an interplay of coalitions— giving rise to corporatist tendencies of direct negotiation, either between organized groups—particularly labor and capital— under the tutelage of the government or between each group and the government."[23]

THE DECLINE OF IDEOLOGICAL SYMBIOSIS IN THE 1970s

With Keynesianism waning and the corporatist traditions largely discredited, the long cycle of the British individualist-communitarian symbiosis has undergone increasing stress. In the 1970s economic growth slowed, and a welfare state consensus that had spanned party identities came undone.

The Conservative Party of R. A. Butler and Harold Macmillan had confirmed the postwar settlement. They neither attacked the welfare state that had grown so dramatically during the Labour government of Clement Atlee nor did they forsake the goal of full employment, even under the mounting pressure of inflation and recession. Although it may seem remarkable today, the Macmillan government was genuinely dismayed when efforts to reduce inflation through monetary policy during the height of the 1958 recession engendered a 2.8 percent unemployment rate in January 1959. And we should keep in mind that the Conservatives under Macmillan introduced the classic British exercise in planning—the National Economic Development Council (NEDC), composed of representatives of unions, private and public management, and the government.

The "one-nation" Tories were undoubtedly committed to the terms of the postwar settlement, notably to expand the welfare state and to achieve full employment. In fact, this commitment of Conservatives and mainstream Labour alike to a common road of mild European social democratic reforms is revealed in the language of British political studies. "Butskellism" (after Butler and Gaitskell) and the less common "MacWilsonism" (after Macmillan and Wilson), represent the high watermark of interparty consensus and the dominance of Keynesian-welfarist-communitarian ideals.[24]

Viewed in this context, the 1970s were a crucial period of increasing economic strain and political fragmentation. Britain's ideological orientation was also undergoing a far-reaching revision. The general phenomenon can best be understood by reference to industrial relations.

Industrial Relations

Throughout the 1960s and 1970s, a succession of Labour and Conservative governments tried with little success to restructure labor management relations to reduce wage costs and industrial conflict, and to increase productivity. These government efforts to reform the industrial relations system are especially interesting because they seem to draw in equal measure upon individualist and communitarian ideals.

Thus, when there was increasing concern in the mid-1960s that the proliferation of informal shop-floor agreements reflected a "breakdown of the normative order," encouraged work stoppages, and contributed to "uncontrolled movements of earnings and labor costs,"[25] Wilson's Donovan Commission accepted as inevitable that divisions of interest at every industrial level would generate multiple informal and contractual agreements. The Commission's recommendation that multi-tier agreements should be formalized, centralized, and rendered enforceable reflected essential individualist precepts: the centrality of contract; an acceptance of an adversary relationship between labor and management as natural; the fragmentation and individuation of interest/need; the role of government as a limited purveyor of environmental conditions to encourage private solutions.

At the same time, British governments attempted to implement corporatist arrangements. In the 1960s, efforts were made first by the Conservatives and then by Labour to encourage union acceptance of voluntary wage restraints via participation in planning institutions inspired by the French model of indicative planning. This further effort at tripartite communitarianism principally involved the National Board for Prices and Incomes. The Board, commissioned to regulate wages in accordance with national interest, was briefly successful with an incomes policy inaugurated in 1965.

The most impressive and significant neocorporatist arrangements occurred, however, after the oil shock of 1973–74. The last Labour government sought to stabilize the economy at once and to involve the Trades Union Congress (TUC) in an expanded agenda of shared responsibility for economic and social policy. The Labour strategy was planned during the trade-union struggle with the Heath government over the 1972 Industrial Relations Act (which mandated the registration of all unions and assigned financial liability to them when their members went on nonsanctioned strikes). The "Social Contract," agreed to by the TUC-Labour Party Liaison Committee in February 1973, called for wage and price controls "within the context of coherent economic and social strategy—one designed both to overcome the nation's grave economic problems, and to provide the basis for cooperation between the trade unions and the Government."[26]

It is well known that the pressure of mounting inflation and a substantial run on the pound quickly removed the more expensive (and, for the TUC, most attractive) elements of the "Social Contract," especially the promises of expanded social services and of industrial and economic democracy. After the electoral victory in February 1974, the new Labour Government and the TUC agreed to a formal (voluntary) incomes policy in 1975. New terms were bargained for each of four annual "phases," with decreasing TUC, trade union, and rank-and-file support. As Stephen Bornstein observes:

> Like all earlier British attempts at incomes policies . . . the Social Contract was unable to last beyond a few years. The increasingly conservative fiscal and social policies of the government in combination with the accumulation of worker resentment and the inability of unions to impose their will on their own shop stewards and members, produced an explosion of wage militancy in the winter of 1978–1979. The strikes, and the stubborn and maladroit manner in which the Labour Cabinet attempted to handle them, were instrumental in undermining the authority of the government and bringing its defeat in the election of May 1979.[27]

The traditional communitarianism that underlay class solidarities had subverted the newer interclass, but nonetheless communitarian, consensus.

Two points seem clear. First, the "Butskellite" period of the Keynesian welfare state involved policies having contradictory ideological resonances. Individualism found expression in the reinforcement of divided interests and the strict application of contract implied by the Donovan Commission; communitarianism found expression in the neocorporatist exercises of voluntary wage constraint and tripartite planning in the national interest for community need, culminating in the Social Contract of the Wilson (later the Callaghan) government. Second, neither ploy was terribly successful. Nor indeed were the statutory restrictions on the trade unions attempted by the first Wilson government ("In Place of Strife") nor by Heath (the 1972 Industrial Relations Act). The individualist approach foundered because of resistance located in private interest and competition; the communitarian approach foundered because corporatist arrangements cannot withstand the extreme pressures of economic crisis. It is perhaps optimistic, therefore, to refer to this pattern as ideological symbiosis. Nevertheless, through 1979, two coexisting and well-balanced ideological motifs oriented British approaches to industrial relations, alternating one with the other. Has the present government continued this pattern?

THE IDEOLOGICAL DIRECTION OF THE 1980s

"What have you changed?" someone asked the new prime minister in 1979, and Margaret Thatcher replied, "I have changed everything."[28] While this was a mere boast, Thatcher unwittingly revealed the central truth of what she really had changed. In response to a question from Anthony Sampson, she noted with characteristic clarity, "I've always regarded the Conservatives as the party of the individual."[29] Thatcher's is perhaps an uncommon interpretation of a party more typically associated with organic symbolism, Disraelian social reform, and a patrician regard for the permanence of community defined by hierarchical and functional divisions. And, of course, there is still the continuity of parliament and parties, and of class divisions and monarchical loyalties. Thatcher has not "changed everything," but Thatcherism does represent a fundamental ideological transformation, in two ways. It is different ideologically, but it is also more highly charged by ideology.

Traditionally, the Conservatives in Britain are less hampered by ideological commitment when they make policy than are their Labour counterparts. Beer once observed that "the Conservatives have been regarded as the party that has no ideas but which can govern."[30] The opposite is closer to the truth today. The Thatcher government has significantly recast the ideological orientation toward neoindividualism.

During the sharp economic downturn in the 1970s, the existing political and economic arrangements were severely jeopardized. The potential fragility of Britain's ideological consensus is most readily apparent in specific areas of ideological conflict: industrial relations, the role of the state in economic management, and the rights and duties of community membership.

Industrial Relations

There are strong indications that the Thatcher Government has altered the hybrid "Butskellite" approach, with some dramatic consequences. As Huw Benyon and Peter McMylor observe:

> From the beginning, Thatcher had been anxious to break the old consensus. . . . the old class compromises were not for her, neither were collective forms of life and relationships. With all *corporate* forms apparently in crisis [such as income policies, etc.], the powerful articulation of *individualism* was made to seem both fresh and plausible. In this way of thinking, the phrase 'right to work' became deflected from its original social-democratic meaning of a *public* commitment to full employment, towards a citizen's right to sell, unhindered, one's labour as *individual* in the market-place."[31]

This ideological shift has involved a fundamental change in the meaning of labor-management disputes. They have become, under Thatcher, an opening for defeating the communitarian character of trade unions and for further removing the government from future corporatist-tripartite planning. Like the Butskellite pattern, this government's industrial relations strategy has two central elements, but both are heavily individualist.

The first element involves three pieces of legislation—the Employment Acts of 1980 and 1982, and the Trade Union Act of 1984—that "individuate" trade unions, thereby substantially reducing the rights with which British trade unions have been collectively endowed since 1906. Taken together, these acts hold union officials financially and legally responsible for a wide range of illegal activities (including large-scale picketing, strikes to protest government activity, and secondary strikes); severely restrict the institution of the "closed shop"; expand the ability of owners to dismiss strikers and union officials; and remove legal immunity from unions and officials who authorize otherwise legal industrial action without meeting particular balloting procedures.

Thatcher's second industrial relations strategy involved planned confrontations with crucial trade unions. Soon after becoming leader, but before the 1979 general election, Thatcher commissioned two internal Conservative Party reports and was considerably influenced by them. In the first, Lord Carrington—who was her Tory predecessor, Edward Heath's energy minister—dispelled a widely held Tory belief that Heath's failed showdown with the miners in 1974, when the Conservatives lost the election Heath called during a national miners' strike, had been a consequence of weak leadership. Instead, argued Carrington, society was being challenged by strategically powerful and self-interested groups of workers in the energy sector. Society was at a disadvantage in that sector's industrial disputes because of the general economic dependence on electricity and because neither miners nor electricity-generating plant personnel could be replaced by the armed forces during a strike.

The second report, a widely leaked document written for Thatcher by Nicholas Ridley, laid a blueprint for a political plan to overcome the technological and organizational problems identified by Carrington. Referring to the likelihood of a "political threat," the Ridley Report urged a carefully orchestrated series of confrontations with unions in the energy sector and in other basic industries. The early encounters would be with the weak and divided unions in the steel industry and would work up to an ultimate challenge to the National Union of Mineworkers (NUM), who had "defeated" the last Conservative government. Appearing first in *The Economist* in May 1978, Ridley's five-point plan had these features:

1. Profit (return on capital) figures should be rigged so that an above-average wage claim can be paid to the "vulnerable" industries.
2. The eventual battle should be on ground chosen by the Tories, in a field they think could be won (railways, British Leyland, the Civil Service, or steel).
3. Every precaution should be taken against a challenge in electricity or gas. The most likely battleground would be the coal industry. A Thatcher government should therefore: (a) build up maximum coal stocks, particularly in the power stations; (b) make contingency plans for importing of coal; (c) encourage the recruitment of

nonunion lorry drivers by haulage companies to help
move coal where necessary; (d) introduce dual coal/oil
fueling in all power stations as quickly as possible.
4. The greatest deterrent to any strike would be "to cut
off the money supply to strikers, and make the union
finance them."
5. There should be a large, mobile squad of police equipped
and prepared to uphold the law against violent picketing. "Good nonunion drivers" should be recruited to
cross picket lines with police protection.[32]

This is not the place to rehearse a detailed narrative of the
year-long miners' strike, but the Ridley plan for remedying the
problems raised by Carrington leaves the unmistakable impres-
sion that both the steelworkers' strike of the winter of 1979
and the miners' strike of 1984–85 followed firm governmental
policy.[33] For our purposes it is enough to suggest that through
legislation to vastly reduce the community rights and collective
identity of unions, through a reversal of meaning in expressions like "right to work," and through well-planned strategies
of political confrontation with leading unions, Thatcher's industrial relations policy has stretched the attenuated ideological
symbiosis to its limits.

Britain and its unions are now decidedly in the individualist
position of adversaries. Trade-union elites can foster natural
competition against management and against other unions,
since they have obligations to a self-interested bargaining unit.
Can government action strategically blend these factors into a
broader concern that would encourage union participation in
tripartite neocorporatist bodies? Or will the government challenge trade unions to fight for their interests against that of the
national community, goading them into strikes that further
deindustrialize Britain, weaken competitiveness, and chill the
investment climate? Britain today does not provide easy solutions to the problems of industrial relations. There are, however, alternative agendas available to policymakers and private
sector executives. Their ideological implications are deep, and
their costs of failure are quite different from policies pursued
today.

Astute government policy could "Germanize" the British

industrial relations system by recognizing the disparate political perspectives and economic interests of laboring people.
The result could be to increase participation of workers and
trade unions in areas of management prerogative. That effort
might help increase the productivity and efficiency of British
firms by linking the interests of skilled, unionized, highly
motivated workers more closely to those of managers and
government officials, whose concern is with economic performance. Indeed, such developments in industrial relations might
generally invigorate Britain's consensual traditions. However,
government can make that happen only by first diminishing
the force of Britain's other ideological tradition of adver-
sarial/contractual dispute, and then by encouraging a balance
of rights and duties more generally regarded as fair through
welfare provision and macroeconomic policy designed to substantially reduce unemployment.

The Role of the State in Economic Management

In many ways industrial relations illustrates the broad pattern
of ideological change associated with the Thatcherite project.
Thatcher's is the first postwar government to deny any obligation to secure "full" employment and to challenge not simply
the cost but the rightfulness of public provision of housing or
health care. Her boast that she has "changed everything" is
clearly untrue, but she has gone quite far in changing the way
people think about a great many things.

The dry facts of policies require a brief review, even though
their ideological meanings interest us more. The Thatcher
record on public expenditure is mixed. The first five years of
the Conservative experiment show that the reduced spending
could not be sustained, largely because a recession triggered
greater income support and unemployment benefits. Spending
grew overall by more than 6 percent in real terms in the four
years up to 1982–83, and by about 1 percent in 1983–84.
Government claims of zero growth for the remainder of Thatcher's second government may be unrealistic. Ideologically linked
policies are visible within the total public expenditure. By the
end of 1984–85, spending on national defense and police programs was 40 percent greater in real terms than in 1978–79;

education and transport have been held roughly constant; expenditure on housing had been cut more than half by 1982–83; income support and health and social services programs have grown, in part owing to the effects of recession and the great difficulty of containing health care costs, whatever the ideology or institutional alternatives.[34]

Economic Performance The macroeconomic record of the Thatcher government is also mixed. An economic recovery that began in 1981 continued through 1985–86. Output grew at about 3 percent annually, and inflation fell from 18 percent in 1980 to 5 percent in 1984. Export growth has averaged 5 percent per year during this period, but the contribution of the foreign balance to general growth was negative during the first two to three years of recovery as a consequence of poor competitiveness and an increase in the value of imported goods and services. Moreover, the contribution of private consumption to the current period of sustained growth in GDP has been less than during the 1975–79 recovery, since it has been associated with a decline of 3.25 percent in the savings ratio, but only a 1.5 percent annual increase in real incomes. Real wage costs have risen throughout the period of recovery and in 1985–86 showed signs of acceleration. In combination with a continued decline in competitiveness, increased pressure on profits was expected in 1986. Finally, at 13 percent the unemployment in the first half of 1985 reached a record postwar level and was not projected to improve by more than 0.5 percent through 1987.[35]

Opinion is divided about what responsibility the government should claim for the modest recovery in output since 1981, and what blame it deserves for unemployment and competitive weakness in manufacturing. For government ministers, the favored analysis is linked closely to the neo-laissez-faire celebration of market forces. As economist Gavyn Davies observes:

Inflation [British ministers] say, has been shown to be primarily a monetary phenomenon, the control of which is compatible with a free-market economy, shorn of prices and incomes controls. Output and employment, they argue, are determined quite independently of fiscal and monetary policy, as is demonstrated by the recovery in output which has occurred "automatically" since 1981. Unemployment, they admit, is still a problem, but only because real wages refuse to adjust downwards. In short, the free market is working, just as they always said it would—except in the labour market.[36]

From this perspective, further wage restraint would benefit the economy by bringing additional downward pressure on inflation and improving competitiveness. These issues grow increasingly salient since, as a recent Economic Report of the European Community notes, "Several important trading partners have now entered a period of virtual price stability."[37] Relations between competitive and noncompetitive sectors should be enhanced. In addition, union resistance to technological changes that influence differentials, or reduce labor requirements, and to the effects of restrictive work practices should be diminished.[38] The Tory political agenda of restrictive trade union legislation augmented by strategic industrial confrontation becomes part of the current Tory macroeconomic approach at precisely these junctures.

Despite the controversial character of the Conservative strategy, a few unproblematic observations may be made. First, governmental management of the economy and conduct of public expenditure show some important continuities across the Wilson/Callaghan and Thatcher governments. When the Labour government in 1976 introduced monetary targets, cut social welfare expenditure to meet loan conditions set by the International Monetary Fund, and began to doubt that its own macroeconomic policy and corporatist stance could control either inflation or unemployment, the metamorphosis from a Keynesian consensus to a neomonetarism had begun.[39] Second, although international exigencies and the weakened British competitive position forced changes in macroeconomic policy, no significant change in British ideology occurred until Thatcher's policies were in place. The Labour Party had clung to the individualist-communitarian symbiosis past the point where even improved economic performance was likely to resolve growing distributional conflicts. Increasingly monetarist in practice, the last Labour government was still Keynesian in sentiment: the battle against inflation would be won by "responsible cooperation" by employers and trade unions who served higher community need and, after the victory, full employment would be restored and the social welfare rights of citizenship would be expanded.[40]

The ideological effect of Thatcher's economic and social policies has been quite different. Monetarism, market forces, and privatization are carefully orchestrating a movement away from the KWS consensus.

Rights and Duties of Membership

Thatcher's social and economic policies have come together to seriously revise British ideology on the rights and duties of membership in the political community. These ideological changes have strained consensus.

Just as the "right to work" has taken on new individualist connotations, so too has the "right to decent housing" been replaced by a statutory "right to buy" that has resulted in the transfer of half a million units of public housing to private ownership.[41] The denationalization of British Telecom and the widely noted inducements to small investors encourage popular acceptance of privatization: a "nation of shareholders" is to be created.

But more subtle aspects of privatization powerfully reinforce an individualist ethos. The National Health Service (NHS) has currently shifted resources into chronic care, a shift fully justified by the poor quality of such services and by an expanded need deriving from demographic changes. At the same time, however, reduced overall funding means weaker service and larger queues in NHS services used by persons who can afford to seek private care or acquire private health insurance. Budget constraints, the shifting of resources, the questioning of NHS capacities, an industrial relations posture in the health services that encourages disputes and the out-migration of nurses and doctors from the public sector, government support for expanded private insurance coverage—all this encourages a further erosion of the NHS, once "the jewel in the crown"[42] of Britain's welfare state.

"Implicit privatization"[43] thus complements budgetary reductions in selected areas of social welfare provisions. Alongside revisions of more traditional citizenship rights mandated by the Nationalities Act of 1981—which restricts the right of many commonwealth citizens to enter the United Kingdom[44]—these policies seriously limit heretofore widely accepted social rights of membership in Britain's political community.

CONCLUSIONS

Britain's ideological symbiosis has been weakened by the Thatcher government's social and economic policies. The society's values have been channeled toward individualism, with reliance on market mechanisms reinforcing a view of the community as a set of self-interested competitive actors. The ideological direction of the 1980s has seen the rise of the "managerial right" with several "self-made men" entering the Cabinet. The demarcation between "Drys" and "Wets" in the Tory Party is a division between the newer bourgeois individualism of the Thatcherites and the older gentleman-squirearchy one-nation Toryism. Thatcher's ideological dominance represents the first time that the Conservatives have even purported to put business interests to the fore, rewarding competition and individualism even perhaps above national interest.

Communitarian norms are further weakened when industrial relations is based on the legalistic dissolution of unions as protected bodies and on strategic combat rather than on corporatist consensus. The labor contract, threats of dismissal, and suits for damages against trade unionists replace the earlier organic cohesion implied by the Social Contracts of the 1970s and cooperative planning. Limits placed on the rights of mainly black nationals to settle in the United Kingdom, reduction in selected welfare benefits, and expanded privatization campaigns diminish rights of membership in the British political community. The remaining rights are market based and individualist: the right to work (if there were sufficient jobs), the right to buy (whatever the quality of housing stock).

Although Thatcherism seems to have restored ideological individualism, the government's behavior does not permit a clear tracking of its ideological direction. Ordinarily, the legitimacy gap between ideological representations and institutional practices emerges when groups of persons pursuing their institutional interests make partly intentional and partly unreflective departures from traditional norms. In Britain, however, such a legitimacy gap seems to have occurred less innocently. A deliberate disjuncture between ideology and government practice has been a fundamental part of the Thatcher experiment.

One of the government's avowed central aims is to withdraw the state from economic management to unleash the salutary effects of free market forces. But the dagger of intervention is only partly hidden behind a laissez-faire cloak. As Peter Hall notes:

> The object of the Thatcher government has been to reinforce the operation of market mechanisms in the hope that they will rejuvenate the economy with a minimum of state intervention. But this aspect of its program has foundered on a critical paradox: in order to restore the economy to a condition in which resources are allocated efficiently by self-regulating markets, the government found it necessary to alter many institutions in the British economy. That, in turn, has required a great deal of state intervention.[45]

The Thatcher government's policies, therefore, not only rekindle an individualist ethos but also send mixed messages. While trumpeting the virtues of laissez-faire, the government intervenes decisively: by managing the nationalized industries from the Cabinet more than ever before;[46] by introducing fundamental changes in the role of local authorities; by privatization. Thatcher's is, as Andrew Gamble put it, "the strong state in a weak economy,[47] and that is not the same as laissez-faire withdrawal from economic management. How should one evaluate Thatcher's ideological message: restored individualism and an engineered legitimacy gap?

First, while a government-sponsored legitimacy gap may be destabilizing, neither the miners nor the Coal Board managers nor the general public seemed to doubt that the recent strike was prompted and conducted by an "interventionist state." Disclaimers only inflamed the situation.[48] More generally, unemployment is viewed by 73 percent of respondents as Britain's most serious problem, and there is growing pessimism about the economy: only 18 percent in a May 1985 MORI poll thought that economic conditions were likely to improve. It may be time for the government to forsake the ideological stance of laissez-faire and accept direct responsibility for the conduct of the economy.[49] It is not impossible to be both procapitalist and interventionist. Such a stance would reduce the legitimacy gap and might restore confidence in government.

Second, the evolutionary changes in British ideologies have proceeded from symbiosis during the period of England's industrial preeminence and Pax Britannica, to growing ambivalence and dissolution during the decline of the Keynesian welfare state during the economic crisis of the 1970s, to neoindividualism and legitimacy gap today. Ideological coherence and solid economic performance may well rise and fall together. The dysfunction of ideology in Britain today may be more intimately connected with Britain's falling from imperial power to the bottom of the second rank of nations than with the Thatcher government's manipulations. Nevertheless, efforts to reinvigorate an ideological symbiosis might prove valuable.

New policy directions might emerge from combining a Tory-sponsored Donovan commission with more extensive use of the National Economic Development Council. More thoughtful and less confrontational treatment of the crucial problems of restrictive union practices and archaic and shallow business investment might thereby be encouraged. Easing the fiscal stance of the government (involving a modest expansion of the PSBR) might have positive consequences for unemployment. If presented well, it could reduce the prevailing sense that the government is shrugging its shoulders about the problem. Finally, public spending should be applied to unify the "two nations": the cash limits on local councils should be raised to permit better maintenance and provision of transport, public housing, and related matters; and privatizations should be applied on economic and organizational, not ideological, grounds.

These mild proposals are suggested as mainstream offerings in the context of a Conservative government in the 1980s. They are very limited, representing only a shallow agenda in pursuit of greater social stability. Britain has probably ceased to be a global or economic power, but it is unnecessary for the nation to remain beset by industrial and social divisions. As one British observer noted recently, "The rational task of modernization in Britain, then, is to make the U.K. a relatively thriving, but nonetheless second-rate, country."[50]

This task would surely be advanced by efforts to foster cooperation within, and enhance commitment to, the national political community by reasserting Britain's traditional ideological balance.

3

FRANCE

Ideological Divisions and the Global Reality

Janice McCormick

The policy which the government put into operation in September 1976—and which it has followed ever since— is dominated by a single consideration: to adapt France to the new conditions of the world, that is, to adapt France to the consequences of the structural changes of which I have recently spoken—the rise in the price of energy and the emergence of the developing countries. It is aimed at assuring the competitive capacity of the French economy, and the conditions of employment, and the standard of living of the French. Today, and for all the years to come, this is the central problem facing France. On it everything else depends.[1] (Raymond Barre)

To extract ourselves from the economic crisis, we must pull out of capitalism in crisis. Since this crisis is capitalism's strategy for recovering profits and restoring its power, we must invent another logic of development towards other ends and with other incentives. We will not get out of the economic crisis which has tended to make France a subsidiary of the USA unless we radically reverse the present trends.[2] (Socialist Party platform)

These two radically different views of economic policy represent the positions of the right and the left that have for so long divided French politics and society. However, closer scrutiny of actual policies reveals a less than rigid adherence to these positions.

The liberal government of Raymond Barre in fact nationalized the French steel industry and denied the American automobile companies permission to build new plants in Lorraine. Several years later the socialist government of Laurent Fabius told Renault, the nationalized automaker, to become profitable, even at the expense of employment. Furthermore, Fabius encouraged French electronics companies to seek joint ventures or licensing agreements with American and Japanese competitors.

How can we explain the unexpected actions of these two contemporary political leaders? A cynical response would be to dismiss the earlier pronouncements as political rhetoric. Others would see these contradictions as examples of the irrelevance of ideology for understanding policy formulation.

I shall argue, however, that the contradictions are really examples of the importance of ideology in France. They demonstrate the tenacity of traditional ideological positions and the difficulty surrounding attempts to implement policies consistent with these beliefs. Both Raymond Barre and the socialists felt that their actions were legitimized by their respective ideologies; in each case they were constrained by adherents of competing ideologies that did not legitimize that particular set of policies.

The common element of both parties is that the government sees itself as the reflection of the general will as defined by Jean-Jacques Rousseau, a will that is superior to that of any business or individual interest. The liberal Barre and the socialist Mitterrand see themselves as interpreters of the national interest, or what in chapter 1 is referred to as community need. Their language is a reflection of their particular ideological tradition, though their policy choices are constrained by political and economic realities.

FRENCH IDEOLOGICAL TRADITIONS

To understand the language and actions of French policymakers, it is important to study French ideological traditions. France may be seen as having two major ideological traditions: one on the right and one on the left. But each of these has two variants: the right has a historical legacy of both authoritarianism and liberalism; the left's authoritarianism is in the form of Jacobinism and its liberalism is in the form of social democracy. Thus, the ideology of the French is neither simply communitarian nor individualist; left and right are mixtures of both.[3]

The French today continue to legitimize their actions in terms of one of these four ideologies. As a result, the nation is deeply divided ideologically at a time when developments in the international competitive arena demand consensus around more communitarian actions. For both the liberal Raymond Barre and the socialist Mitterrand, that consensus has been elusive. Therefore, in France, where power has alternated between left and right, and where there is no political consensus, it will continue to be difficult to implement policies that would make the country competitive in the world economy.

Authoritarianism

The authoritarian ideology has its origins in the *ancien régime*. According to the theoreticians of the absolutist state, the role of the state was to "straitjacket" the nation and control factions; its imperative was to represent the common good, as determined by the king, above all special interests. The king reigned and governed by the grace of God. Below God's chosen leader for France, the social order was clearly hierarchical, dominated by the nobility and the clergy. In practice, however, the central state also sold offices and titles to generate revenue, thereby maintaining stability by providing an avenue for social mobility. The stability of the system also depended on the subservience of the lower classes; under feudal communitarianism, they were protected, supported and given a minimal education.

The economic policies of the absolutist state were not necessarily conservative. Colbert, Louis XIV's illustrious minister,
encouraged the development of productive wealth, and mercantilism flourished under the protection of the state.

This peculiar variant of authoritarianism left two lasting
marks on the political and social order of France. The first is
centralization: all subsequent political regimes, of whatever
ideological bent, have struggled with this legacy. The central
bureaucracy developed a dynamic of its own, and its power
was reinforced by later regimes of both the left and the right.
Second, Louis XIV created a dependence on the all-powerful
state, and Frenchmen came to rely on the central state to
resolve conflicts that could have been handled more effectively
at the local level. This view of the state as protector and arbiter
has permeated French politics for the past three hundred
years.

The development of capitalism, however, made it increasingly obvious that absolutist institutions, established in an era
when the social order could be described in terms of estates,
no longer corresponded to social reality. An Enlightenment
thought came to permeate French society, the legitimacy of the
absolute monarch declined. A new ideology had established its
hegemony within the ruling elite, an ideology that in the
nineteenth century was to flourish as liberalism.

Liberalism

The French liberal tradition has its intellectual origins in the
individualism of the Enlightenment. Anchored in a belief in the
natural rights of the individual, French liberal theory supported a technocratic and meritocratic state to protect the
individual citizen from arbitrary regulations. This tradition
emerged on the right in opposition to the authoritarian tradition described above.

Historians have described the years 1789–92 as the liberal
period of the French Revolution, for one of the key political
issues at the time was the establishment of private property
free of feudal trappings. As a result, ownership of property
became absolute, but for the vast majority its just distribution
was of no interest. Furthermore, in these years, internal free

trade was established, though France as a whole remained protectionist.

Certain early laws reflected this strong liberal orientation. Associations that would restrict the free flow of labor, for example, were outlawed.

The liberal tradition was weak in France, however, for several reasons. First, nations with a strong feudal past have historically found it difficult to establish a republican form of government; France was no exception. Second, French liberal intellectuals have always been divided: they cannot agree on a form for the state, nor on an economic system. At the root of their differences has been disagreement over which citizens are to be equals. Their failure to address the question of social equality, and their mistrust of popular classes, destined liberalism to be positioned on the right of the political spectrum. Finally, liberals were besieged from both the left and the right, as they would be throughout the nineteenth and twentieth centuries.

Jacobinism

The Jacobin tradition, which emerged in reaction to the perceived failings of liberalism, is a peculiarly French ideology, a mix of democracy and authoritarianism.

The Jacobins defeated the liberal government in 1793, and attempted to establish a republican government based on equality and fraternity. Believing in an equality of result and not of opportunity, they supported requisitioning private property to benefit the disadvantaged. Like the authoritarians of the right, the Jacobins distrusted emerging capitalism and individualism, preferring elements of communitarian absolutism. They opposed existing representative institutions, arguing instead for direct democracy and universal suffrage. The Jacobins did not tolerate political pluralism, and the use of any means to protect the nation's interest was deemed justified. Furthermore, the Jacobins believed in a separation of church and state, a belief sustained for nearly two centuries, during which all French republics were anticlerical and the Church antirepublican.

The Third Republic (1871–1940) represented a compromise,

albeit temporary, of divergent liberal and authoritarian groups. The compromise has been called a "republican synthesis," because all of the factions agreed to accept the legitimacy of the political institutions. Their agreement was based on an economic and social equilibrium of slow growth, one that would not threaten a strong bourgeoisie which, in alliance with the peasantry, would control the excesses of capitalist competition. Thus the social status quo was preserved. Excluded from this arrangement was the industrial working class, a fact that pleased the new Jacobin defenders of the proletariat, more interested in violent revolution than reform.

The rhetoric of liberal politicians extolled the virtues of the free market but, in practice, France was insulated from competitive pressures, since its borders continued to be closed to foreign products. Furthermore, internal competition was weak, due to a declining birth rate and low market demand. Most businesses remained small and poorly organized.

The leaders of the Third Republic opposed an interventionist state. The only legitimate role for the state was to guarantee national security and to provide the conditions for commerce. Until World War I, the French economy prospered under this liberal compromise; gross national product, productivity, and industrial output all grew about 2 percent annually. But after the war, the Liberals came under continuous attack from both the right and the left. The right sought strong government to return France to greatness and moral superiority, and the left criticized the social injustice of the regime.[4]

Social Democracy

The French social democratic ideological tradition is the last to emerge and the weakest. It is the only major ideological tradition not to have had a chance to fashion its own political institutions. Positioned between the authoritarians and liberals on their right and the Jacobins on their left, the social democrats were often merely a reactive force to the two extremes.

After the Paris Commune, social democracy emerged from the left-wing debate about reform versus revolution. Like the Jacobins, social democrats were anticlerical and opposed to the social inequality of the Third Republic. Like the Jacobins, they opposed the consequences of the industrial revolution: the greatest supporters of both left-wing groups were the working classes. Both couched their rhetoric in moral terms but, unlike the Jacobins, the social democrats resisted economic panaceas. And unlike the Jacobins, the social democrats supported the political institutions of the Republic. They have been in power three times in the twentieth century, but never for long. Their most important victory was the Popular Front of Leon Blum in 1936, though their Jacobin allies, the Communist Party, refused to participate in the government. This social democratic experiment, however, was short-lived, attacked from both the left and the right, and finally upset by international events.

THE POSTWAR CONSENSUS—MODERNIZATION

In the midst of ideological chaos, the liberal Third Republic came to an end with the military defeat of France in 1940. Criticized as selfish, individualistic, and weak, liberalism was discredited. Worse, in the eyes of most Frenchmen, it had led to the economic and military inferiority of France, something intolerable within the context of all four ideological traditions.

The failure of the liberal experiment enabled the postwar politicians to undertake an audacious program of modernization of the social and industrial infrastructure. Coordinated planning under the guidance of technocrats became legitimate and, with the creation of the European Economic Community (EEC), France was now more open to foreign competition than it had ever been. In effect, "a Gallic style of economic management that blended state direction, corporatist bodies and market forces,[5] constituted a consensus around the idea of international greatness, if not around capitalism.

As with other Western nations struggling to find new ways to coordinate their economies for rapid reconstruction in the postwar era, the French drew upon elements of their traditional ideologies to legitimize their actions. As one political scientist has argued: "The Gallic form of liberalism combined a certain reserve about competition with a protectionist state."[6]

As long as high growth rates were sustained, the consensus around capitalist institutions, tempered by a highly interventionist state, was preserved. Problems arose after the 1973 oil crisis as growth rates declined.

GROWTH AND INDUSTRIAL POLICY UNDER POST-OIL-CRISIS LIBERALISM

The most important political battle of the past decade has been that of growth: how to sustain it and how its benefits would be distributed. Now, since the victory of the "modernizers" in the 1950s, only a minority of the French remains suspicious of the need for growth. Therefore, the current debate is not whether to seek it, but how.

Elected president in 1973, Valéry Giscard d'Estaing was in many ways a nineteenth-century liberal. And the rhetoric of the government headed by Raymond Barre (1976–81) was clearly in the tradition of the turn-of-the-century liberals. Barre argued: "The state should do the least possible. When it intervenes, it should only help to do things and help to get things done—and only in areas where market forces have proven insufficient."[7] Furthermore, he ruled out protectionism, not wanting to insulate France from foreign competitors.

The new liberals argued that France must have an open economy, competitive in international markets. To succeed in these markets, the industrial infrastructure had to be made healthier by the application of a good dose of hard competitive medicine. Unproductive firms were to be allowed to close; layoffs were to be permitted; nationalized firms were not to run deficits, and their prices were to be allowed to increase in line with costs. As in the 1950s, the new liberal government wished to use the state to support high-growth industries with strong export potential. The key to its strategy was an austerity program designed to stabilize costs and to increase profits. The instruments of this liberal policy were a strong franc, uncontrolled prices, and "voluntary" wage controls. These, combined with monetary restraint and credit controls, it was believed, would reduce inflation. And unlike previous governments in the postwar era, which relied on inflation to keep employment levels high, it was argued that only the growth of healthy competitive firms would lower unemployment.

The Test of Liberalism: Industrial Policy

Despite its liberal rhetoric, the Barre government was reluctant to allow private interests to define the public good. Implicit in government actions was a belief that the state was still the best allocator of resources, and a better judge of need. Therefore, private business remained under the watchful eye of the state. Financing continued to come either directly from the state or from state-owned banks. Furthermore, the governments of this era introduced new restrictions on layoffs. For example, companies were required to provide nearly full salary for one year to those laid off.

The Barre government felt that the French political climate limited its policy options. With close to 50 percent of the electorate, the left-wing parties and their trade-union allies vociferously opposed all layoffs, and they called for government bailouts of declining companies. The liberal government feared both trade-union and electoral reprisals.

The steel industry. In 1977 the French steel industry, suffering from overcapacity in many inefficient facilities, faced another year of losses. The two principal producers had not shown a profit in years.

Under previous governments the state had intervened, forcing the companies and the trade unions to agree to the gradual reduction of capacity. In each case, it was generally assumed that the state would subsidize the costs of the adjustments. However, with the advent of a liberal government many in the industry feared that the companies would be allowed to fail, with massive job losses the result.

Under the initiative of the government, the steel trade association negotiated a restructuring of the industry as well as a retraining plan for those who would lose jobs. Though the government would pay for the plan, Raymond Barre made one additional demand: for their mismanagement of the industry, he forced the resignations of the presidents of the steel companies.

In exchange for state aid, the companies were forced to take prodigious writedowns of their stock and the nationalized banks were asked to underwrite the companies' losses, thereby effectively nationalizing the firms.

The decline of a national champion—Renault. Both Gaullists in the authoritarian tradition and the liberal Barre government supported active state intervention in certain industrial sectors. In some industries, they all argued, national interest demanded that French firms be protected from foreign competition. The history of Renault is illustrative.

Nationalized in 1947 to punish its owner for collaboration with the Nazis, Renault became the French model of a well-managed company at the service of the nation. Although top management was appointed by the government and representatives of several ministries served on the board, Renault was granted autonomy in its strategic and marketing decisions. "The French were able to direct the long-run policies of Renault to conform with what the government perceived as the national interest. At the same time, the government generally avoided interference in day-to-day decisions."[8]

Wages and benefits at Renault were consistently 10 percent to 20 percent above those of other automakers, and Renault's social policies were seen as trendsetters for the nation. For example, Renault established a works council before a law required it, and was the first employer to bargain with the unions at the plant level. Peugeot and Citroën, in contrast, were old-fashioned family firms with hostile labor-management relations.

The postwar governments were anxious to build a strong French automobile industry. High tariffs were imposed on imported cars prior to 1959, and the tax and credit incentives available to French car buyers discriminated against foreign manufacturers. Even after the creation of the European Economic Community, the French government closely monitored the domestic car market. In 1963 de Gaulle resisted Chrysler's attempt to increase its ownership of Simca, though in the end EEC pressure forced him to allow the takeover. On several occasions the government also refused to allow Ford or General Motors to build assembly plants in France, even in Lorraine, a region where in 1980 unemployment was especially high. And later, when the competitive threat came from Japan,

Giscard ruled that Japanese cars would be limited to 3 percent of the market, a decision in clear violation of trade agreements as well as of the "free trade" rhetoric of the regime. One government spokesman described how customs officials personally inspected each car as it was unloaded at the port: "Most either failed inspection or were held up so long that it was unprofitable for the Japanese to continue to send so many."[9]

For many years the automobile firms were both model employers and the largest exporters. However, a combination of strategic choices, management practices, and government policies weakened these firms. In the post-oil-crisis period, both Renault and Peugeot chose to expand capacity and to acquire other firms in the industry. Renault also continued its globalization strategy (every year a new country, a new factory, and a new model), in the process acquiring American Motors Corporation in the United States. Furthermore, faced with the prospect of high unemployment, the government pressured Renault to buy Peugeot's unprofitable truck division, and it encouraged the two automakers to expand production in regions of France that were targeted by the state for industrial development.

In a shrinking world market with intensified competition, an acquisition strategy proved costly. Both companies became heavily indebted. Supported within their domestic market by government loans and under government pressure not to provoke social unrest by plant closings, both Renault and Peugeot joined the ranks of producers of the world's most costly automobiles.

The End of Liberalism

The economic consequences of the liberal experiments of the 1970s were generally good. Exports had increased and, though growth was slow, France outperformed its EEC trading partners. The franc held firm while the growth of the money supply slowed. At the same time, France had the smallest budget deficit of any Western nation.

Some of the consequences, however, were less favorable. Private investment continued to stagnate. And although France had acquired a competitive position in several industries—

armaments, nuclear development, aeronautics, and space equipment—these were all industries heavily dependent on state financing. Furthermore, inflation remained above 10 percent, and unemployment continued to rise.

The liberal government had political difficulties implementing many of its policies, as the failure to close unproductive plants in the steel industry demonstrates. The government had two principal problems. First, like earlier liberals, they represented only a small minority of the French electorate. Second, since there were no traditions or mechanisms for achieving consensus, like earlier liberals the government feared social unrest among the working classes that generally supported the left. In the end, it was this fear that kept the Liberals from implementing many of their favorite ideas.

However, the greatest failure of the liberal government was ideological: it failed to learn the lessons of earlier liberal experiments. Giscard and Barre failed to recognize that the French believed in *grandeur* and social justice more than in the intrinsic merits of competitiveness. In 1981 the Socialist Party was thus well positioned to plead the case for these traditional values.

SOCIAL DEMOCRACY IN POWER

François Mitterrand ran an astute campaign as the potential leader above the fray of day-to-day politics. He criticized the liberals for their austerity policies that had increased inequalities, arguing that they represented selfish individualism rather than the general will. The French electorate no longer wished to hear about economic weakness and decline. In electing Mitterrand president, the French expressed their preference for traditional French values that had so long made the nation great. Liberalism in the 1970s was an attempt to heal the ills of Gaullist statism; socialism in the 1980s would try to heal the ills of liberalism.[10]

In 1981 Mitterrand came to power in alliance with the Communist Party, the heirs of the old Jacobin tradition. His platform was a blend of social democratic and Jacobin ideologies. The social vision of justice and equality would prevail over the economic order, and political power would be used to achieve greater equality and to redistribute income. Drawing from the Jacobin tradition, the left criticized capitalism, arguing that social change would be achieved by class struggle. In a seeming contradiction, the socialists in a social democratic tradition believed that the transformation of society could be achieved through state mechanisms. Most important, though, both intellectual currents coexisted within the coalition government.

France could be great again, argued the left, even though the rest of the world was in the midst of a recession. French growth, it was believed, could be stimulated through a series of Keynesian macroeconomic recipes accompanied by redistributive reforms.

The policies implemented by the left, once in power, have been seen by some as a gradual retreat from socialist ideals. However, the retreat from their anticapitalist and redistributive campaign promises can also be seen as a return to other traditional French ideological tenets. Much like the modernizers of the 1950s, the socialist government of the 1980s came to believe that France's *grandeur,* and its international position, were threatened by policies that ran counter to those of the rest of the developed world.

During the first year the new administration retained popular support for what was to be the transition to socialism. During this first phase, the coalition sought to implement its campaign promises with a series of redistributive measures. It increased minimum wages and transfer payments to stimulate consumption, particularly by the least advantaged. Furthermore, by nationalizing five major industrial groups and two financial holding companies, the new government hoped to revive the economy.

An explanation of the public support for these reforms, especially the costly nationalizations, is to be found in the traditional anticapitalism of the Jacobin as well as the social democratic traditions. Both communists and socialists considered the ownership of personal private property to be sacred, but generally they mistrusted business. Both Socialist and Communist Parties believed that it was the role of the state to protect its citizens from the effects of capitalism.

Other reforms of this first phase of the left in power were equally popular. Labor law reforms, for example, reinforced the power of the trade unions, while new legislation was enacted to protect the rights of foreign workers. Social security coverage was increased and greater protection was extended to the disadvantaged.

There were, however, two problems with this series of reforms. First, the socialists alienated the traditional liberals, even though they needed their support, especially within the business community. On the one hand, their political pronouncements were reminiscent of the 1794 Jacobin Terror: "big capital will pay" and "some heads will fall"; on the other hand, they expected French business to demonstrate confidence in the government by investing in their firms. But companies were not investing; investment declined 10 percent in 1981, and the outlook for 1982 was worse.

The socialist coalition government faced a second, more serious, problem deriving from the first year's policies. The competitive position of France in the international economy had seriously eroded; the global context was again closing in on France, forcing a new ideological synthesis. While its foreign competitors were lowering their inflation rates, France's rate continued to rise. And as a consequence of the French stimulation of consumption, which could not be met by French goods, foreign goods flooded the French market. French trade thus suffered severe deficits and the franc weakened steadily.

It was increasingly obvious that this version of the socialist ideology, heavily tinged with Jacobinism, was impossible in a capitalist international environment. For the French economy to survive, the government would have to play by the existing international rules of competition; a mere act of ideological faith could not change them. Whether individualist or communitarian, the ideology had to conform to economic reality. Rights had to be balanced with duties to achieve a consensus around a coherent conception of community need in which the health of business was critical to the national interest.

Disastrous economic results were accompanied by electoral reversals. The time was clearly ripe for a change of direction.

Industrial Policy under Socialism

In 1982, with gradually increasing severity, austerity policies were implemented. They were oddly reminiscent of those advocated, but scarcely implemented, by the previous liberal government. Wage and price controls, decreased government spending, and higher personal but lower business taxes were enacted to cool down the economy. In the name of a return to *grandeur,* a "national effort for the economy" was necessary; and every citizen would be required to make sacrifices to make French goods and businesses competitive.

Strong private firms and increased industrial investment were the new priorities. Success in high-technology industries was declared to be "the great affair of the century." And, unlike the industrial policies of the 1950s modernizers, and in spite of socialist theory, this time the impetus for change was not to come from the state but from entrepreneurship assisted by private venture capital. According to Prime Minister Fabius, the four weaknesses of French industry were investment, training, research, and marketing, and he argued for a narrower role for the state to foster an environment where these could improve.

To the surprise of many, including their communist coalition partners, the socialists allowed many firms to close unproductive facilities and to fire workers. Even the newly nationalized firms were told to cut costs, and steel companies that had attempted to do so under the liberal government were now under socialists told to go ahead. "There can be no salvation without modernization," declared Mitterrand, and despite protests the government policies have helped firms become more competitive.

Socialists and the auto industry. When Mitterrand was elected president, the two French automakers were overmanned and in serious financial difficulty. PSA—the new Peugeot, Chrysler, Citroën conglomerate—reorganized, hired new management, and approached the government with a new rationalization plan that would involve the layoff of 15,000 employees. After long negotiations with the government and the trade unions, it was agreed that 11,555 jobs would be eliminated. This plan was implemented, despite occasional strikes by trade-union dissidents and immigrant workers.

Renault also faced serious problems. In the first year in power, they had further encouraged Renault's growth and acquisition strategy by maintaining government financial support. But Renault was also forced to make some poor acquisitions. As part of its attempt to save the French machine tool and farm machinery industries, for example, the government forced Renault to buy several bankrupt firms in these industries. Not surprisingly, Renault's balance sheet worsened.

Renault's auto business seriously declined in the early 1980s. Its French market share dropped from 38 percent in 1981 to 33 percent in 1984; its share of the European market shrank from 13 percent to 11 percent in the same period.[11] To handle its overcapacity, Renault's newly appointed boss, Bernard Hanon, carefully negotiated "soft layoffs" with the trade unions. A combination of early retirements, job transfers with retraining, and repatriation bonuses for foreign workers was worked out. But, to the embarrassment of Hanon, Renault's largest union, the CGT, repudiated the agreement at the last minute.

When Fabius became prime minister in the summer of 1984, he declared that social reform and welfare would not be at the expense of sound management practices and profitability. A new government survey concluded that, by 1988, the auto industry must reduce its labor force by 80,000 to be competitive.[12] And when Renault announced a record $1 billion loss for 1984, Hanon was abruptly fired. His replacement, the former president of Pechiney, had returned that company to profitability and was generally perceived as a sound businessman, not as a civil servant. Thus, although the government had used Hanon as a scapegoat for many years of business and government mistakes at Renault, it sent a clear signal to the managers at Renault that the tide had turned. Under the new socialist industrial policy, the nationalized firms were to be examples of competitiveness, not of social welfare.

The Socialists and high tech. In language reminiscent of de Gaulle himself, François Mitterrand called the development of a successful French electronics industry *la grande affaire industrielle* of the century, which the French must win to maintain the economic independence and the cultural identity of France. The French had cause for concern. For decades, the government had pumped money into high technology and had developed innumerable plans for its computer and electronic components industries. Still, the French industry remained unprofitable, and the gap between the French and their Japanese and American competitors was widening. In 1980, only 6 percent of total French business turnover was in electronics, compared to 46 percent for the United States and 20 percent for Japan. In 1982, France imported most of its electronics from the United States and Japan. Its trade deficit in the industry was 11 billion francs. The French realized that without their own high-tech production they could not expect to be a world industrial leader.

The government's response followed France's traditional interventionist pattern. *A filière électronique* was proposed in which plans and financing of upstream products like semiconductors were to be linked to those for downstream products such as computers and consumer electronics. In this way, government policymakers assumed that it would be possible to maintain a French line in all electronics products. Very early, however, it became clear that this plan was impossible to implement, for it lacked business logic: the links between the various industries were more theoretical than real. Moreover, it was far too costly for France to maintain or create a presence in all electronics industries.

The major electronics companies—Bull in computers, Thomson in consumer electronics, and CGE (Companie Générale d' Electricité) in telecommunications—were all nationalized in 1981, and new managers were appointed by the government. The companies were encouraged to exchange certain divisions to eliminate competing product lines. Fortunately, however, the government very early abandoned its attempts to establish a *filière électronique*. Remarked one manager, "It was the idea of some bureaucrat who had never set foot in a company."[13]

Some of the newly appointed managers were a different breed of socialists. Many had business training and experience, and most of them were committed to reducing their dependence on the state by making their companies profitable. The first challenge they faced was cutting costs while improving productivity and fostering an environment conducive to innovation. Thomson's president, Alain Gomez, for example, decided to set a new tone by reducing the corporate staff; several hundred managers were told to seek employment in one of the subsidiaries. After one year only one third of the staff remained at the plush corporate headquarters. To head the key divisions, new managers with tough performance standards were hired from private firms such as Texas Instruments.

But the government's policy of managerial autonomy for these companies was not absolute. When Gomez attempted to sell an unprofitable medical instruments subsidiary to an American firm, the government stopped him. If Thomson had sold the subsidiary, France would no longer have a national producer of medical instruments, something the socialists deemed to be in the national interest.

Similarly, the government was concerned about the videocassette recorder industry. Since France had no national manufacturers, Japanese VCRs were selling well during the 1982 Christmas season. Concerned about its balance of trade, the government delayed the Japanese machines in customs to keep them off the market, in much the same way that Barre in the mid-1970s had prevented an influx of Japanese cars. Ironically, the state-sponsored delays were a hardship for Thomson, since it was selling some of the Japanese VCRs under its own label. Thus once again French industry suffered from protectionist measures introduced ostensibly in the national interest.

After the first few years, the socialist attitude to foreign penetration of the electronics industry shifted. Bull and Thomson have been allowed joint ventures and licensing agreements with both Japanese and American companies. With the example of the successful Japanese strategy of late entry into electronics, French managers convinced the state that it was cheaper to buy the dominant technology than to develop a uniquely French one.

The results have been promising. Thomson's losses fell from $260 million in 1982 to $14 million in 1984, and CGE remains very profitable. Bull is doing less well, but it, too, has cut its losses.[14]

The changed climate in these companies, however, is more striking than the improved performance. The old sclerotic managers have retired or been replaced. And, at all levels, employees are forced to be concerned about productivity, competitiveness, and efficiency. In many cases, they are even paid and evaluated on the basis of their performance.

The French have chosen to develop competitive firms, even

if it means layoffs, risky long-term investments, and foreign links. France's late entry into high-tech industries, combined with ineffective or damaging public policies, however, has put French firms at a competitive disadvantage. Nevertheless, the new managers are doing their best to manage by the traditional capitalist criterion of profitability. And most important, there is now a consensus that this is in the national interest, a consensus forced by the reality of global competition.

The Lessons of Socialism in Power

In the spring of 1986, the socialist government faced its biggest challenge—an electoral one. The explanations for the decline in support for the socialists include the bizarre revival of the nineteenth-century anticlerical debate. In the 1960s, de Gaulle had restored state funds to Catholic schools. But when anticlerical socialists in 1983 introduced a bill in the National Assembly to fully integrate Catholic school teachers into the national education system, over one million protesters took to the streets. A mix of liberal individualists, Catholics, and social democrats, they accused the socialists of "collectivist Jacobinism" bent on destroying the individual citizen's right to choose a form of education for his children. The event illustrates how the socialists had forgotten that the French social democratic tradition was also strongly individualist.

The second reason for the loss of support for the left has been a wide public disappointment over the decline of French *grandeur.* Although Mitterrand's foreign policy has continued in the Gaullist tradition of French greatness, as the alternative to the two superpowers, his domestic policies have demonstrated only weakness. In the short run, France has experienced record unemployment, lower growth, and higher inflation than most of its trading partners. And if the French voted Giscard out of office for his insensitivity to these domestic aspects of *grandeur,* there is no reason to believe that they will be more tolerant of Mitterrand in the presidential election of 1988.

The socialists, however, are not entirely to blame for these problems. Given their inexperience at governing, the socialists not surprisingly had some difficulties implementing their ideology. Unfortunately, their experimentation took place during a world recession and in the context of intensifying world competition. Furthermore, some of their early Keynesian policies had serious, and damaging, repercussions for business and the entire French economy. But their willingness to reverse direction when their policies were shown to be too costly demonstrated their flexibility and pragmatism. In the end, the Socialists, too, oriented the national interest toward competitive business.

The balance sheet is not all negative. The socialist experiment has had an important impact on the political and ideological configuration of France. First, the left has learned a lesson about international economic interdependence, and it seems that the French electorate has learned the same lesson. In the future, ideologies and policies whose major premise is the isolation and protection of France from the world will be treated with considerable skepticism. Quite bluntly, the electorate has witnessed the failure of these policies. Faced with the continued erosion of its electorate and of traditional Jacobin beliefs, even the communists are now discussing "new criteria of competitiveness" instead of the traditional defense of declining French industries. The only remaining isolationist groups in France today are on the far authoritarian right.

A second important lesson of the socialist experiment centers around French attitudes toward business. In the past, a majority of French citizens mistrusted business and disdained profits. Today, the French of all ideological schools are reconciled to, if not completely supportive of, business. In political debates, all three leading opposition candidates, like the socialist prime minister, stress the importance of free competitive enterprises. Mathematics, instead of philosophy and the classics, is now the most popular high school major, schools of business are flooded with applicants, and socialist heads of nationalized companies are seeking financing on the international capital markets.

In spite of decades of anticapitalist rhetoric, the socialists have succeeded in reconciling France to the legitimacy of business. But they have done so in the name of *grandeur,* or French national interest, not by calling up the liberal ghosts of Adam Smith's invisible hand.

THE FUTURE OF FRENCH IDEOLOGY

Ideology has not lost its salience in French politics: it continues to set the parameters for acceptable policies. France is still divided between the left and the right, but the positions share more premises. Beliefs appear to converge around an ideology aimed at global competitiveness, although national opinion is still divided about whether that ideology is individualist or communitarian.

Growth, *grandeur,* and an important role for the state are values shared by all ideological schools. But the ideological groups are still separated by their priorities and their allocations of rights and duties. The left continues to emphasize social justice and equal distribution; the right prefers individualism and equality of opportunity. And though these differences may be based more on history than on any current reality, they continue to be reflected in the behavior of the French electorate.

Herein lie the key dilemmas for the French political system. Discourse has remained ideological to the point of potentially damaging French industry, but the profitability of French companies is better than it has been in years (see *Exhibits 3–1* through *3–6* at end of chapter). Managers are now freer to make necessary layoffs. Yet many managers have not increased their investments to levels expected by the state, and investment rates remain below 1980 levels (*Exhibit 3–5*). Some leaders of French management have said that many managers are waiting until the political right returns to power, hoping for a more favorable business climate. What these businessmen seem to have forgotten is that investments, as well as profits, were lower under the previous regimes.

When public debate about key social and economic issues is conducted at an ideological level, realistic options are not presented to the electorate. In the past, this has resulted in irresponsible campaign promises and unrealistic popular expectations, which render governing impossible. Furthermore, both Barre and Mitterrand were forced by objective economic and political realities to do things that were not compatible with their respective ideologies. And without a consensus around national policy objectives, it has been more difficult for them to develop practices that will help France respond and adapt to world competition. The socialists may have laid the foundation for that consensus, but France has not thereby been given the internal stability necessary to meet the challenge.

The governing majority was defeated in the spring 1986 legislative elections. Even with a return to a form of proportional representation, the political party of Jacques Chirac is likely to prevail. Interestingly enough, Barre has not specifically criticized the current economic policies of the socialists. To be sure, he faults them for the weak currency and their loss of business confidence, both of which weaken companies and lead to high unemployment. But, if he were in power, his policies would differ only slightly from those of the government.

Chirac, on the other hand, has described himself as a "supply-sider," and he has said that one of his priorities would be the denationalization of many firms. Unless carried out slowly and cautiously, this could be a very costly reversal, undermining many of the very successful strategic and managerial reorientations that have taken place since 1981. It is unclear whether the French capital markets could absorb such a flood, and whether the nationalistic French would allow major penetration of foreign capital.

Both right-wing contenders, Barre and Chirac, have heavily criticized the socialists for seriously limiting managerial flexibility. The inability to lay off excess employees is a major source of French uncompetitiveness, they argue. What they neglect to add, as we have seen, is that the earliest and toughest limitations on layoffs were enacted under the right-wing government of Prime Minister Chirac and the liberal presidency of Giscard.

Once again the financial health of a business enterprise would be secondary to an ideological interpretation of the public interest. The combination of political pragmatism and ideology continues to baffle Anglo-Saxon observers.

Exhibit 3-1

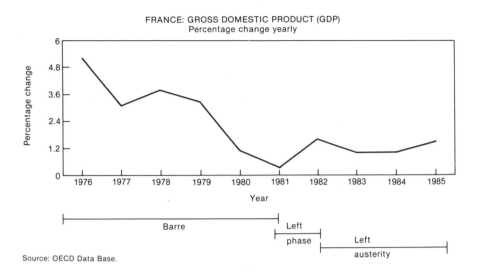

FRANCE: GROSS DOMESTIC PRODUCT (GDP)
Percentage change yearly

Source: OECD Data Base.

Exhibit 3-2

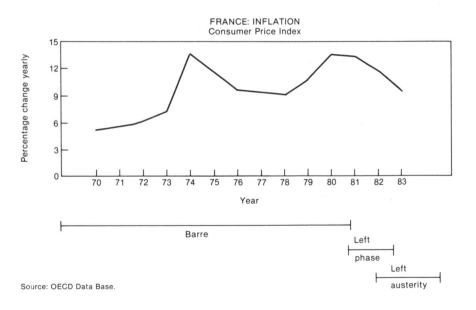

FRANCE: INFLATION
Consumer Price Index

Source: OECD Data Base.

Exhibit 3-3

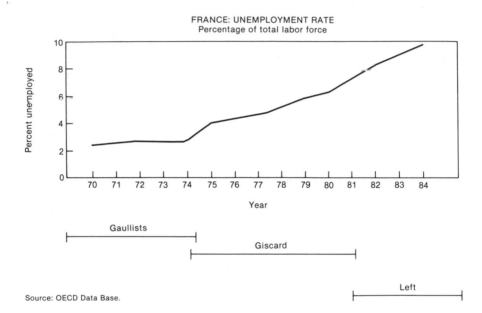

FRANCE: UNEMPLOYMENT RATE
Percentage of total labor force

Source: OECD Data Base.

Exhibit 3–4

PRIVATE INVESTMENT

Index 1970 = 100		
Giscard	1970	100
	1974	118
	1975	108
	1976	118
	1977	110
	1978	112
Barre	1979	112
	1980	118
Left	1981	110
	1982	111
	1983	100
	1984	101
	1985	110

Source: Compiled by author.

Exhibit 3–5

MINIMUM WAGE TRENDS

Percent Annual Increase		
Giscard-Chirac/Barre	1974–76 average	19.0%
Giscard-Barre	1977	12.7
	1978	12.9
	1979	12.5
	1980	
Socialists-phase 1	1981	18.1
	1982	17.6
Socialists-austerity	1983	12.2
	1984	

Source: OECD Economic Surveys, *France.*

Exhibit 3–6

PROFITS

Companies' Percent of Value Added		
1976	26.4	
1977	27.0	
1978	27.5	Right
1979	25.8	
1980	24.6	
1981	23.7	
1982	24.1	Left phase 1
1983	25.0	
1984	27.8	Left austerity
1985	29.0	

Source: Compiled by author.

Exhibit 3–7

FRANCE: IDEOLOGICAL DIVISIONS AND THE GLOBAL REALITY

Profits		
Companies' Percent of Value Added		
1976	26.4	
1977	27.0	
1978	27.5	Right
1979	25.8	
1980	24.6	
1981	23.7	
1982	24.1	Left phase 1
1983	25.0	
1984	27.8	Left austerity
1985	29.0	

Source: Compiled by author.

4

GERMANY

Competing Communitarianisms

Christopher S. Allen

For at least two centuries, ideology in Germany has been strongly influenced by collective institutions and forms of social organization. From the remnants of feudalism that lingered in the numerous German principalities of the late eighteenth century, to the increasingly dominant role of the Prussian (and, after 1871, German) state in the nineteenth, to the Weberian distinctions between *Gemeinschaft* and *Gesellschaft,* and to the European continental public law tradition that has encouraged the formation of institutions for reconciling private and public interests,[1] a communitarian paradigm has found solid footing in German society. More important for this volume, the German pattern stands in sharp contrast to the individualism of the Anglo-Saxon countries.

Historically, Germany has experienced more than just one form of communitarianism. Since the nineteenth century, German institutions have nurtured and shaped several ideologies that have contended with one another for economic, political, and social influence. Generally, these competing collectivist

79

ideologies have overridden the far weaker strands of German individualism because government, business, and labor in Germany have sought and found legitimacy for their actions by fulfilling the needs of the community as their first priority. Satisfying the needs of the individual was perceived as being secondary. However, within German communitarianism there have been and are serious tensions.

Events following World War II increased the influence of individualism in a country in which hitherto it had been scarcely visible. But the increase in individualism after 1945 is superficial, not at all a fundamental shift away from historical German communitarian ideology and practice. The real change in postwar West Germany is that its major institutions are dominated by an ideology of nonstatist rather than statist communitarianism.

HISTORICAL DOMINANCE OF IDEOLOGY

Communitarianism evolved in Germany somewhat differently than in other Western European nations. Although it too traced its origins from feudalism, the German version took a more fragmented form. Each of the numerous principalities during the late eighteenth and early nineteenth centuries had its own collective institutions, and each reflected a variant of communitarian ideology. National political unification did not occur until 1871.

Before 1871, the province of Prussia was clearly dominant. Possessing a more authoritarian communitarian ideology and practice, Prussian leaders during the early nineteenth century relied on political might and economic strength to achieve increasing hegemony over the other German states. One early example of Prussian economic strength was the establishment in 1834 of a customs union (*Zollverein*) that began to regularize trade among many of the larger principalities, thus helping to pave the way for national political unification thirty-seven years later.

Drawing upon the theories of Fichte and especially Hegel,[2] Prussian leaders blamed their loss of European influence on Napoleon. The remedy for their economic and political fragmentation was to centralize power within a national state. In fact, Hegel argued that only through a strong state could individuals find fulfillment. Opposition to Prussian dominance came from the other provinces and from wary private and parapublic organizations.[3] Not surprisingly, individualistic impulses proved extremely weak in this type of environment—witness the failed liberal revolution of 1848. From these piecemeal beginnings, communitarian ideology in Germany grew deep and tenacious historical roots.

Germany was a late industrializer, some seventy-five years behind Britain, and even thirty to fifty years behind the U.S. textile industry. In the mid-nineteenth century it regarded itself as a victim of "economic backwardness."[4] Indeed, the persistence of feudal elements well into the nineteenth century dramatically retarded the emergence of independent entrepreneurs. It therefore appeared increasingly unlikely that the Germans could generate sufficient capital for economic development by relying on the spontaneity of markets and on individual investors. In short, if Germany wished to compete with countries already playing a leading role in the world economy, it could not afford to do so by waiting for the free market to extend a helping unseen hand. To Germany's economic and political elites, an industrial policy that specifically addressed the challenge of "catching up" with more advanced nations was required.

An initial inflow of foreign, largely British, funds led to the development of German investment banks, accompanied by investment capital provided by the Prussian and (after 1871) German government. Banks, industrial cartels, and the state decided which sectors were to evolve, adapt, and develop. Thus did Germany's rail, coal, steel, chemical, and electrical industries achieve dominance. In the late nineteenth century Germany became a "first mover"[5] in the industries of the "second" industrial revolution.[6] Germany's industrial development, like that of Japan, was one of "organized capitalism," as Rudolf Hilferding described it during the early years of this century: banks, cartels, and large corporations played an even larger role than the powerful imperial German state in shaping the communitarian framework within which businesses adapted to competition. This pattern, once established in the late nineteenth century, continued to play a significant role throughout the twentieth century.

Just as Germany initially lacked the necessary capital to generate economic growth, so too did it confront a shortage of industrial workers. When German heavy industrial expansion shot forward in the 1850s and 1860s, German firms in the Ruhr (by then under Prussian control) faced a desperate labor shortage. The region's employers recruited thousands of peasants from Prussia and from Poland to work in the coal mines and the iron foundries. German trade unions arose. Their ideology was communitarian but of a decidedly different stripe from that of German industry. The general economic and social dislocation produced by rapid industrialization, the attraction for German workers of the ideas of Marx and other German Socialists, and the fact that these peasant/workers collectively faced the same kind of subordinate relationship with their new industrial employers as with their old feudal ones meant that the Socialist trade unions would be the collective expression of the working class in the market arena against the capitalist owners.[7] The ideology of the trade unions and the newly formed Social Democratic Party (SPD) was also underpinned by the desire for political democracy which the Prussian (and, after 1871, German) leaders tried to suppress.

By the end of the nineteenth century, employers and the German state's political leaders were fearful that the nation's rapid industrialization would be impeded by adverse world economic conditions, by the increasingly militant trade unions, and by the expanding Social Democratic Party as it gained strength in the *Reichstag* (Parliament). In the late 1870s and the early 1880s Bismarck responded in two ways. He banned the SPD with his "anti-Socialist" legislation, and he initiated numerous welfare state measures, thereby stealing some of the labor movement's thunder by developing one of the earliest systemic forms of *modern* communitarian institutional practice.[8] Bismarck acted both because of his concern for the country's political economy and because he doubted whether individual industrialists would be able to see beyond their own specific interests to those of the economy as a whole.[9]

The outlawed SPD grew still stronger as an underground movement in the 1880s, then was made legal again in the 1890s.

While Bismarck's intervention was a maneuver to co-opt the nascent German left, its legacy remained within both the "political arm" and the "labor arm" of the organized working class.[10] The state's action in the 1880s imposed heavy restrictions on the working class, but it also provided considerable benefit in the form of social insurance and welfare programs, a fact not lost on the leaders of the German left. Trade-union leaders thus came to believe that if they failed to attain the goals they considered most important by their struggles in the labor market, they could then turn to political action via the SPD and the state.

By the first decade of the twentieth century the unions had lost some of the communitarian belief in worker control held by the labor movement in the 1870s and 1880s. By identifying their fate with their respective firms, many of whom (in concert with the German state) became increasingly militaristic, the trade unions and Social Democratic Party were ill-placed to challenge the direction of the political economy.[11] Major portions of the trade unions and the SPD supported the declaration of war in 1914, a decision that caused a deep split on the left, both within Germany and internationally,[12] and proved a disaster for German society. When the Kaiser abdicated after World War I in 1918, the democratic Weimar Republic, having precious few defenders, was hurriedly erected.

In Weimar Germany the ideological cleavages were mostly among competing conceptions of communitarianism. Initially, the Weimar government was controlled by the reformist Social Democratic Party, which thought that by attaining the "commanding heights" of the economy, it could attain a social democratic society. During 1918–19, militant independent Socialists demanded workers councils (*Arbeiterraete*) in all factories to democratize decisions within the firm, but instead the SPD-led Weimar government institutionalized the less threatening works councils (*Betriebsraete*), which left power in the hands of management.[13] The Communist party's determination to seize state power became increasingly unattainable as the party lost sight of distinctions between German interests and Soviet ones. The Catholic Center Party hoped to alleviate the growing class conflict by calls to Christian brotherhood. The conservative large industrialists, who were plainly uncomfortable with the unstable Weimar democracy, preferred a more authoritarian and hierarchical society. Finally, the Nazis seized state power to attain some mythical and glorious past. Hitler's totalitarianism—clearly the most extreme form of communitarianism and one that obliterated all other competing visions—was made possible by the collapse of the Weimar democracy, itself weakened further by the total inability of opposition parties to unite to challenge the Nazis; by a severe depression that devastated an economy already vulnerable because of its lack of natural resources, its export dependence, and an extensive welfare state; and by Nazi Germany's xenophobic siege mentality, intensified by its hatred for its central European neighbors and all "inferior" races.

Without doubt, then, Germany's ideological history until 1945 was dominated by communitarianism. A strong state and a strong oligopolistic private sector derived from Germany's need to industrialize rapidly in the nineteenth century. Modernization was thus imposed before traditional feudal communitarianism had declined and before Western individualism had become an alternative.

INDIVIDUALISM IN CONTEMPORARY WEST GERMANY

For Germany, 1945 marked a great divide. To the geographic, economic, and political divisions was added a new ideological division when individualism increased its penetration into West Germany. Individualism grew in Germany after World War II, first and most obviously through the role of the United States as an occupation power. In seeking to resuscitate the destroyed German economy, the American economic advisors relied on their own conceptions of how a national economy was to function. As they did in Japan, the Americans, relying on an antitrust ideology, broke up some of the large economic units.[14] And, due to the Nazi abuses, the central government had been thoroughly discredited as the dominant economic and political actor. In 1949 the framers of the Federal Republic introduced a federal system of regional governments (the *Laender*) because they feared that a centralized public sector could again be used by an undemocratic movement for evil ends.

The democratic order that began in 1949 owed much to the small classical liberal Free Democratic Party (FDP). Except for the Christian Democratic Union-Christian Social Union (CDU–CSU) majority (1957–61) and the Social Democratic-Christian Democratic "Grand Coalition" (1966–69), the FDP has participated in *every* cabinet since 1949, and it has almost always controlled the important Economics Ministry. When Helmut Schmidt was chancellor of the Federal Republic during the late 1970s, the left wing of his own Social Democratic Party argued that his policies were too conservative. Schmidt offered as his primary defense the FDP's presence as the minority member of his coalition. He claimed that, in the interest of the coalition, less collectivist policies would have to be employed. Schmidt's moderate course led to the FDP's being called in the early 1980s the "tail that wagged the (SPD) dog." So the FDP was not merely a junior partner of the SPD from 1969 to 1982 but a major force in the coalition. Just as the FDP restricted the statist communitarianism of the SPD, it also inhibited the more active nonstatist communitarianism ("organized capitalism") of many Christian Democrats.

The "Social Market economy" (*Sozialemarkwirtschaft*) of the center-right CDU/CSU–FDP coalitions during the 1950s and early 1960s also placed greater emphasis on the individual. Its goal was a socially responsible capitalism. The Social Market economy saw a modern welfare state grow and provide collective benefits for money. But it also saw more mobile individuals, the growth of mass production industries, and the development of American style consumerism in West Germany.

Germany's geographic position on the USSR's frontier reinforced the procapitalist (and fervent anti-Communist) tendencies of the early 1950s, serving as a sharp brake on economic and political innovation beyond the initial welfare state benefits of the Social Market economy. Conservatives simply pointed to East Germany, described by many as either the "Soviet zone of occupation" or the "so-called" German Democratic Republic, as a profoundly negative example of socialism. The Cold War thus had considerable impact on West German domestic politics. For example, the trade-union confederation, *Deutsche Gewerkschaftsbund* (DGB) and the Social Democrats wanted to nationalize industries that had collaborated with the Nazis. The trade unions also wanted full participation (*Mitbestimmung*) for workers and unions on the boards of directors of all major West German corporations, and influence on the shop floor via the works councils (*Betriebsraete*). But these demands were quickly beaten back in the more conservative climate of the late 1940s.

Given the flowering of individualistic impulses, it is not surprising that outsiders saw Germany as more individualistic than it was. When the American advisors attempted to apply strict antitrust guidelines in the late 1940s, they failed to realize that, for the Germans, large firms were the norm and not the exception. Yet when U.S. policymakers wanted to see an economically strong West Germany in the mid-1950s, they were quick to forgive West German industrialists for returning to old and familiar forms of "organized capitalism." Again the analogy to Japan is relevant. For, in praising the West German "economic miracle" of the 1950s, American observers saw individualism and not the more accurate communitarianism, which by then was largely nonstatist.

Americans—and those Germans who saw America in an especially favorable light—overlooked the more collectivist forms of social organization that prevailed, particularly in the private sector. In essence, the dominant communitarian ideology in Germany was far from dead. Even though the central state had declined in importance in postwar West Germany, the banks and industry associations (*Verbaende*) continued to play a crucial role in economic change. Collectivist institutions such as employer associations and unions had competed with one another during the late nineteenth and early twentieth centuries, and the same competition reemerged after 1945. The unions and the Social Democratic Party continued to offer their respective visions during the 1950s and 1960s; they were still Marxist at first but became more moderate in the late 1950s and early 1960s. Yet they were never able to overcome the obstacles to rebuilding a strong statist communitarian ideology until their qualified successes during the center/left coalition of the 1970s and early 1980s.

NONSTATIST COMMUNITARIANISM IN WEST GERMANY

A nonstatist vision of communitarianism prevails in West Germany today. Its practice is readily apparent in the framing rather than the directing role of the state in economic management, in labor relations, and in the rights and duties connected with collectivist versions of prosperity. By implication, this means that considerable power resides in the institutionalized, yet still private, sector: the organizations of entities such as banks and the *Verbaende.*

Role of the State in Economic Management

Economic competition in Germany has always been intimately bound up with the international issues of obtaining sufficient natural resources and gaining access to world markets. The heavy dependence of the nation's large corporations on exports made it essential that industry work closely with the banks and the state to better Germany's international position.

Germany controlled its industry through charter, that is, state ownership, during the imperial period, the Weimar Republic, and the Third Reich. The most well-known example of this private sector–public sector collaboration was Bismarck's "arranged marriage of iron and rye"[15] in the late nineteenth century. Together with the Ruhr steel barons and the Prussian grain-growing feudal lords, Bismarck embarked upon a policy of strategic protectionism that temporarily sheltered these industries from international competition. Bismarck's goal was to reconcile antagonistic elements in German society. More important, however, the policy fostered demand for the growth of the railroads because grain had to be transported from Prussia to the West, and the building of the railroads required massive quantities of steel and bank capital. The ultimate purpose of these and other policies in newly emerging sectors was to insure that Germany would be able to compete internationally.

Germany's policies during the late nineteenth and early twentieth centuries mirrored those of late twentieth-century Asian nations. All industrialized late, were poor in resources, and depended heavily on exports.

Since 1945 the *central* state's direct involvement in the control of firms and industries has been sharply curtailed. More limited relationships prevail: partnership between the central government and industry is now quite common in steel, oil, shipbuilding, automobiles (VW), and electronics, and strategic regulation is even more common.

Regulation in Germany always has some strategic national purpose: an active labor-market policy to smooth the movement of workers from one industry to another; the development of a craft-based apprenticeship system to maintain needed skilled workers; the funding of a ministry of research and technology to help industry develop promising new products; and the demand that the ailing steel industry decrease its capacity. German business does not adopt an antagonistic attitude toward these measures because it perceives that the state's regulation is undertaken for the long-run economic good of the firm or industry.

In essence, the present role of the central state is a "framing" one[16]: through its active monetary and fiscal policies it helps shape the arena within which the private sector can best compete internationally.

Despite the obvious decrease in the role of the central government, the definition of community need in contemporary West Germany still takes place in largely communitarian terms. Three large banks play a dominant role in the raising of capital as they continue to hold major voting blocks of shares in the large German firms. *Bundesvereinigung der Deutschen Arbeitgeberverbände* (BDA), the employers' association, the Federal Association of German Industry (BDI), and certain industry-specific associations have stepped into the vacuum created by decreased central state activity. Generically they are known as the *Verbaende*.

The regional governments (the *Laender*) have become a major source of power in postwar West Germany. In conjunction with industry associations, these *Land* governments have evolved a network of "parapublic institutions" and "private interest governments"[17] that are profoundly communitarian but do not involve the *central* state as the dominant force. The *Laender* partially own certain firms, develop regional growth plans, and set educational requirements that meet the needs of the region's inhabitants.

The regional governments will become even more important. Germany's strategy for economic adaptation relies on manufacturing high value-added products in traditional industries, using a combination of applied technologies and highly skilled and flexible workers.[18] Mass production industries will become increasingly less dominant as Germany develops its version of high technology. Since the regional governments best know the needs of business and industry within their areas, they can most quickly implement policies for mobilizing and training Germany's only real natural resource—its highly skilled workers.

The West Germans have tried to involve all the major segments of society in the shaping of community need, although this has not always proved successful. Since the mid-1970s, the labor movement has walked out of the "concerted action" negotiations among unions, government, and business. And in 1986 a law was passed restricting unemployment benefits for locked-out workers. German institutions have not yet found ways to assimilate the members of the Green Party and other "alternative" elements in German society who question the very fundamentals of industrial capitalism. Yet most elites in Germany also feel that the Greens can eventually be assimilated in one way or another.

Perhaps the difficulty in defining community need during the late 1970s and early 1980s comes from Germany's attempt to combine a developmental national strategy—left over from its late industrializing period—with a distributional national strategy—left over from the postwar boom years.[19] Although the current period may not be a smooth one, few contemporary West Germans accept the notion that the definition of community need requires a stark choice between growth and equity. The concepts of economic, political, and social rights lie deep within the fabric of German society and will not easily be uprooted. At the same time there is a tradition of duty and a realistic recognition that international competition is necessary. Labor, for example, is well aware of low-cost (and low-wage) Asian competition. Nevertheless, the communitarian mechanisms of government, business, and labor seem to be much better prepared to deal with these tensions than their counterparts in Britain.[20]

Labor Relations

Relations between labor and management and between business and government are more strongly influenced in Germany by an institutionally mediated consensus than by the postwar impact of individualism. Many American advisors arrived in West Germany with the goals of establishing an American-style industrial relations system and embedding collective bargaining. The Americans were surprised to learn that these two goals were not only difficult to establish but that the terms for them did not even exist in the German language.

West Germany did develop a wage-bargaining system but the state-sanctioned works councils and codetermination played a more important role than open bargaining between contract partners. Employers and workers were left to establish the terms and functioning of that relationship within the private sector but in ways that were institutionally bounded. The tightly organized incomes policy arrangements, active statist models of corporatism[21] that developed in other Western European nations, enjoyed only a short life span in West Germany: from the late 1960s until the mid-1970s.

More commonly, IG Metall, the influential metalworkers' union that represents roughly one third of all organized workers in Germany, bargained first with the employers to set a pattern toward which the less powerful unions could then aim. BDA, the influential employers association, developed an elaborate system of consensus so that all members would follow these same guidelines in their dealings with the unions, on pain of paying sharp penalties for noncompliance.

Each of the two collective organizations had its own mechanisms for seeking and maintaining consensus in ways that hardly resembled American-style labor-management relations. The arrangements that characterized employer/union relationships were contractual, yet powerful institutional pressures retarded any rapid acceptance of adversarial Anglo-Saxon patterns of industrial relations.

The German labor movement and SPD continued to stress their prewar tendency toward equality of result. These Germans saw economic gains only as they benefited workers as a class rather than as individuals. Yet the German democratic left favored a collective demand for equal opportunity, whether by increasing worker participation in shaping industrial change or by increasing workers' purchasing power. Their goal was not for individuals to rise out of their class but for them to rise collectively with their class. For the left, the new institutions were not simply mechanisms for economic distribution, they were also vehicles by which working people could help shape economic growth. During the 1970s and 1980s, German unions achieved minor successes in the machine tool, automobile, and printing industries when they bargained on the issue of innovation.[22]

The heightened demand for equality by the left, however, was not able to override the old faith in hierarchy that remained strong among the conservative forces dominating economic and political life during the 1950s and early 1960s. In a country in which large firms were the major economic actors, persons who wished to succeed were promoted to leadership positions only by working diligently and patiently within their organizations. By the same token, individual mobility and equality of opportunity were retarded in the public sector by the well-entrenched civil service and the inegalitarian educational system. The student revolts and subsequent educational reforms of the late 1960s and early 1970s somewhat opened up the educational system. As late as 1968, West German elites in both the public and private sectors were still recruited from only 10 percent of the population.

Collective Property: Rights and Duties

A long history of feudal relationships has marked property with a communitarian dimension in Germany. Property was owned by ruling families in the nineteenth-century principalities, and the "subjects" had certain well-defined rights and duties.

The very concept of entrepreneurialism had a much more collective dimension for the German economic and political elites in the nineteenth century than it had in the United States. In 1888 the Chemical Industry Association (VCI), fully aware of the long-term technological requirements of the chemical sector, decided to allow the financial fruits of discoveries to accrue to the innovating firm, but VCI allowed the technology itself to be diffused to other firms in the sector almost immediately.[23]

The state, particularly under the leadership of Bismarck, also acted as a steward for the interests of collectively owned property during the late nineteenth and early twentieth centuries.[24] By its public ownership of the railroads, electric power, and communication, the state made it quite clear that the functions of this property served the direct interests of the citizens.

Just as property, and the rights thereto, were owned collectively by the private sector and the state, so too were they considered to be collectively owned by the labor movement, but with a different thrust. The speed and pace of industrialization during the late nineteenth and early twentieth centuries and the fact that there was little property ownership among the working class led German workers to hold a communitarian view of property. Many American workers rejected early American Socialist calls for the collectivization of private property because they thought it meant that they would lose their modest homes. German workers took a different stance. Because the private sector and the state in Germany had viewed property in "organized capital" or statist terms, because economic and political constraints made individual property ownership very difficult for many, and because land to own was simply not available, German workers demanded certain rights to collective property: nationalization of key industries, greater welfare state benefits, adequate public housing, and participation in the management of firms.

The deal that was eventually struck allowed citizens access to collective private and public property in return for following certain well-defined rules. This solution took tenuous hold during the Weimar period, then came completely apart during the Third Reich. Although the public ownership of property has been curtailed somewhat since 1945, and although the introduction of a stable democratic order has made certain duties of citizenship less onerous, the relationship between property and rights and duties remains heavily communitarian.

The generous West German welfare state benefits also remain, despite the economic downturn in Germany since the early 1980s. Rather than emphasizing means-testing as the Reagan administration now does, the Germans have retained universal welfare state coverage, a pattern of spending seen to have an overall positive economic function.[25] In addition, worker participation in management at the levels of both the shop floor and the board of directors; the recent agreements between the employers and the metalworkers' union over flexible work assignments; the absence of union demands for protectionism; and union sensitivity to the importance of international competitiveness offer testimony to the unions' understanding of and reliance upon both rights and duties rather than on Anglo-Saxon style adversarial contracts.

Yet it should be emphasized that, despite all the measures to involve unions and workers in major decision-making processes, the ultimate control of the key decisions remains quite clearly with the firms and private-sector institutions that dominate the private sector.

THE COURSE OF ECONOMIC ADAPTATION

By any sound comparative criteria, the German economy is the leading economy of Western Europe, its unemployment is only slightly higher than the "successful" American economy, and most of its export-oriented industries have done remarkably well, retaining key niches as the dollar has fallen in value.[26]

Sectors in the German Economy

One of the major characteristics of West Germany since 1975 is that groups of industries in the economy exhibit sharp differences in performance. The sectors fall into three groups. One group of industries is profoundly threatened and will most likely be radically contracted, if it does not disappear altogether. Steel and textiles are good examples, as in almost all industrialized nations. A second group of newer industries has been the most spectacular and fastest growing: computers, microelectronics, and consumer electronics. But the West German economy tends to be dominated by a third group of what we can call "fulcrum" sectors: machine tools, chemicals, automobiles, and industrial electronics. They are more "mature"[27] than the high-tech industries of the second group, but because they are still crucially important for the health of the national economy, they must be restructured.

These sectoral distinctions are particularly important for understanding German innovation. The performance of the fulcrum sectors has been much more competitive than the conventional wisdom would have it. Their "hidden" economic strength lies in the nature of production in these industries, where the application of high technology in the "unexciting" machine-tool sector reveals much more innovation and change than appear at first glance. In the electronics sector, Bosch and Siemens, on the one hand, should be seen separately from AEG on the other. One of AEG's many "mistakes"[28] was that it departed from the traditional strength of German electronics (industrial applications via specialized processes) and entered the consumer business without a clear strategy. Bosch and Siemens, however, have excelled by using "flexible system manufacturing"[29] via high value-added products aimed at certain niches in the world market. Moreover, the continued high quality of most of these products allows these firms to retain their export markets even as the dollar-DM exchange rate is reduced. Daimler Benz and BMW are familiar users of this strategy to Americans. Opel, Ford, and VW have had more difficulty as mass producers in adopting these new patterns.[30]

Yet the full extent of innovation and change in these sectors cannot be managed by the limited capacities of individual firms. They need the assistance of banks and industry organizations that can take a broader view of the environment in which these firms must compete. By the same token, this industry-specific nature of innovation cannot be adequately handled by clumsy macroeconomic policies. The fulcrum industries are successful in innovating because forces within, or close to, each sector can produce change at the industry level.

Components of "Organized Capitalism"

The distinction between microeconomics (the level of the firm) and macroeconomics (the level of the entire economy) may have to be supplemented by understanding how change takes place at the mesoeconomic (industry) level.[31] The strength of the mesoeconomic school's analysis is that it goes beyond the more static industry studies that have popped up since the debates about *Strukturpolitik* (and American industrial policy) arrived on the scene some years ago.[32] Peters and Preston, leading proponents of mesoeconomics, attempt to see this level of analysis as a strategy linking particular sectors with targeted policies that resonate both downward to the micro level and upward to the macro level.

Mesoeconomic policy in Germany is the contemporary form of "organized capitalism," the framework within which an industry's firms can adapt to changing international competition.[33] It is being executed, not by the national government, but by four sets of private and/or regional institutions: banks, industry organizations, *Laender* governments, and the skilled-worker-dominated trade unions.

Shonfield pointed out some years ago[34] that the structure of the West German banking system allows these vertically integrated institutions to own large blocks of stock in most major corporations in Germany. They can therefore stand above the (microeconomic) fray and understand how particular industries can best be shaped. By owning stock in all large German firms and by their positions on the boards of directors they are able to channel the direction that firms and industries will take toward economic adaptation. The major point to be stressed here is that these banks have massive capacities to intervene on a *sectoral* basis.

Germany's banks have historically been the primary source of its investment capital. One strategy pursued by the Deutsche Bank has been to establish five "in-house" venture capital firms. Each has complete autonomy to explore investment possibilities, but when one presents the bank with a likely target, officers can quickly mobilize the bank's considerable resources.[35] Germany was never first on the industrial scene. Its institutions were designed to maximize the advantage of the

latecomer, by finding unfilled niches. Bank officials see no
reason to extensively foster small firms now when they have
never played a large role in Germany's economy. The primary
importance of the small firm is its function as a supplier to
some of the more well-known large firms. Because large firms
have great ideological legitimacy, the executives within them
have a stronger incentive to transform these large firms to meet
changing patterns of world competition than to let them fail
and start smaller ones afresh. The banks realize that the costs
of the latter policy would be unbearable for German stability.
Thus, it may be much too soon to rule out the innovative
capacity of large German institutions (banks and large firms)
before this phase of industrial innovation has run its course.
An aide to Deutsche Bank Chairman Wilfried Guth said, of the
relationship between the banks and innovation in Germany,
"The Deutsche Bank was founded in 1870. In other words, one
year before there was a Germany there was a Deutsche Bank."
He paused and continued, "Regimes come and regimes go, but
we will always be here."[36]

Industry organizations also play a crucial role in shaping
sectoral economic policy. The term *Rahmenbedingungen* (inad-
equately translated into English as "framework policies") is
used frequently in discussions of the role of these sectoral-level
institutions. The difficulty of translating the term into English
suggests an important ideological distinction between American and German versions of these organizations. Industry organizations in the United States are often special-interest groups
or lobbying organizations whose main function is to limit
defensively the damage of public-sector policies or to protect
against unfair competition from comparable industries in other
countries. In Germany, on the other hand, industry organizations distinguish between *Strukturpolitik* and *Ordnungspolitik*[37]
in their relationship to government. *Strukturpolitik* is difficult
to translate; its closest English approximation is "industrial
policy." *Ordnungspolitik* is also difficult to translate precisely;
"policies of order" is the closest English translation. This term,
too, suggests an ideological difference between the strategic
role of these institutions in Germany—setting the "framework" for industrial "order"—and the essentially defensive
or lobbying role of their counterparts in the United States.

Strukturpolitik is to be avoided because it allows the public sector too much involvement with the direction of the industry. *Ordnungspolitik* is preferable since firms and industry organizations play the dominant role. *Ordnungspolitik* was at work in the chemical industry's careful planning at the sectoral level to change its raw materials base from a dependence on coal in the early 1950s to a dependence on oil by the 1960s and 1970s. The industry is currently investigating whether it can make a comparable switch to depend more extensively on biotechnology.

The third component of West Germany's strategy for industrial adaptation is the regional (*Land*) governments. The *Laender* of Baden-Wuerttemburg and Bavaria have taken major industrial-policy initiatives toward transforming the economies of their regions.[38] They arrange creative public-sector financing, promote exports, and commit significant funds and policies toward vocational education so that the public sector can create the proper framework for innovation and change. This public-sector change at the "mesopolitical," not at the "macropolitical," level deserves notice. Because the Kohl government seems unable to translate the regional successes of fellow conservatives—Baden-Wuerttemburg and Bavaria are governed by the CDU and CSU, respectively—into comparable policies at the national level. In fact, the *Land* governments in North Rhine-Westphalia and Bremen, where the SPD is in power, seem to be more interested in adapting these mesopolicies for regional ends than is the Kohl government in adapting them for national purposes. Successes for the SPD in these *Laender* could be important for the national SPD when it attempts to return to national political power after the 1987 election.

A fourth component of innovative economic adaptation is the skill base of German workers. Long a crucial factor in Germany's economic strength, the role these workers play has often been overlooked by those who wish to innovate as quickly as possible. West German employers and regional governments—if not the Kohl government—have refrained from embarking on British and American "union bashing" because they realize that unionized workers are skilled workers, and that Germany's fulcrum sectors need them to adapt and remain internationally competitive. And, because they are organized on an industry (not company) basis, they can better see how their skills can contribute to industrial adaptation. The German unions have a large stake in the upgrading of worker skills. For decades they have provided input into the vocational education system. Germany's use of skilled workers in flexible-system manufacturing[39] (high value-added products in fulcrum industries that combine applied technologies and skilled workers) should be juxtaposed to declining U.S. strength in high tech. Only then can the question of which country has the more successful model of adaptation be answered.

Piore and Sabel's suggestion of Germany's "hidden adaptiveness" is reinforced by another recent study. Horst Kern and Michael Schumann, German industrial sociologists,[40] have argued that the role of unionized skilled workers is a crucial reason for innovation and adaptation in the chemical, automobile, and machine-tool sectors.[41] Unlike Piore and Sabel, who stop short of speculation, Kern and Schumann argue that these adaptations represent an opportunity for the German labor movement to build a "producer consciousness"; they believe that labor can play an important role in restructuring the economy by shaping progressive economic and social change. Whether the flexible system could be applied to the entire labor movement or would be viable in only a few sectors remains unclear. The labor movement is also part of Germany's *Ordnungspolitik*, thus giving it a legitimacy in helping frame community need. One example is the German labor movement's unwillingness to resort to protectionist demands. Because the trade unions have realized that one in every three manufacturing jobs depends on exports, they are committed to a strong export position for German industry. In these circumstances, the German labor movement's claim to speak for all workers makes labor far less likely to be branded as a "special interest."

POTENTIAL DARK CLOUDS

Several factors could adversely affect adaptation in Germany. Germany remains extremely export-dependent. Thus, any recession in the world economy would place great strains on firms in Germany's fulcrum sectors. Also, Germany has few natural resources, so any new oil shock or similar resource scarcity could leave the cost structure of German firms and industries in drastic disarray. Thus Germany has had to rely on a vast nuclear power industry. The emphasis on this controversial source of energy has represented a difficult choice for policymakers, unions, and particularly the Greens. Nuclear power has drawn militant opposition from the Greens and other "alternative" forces in society who argue that nuclear power represents an environmental time bomb. In addition, much of the new technology used by large industries has been highly capital-intensive. It therefore displaces many highly skilled workers who strongly resist the trend but produces high-paying jobs for the workers that remain. Some workers argue for a more economically sound development in which goods and services are produced so that jobs are created rather than destroyed. This last demand has been a centerpiece of the Greens' program, although they do not specify the concrete steps Germany should take to attain it.

Germany's pattern of high wages and welfare state spending is unlikely to decrease sharply. Although high wages are correlated with the high skill levels needed for flexible-system manufacturing, there are obviously competitive limits on labor costs. The relationship between how many German sectors could use this flexible-system model and how many would have a large number of structurally unemployed skilled workers might be another limiting factor. Steel and textiles are nonfulcrum sectors that have lost a considerable number of workers in the past decade. Whether the vocational education system can adequately train workers, and whether the fulcrum sectors can generate enough skilled jobs to avoid future difficulties remain unclear. Unemployment levels are currently only slightly higher than in the United States, but Germany's stronger commitment to provide benefits may become a burden for the present government. The perspective of the labor movement could be a problem if labor were to insist on reducing the work week to thirty-five hours (a current concern) without realizing the importance of finding its role in the process of innovation. Lastly, the Greens' overall impact on German capitalism remains uncertain.

SUMMARY AND PROSPECTS

Certain collectivist institutions shaped the emergence of both rapid industrialization and the formation of a German nation-state[42] in the late nineteenth century: large vertically integrated banks; cartels, often sanctioned by the new central government to compete with nations that had industrialized earlier; provincial governments and agencies that tried to challenge the often high-handed Prussian-dominated central state; the associations and groups of businessmen, farmers, artisans, and professionals (among others) that articulated the interests of their members to regional and national governments; the trade unions that emerged during industrialization by drawing on the producer traditions of the preindustrial feudal guilds; and the public-sector, social-welfare institutions established by Bismarck to counter the radical demands of the unions and the newly formed Social Democratic Party (SPD).

Events beyond German borders during the nineteenth and the first half of the twentieth centuries shaped the behavior of these statist and nonstatist collective institutions within German society, and thus helped form German ideology. The early industrialization of Britain, increased hostility with Germany's western and central European neighbors, the scramble for foreign colonies and their valuable raw materials (a contest in which Germany was the disadvantaged latecomer), World War I, the Great Depression, and the disaster of World War II, all provoked a profound and continuing sense of external threat among German political and industrial leaders as well as among the public at large. The institutions mentioned above claimed to respond to German needs to preserve and protect itself in a hostile world. By the onset of the Third Reich, these public and parapublic institutions had achieved wide social penetration—if not always legitimacy.

The post–World War II period, however, witnessed major institutional changes that have altered the structure and patterns of German life. Since 1945 these changes have made certain communitarian trends less visible than during the pre-ceding years. Despite these changes, there remains—as in Japan—a far more resilient communitarian ideology than many observers in both Germany and the United States realize. A misperception has emerged that contemporary German ideol-ogy has moved in a less communitarian direction in conse-quence of increased American influence, a vibrant capitalist economy, closer integration with other Western nations, and the pivotal role of the individualistic Free Democratic Party (FDP). On the contrary, communitarian ideology remains extremely strong, particularly in the private and parapublic institutions of West Germany. Policymakers who try to encour-age American-style individualistic solutions in a society that retains strong collective traditions in both public and, espe-cially, private sectors will probably prove increasingly ineffec-tual and perhaps even dysfunctional.

American perceptions to the contrary, Germany is and has always been dominated by both communitarian practice and ideology. The reasons for this are clear, given the economic and political patterns that have taken shape since the late nineteenth century. Indeed, the contemporary economic chal-lenges facing the Federal Republic can be met by utilizing communitarian practices more effectively than by replacing them. This issue is especially important if West Germany is to manage the conflicts that may result from more adverse eco-nomic circumstances. Germany is a highly organized society that has only slight tolerance for error. Thus ideological con-sistency is particularly important, especially as ideology relates to economic adaptation in managing West Germany's crucially important sectors: automobiles, chemicals, industrial electron-ics, and machine tools.

For Germany to adapt successfully to the changing world environment in the 1980s and 1990s, its combative (in German terms) industrial relations of recent years must be amicably resolved. Both the private sector and the labor movement must recognize the legitimacy of the other's communitarian views. It appears that Germany can best shape its comparative advan-tage by moving away from mass production of simple technol-ogy goods, relying instead on specialized manufacture of products of advanced technology. But to do so requires secure and highly skilled workers. That, in turn, will require increased worker participation in enterprises by fully using existing social structures. If Germany is to retain its economic strength, it will be by institutionally limiting and resolving the conflicts among business, labor, and government. In short, if innovation is to come in Germany, it will take a communitarian form, not an individualistic one.

5

THE UNITED STATES

The Costs of Ambivalence

George C. Lodge

From their beginnings in the seventeenth century, Americans have been divided in their devotion to the ideologies of individualism and communitarianism. They have unquestionably preferred the former—it is in fact the crystallization of the American Dream—but they have moved pragmatically toward the latter to confront problems and seize opportunities. If we look back on U.S. history, this ambivalence may have been beneficial: it committed Americans to that peculiar combination of pluralism and unity, conflict and consensus, personal freedom and national strength, that has contributed much to their preeminence as a community. If we look forward, its benefits are by no means as clear.

For half a century a crescendo of events in the real world, domestically and abroad, has accelerated a drift toward communitarian practices. At home this has included the Great Depression, the rise of the large publicly held corporation, the growth in the size and functions of government, the rising expectations of the citizenry, and the insights of ecologists; in the world it has comprised: World War II, the Cold War, the oil shock, and East Asian competition. The last of these is particularly poignant: for the first time there is considerable evidence that some communitarian nations are more competitive than the United States.[1]

These events have forced departure from preferred traditions. To respond to them, government, business, trade unions, and other institutions have been required to behave differently. The departure, however, is often confused and retarded by a kind of guilt. Americans feel forced to act in a way that many feel is un-American; for some, irreligious.

If the exigencies of the real world require ideological change, and if the alternative is competitive deterioration in the world economy and disintegration at home, then ambivalence concerning the transition to a new ideology becomes costly. And if U.S. institutions continue to move toward communitarianism without Americans' fully appreciating the ideological implications of what is happening, there will be the further costs of inadvertence. These costs—social, political, and economic— are characteristics of what I have called elsewhere the American disease, a psychological disorder similar to that afflicting some young people who, refusing to face the reality of adulthood, escape into illusion and fantasy.[2] The treatment for persons suffering from denial of reality is remarkably similar to that for a community as a whole. It requires confronting experience and seeking out those elements that are most compatible with current reality, with what in this book we have been calling "the relevant context," elements that when strengthened and bound together are useful in shaping purpose and effective behavior. Concurrently, it is rejecting or suppressing those traditional elements that have been bypassed or are irrelevant to contemporary reality; it is saving the best of the old while moving toward the new.

THE HISTORICAL CONTEXT

Individualism

When the several American colonies were founded, their roots lay in various reformed versions of medieval communitarianism.

In Massachusetts a Puritan theocracy was committed to the foundation of a religious utopia freed from Old World corruption—"a city upon a hill," John Winthrop called it. Strict laws banned strangers from the pristine settlements, and the champions of God did daily battle with Mammon.[3]

Business flourished, however, and by 1700 the merchants of Boston had breached the old lines. Economic growth required trade with Europe; shipyards and other production facilities required workers. The new entrepreneurs resented the strictures of the traditional religious hierarchy; they were bad for business. Persecution "makes us stinke every wheare," the business-minded George Downing wrote Winthrop.[4]

During the next two hundred years, largely as a result of the workings of economic enterprise, Locke's principles of individualism came to be a complete rationale for the behavior of American institutions.* To tame and exploit a vast wilderness of unlimited resources and huge rewards was a task that meshed perfectly with the idea of individual fulfillment through aggressive and self-reliant struggle. Society was easily explained as loose congeries of individuals, not as the organic, hierarchical whole of the Middle Ages. The very nature of the colonial environment tended to guarantee that those who came to these shores and survived would be those who were willing and able to live by the ideas of individualism. The ideology was an inextricable part of the Declaration of Independence and the Constitution, where the sanctity of contracts and the promise of equality strengthened it.

Implicit in early America's conception of property rights was Adam Smith's view that each individual's use of property for his own self-interest would help make the good community. Smith combined the ideas of individualism and property with economic profit, demonstrating their advantages for the community as a whole. The main device to assure this happy outcome was competition: staunchly self-interested property owners were to use their property to compete in satisfying

---

*Locke's views were, of course, amended and popularized by many others. The thoughts of Montesquieu and Edmund Burke also greatly influenced the country's founders.

individual consumer desires in the marketplace. From such a natural law of human behavior would come an efficient economy and a good community.

Thus, two of the components of our individualist ideology—the rights of private property, and the mechanism of competition to control the uses of property—fell naturally into place. In such a setting, the role of government was clearly limited to protecting a person's body and property. Moving beyond this limitation would constitute an interference with the natural working of things and so curtail freedom and liberty. Federalist Paper No. 51 spoke of the need to design controls over the power of government so "that the private interests of every individual may be a sentinel over the public rights."

The need for inventions, new techniques, and ingenuity to exploit the vast resources of America with only a handful of people was a powerful natural spur to the urgent pursuit of science for practical ends. Americans followed the Newtonian way and took nature apart to learn how to use and control it, so the fifth component, scientific specialization, would also flourish. There was a clear belief that one could tinker at will with the parts and that somehow the whole would still be there, taking care of itself.

Locke's personal importance in revolutionary America can scarcely be overestimated. "Most Americans had absorbed Locke's works as a kind of political gospel," says Carl Becker.[5] Josiah Quincy, Jr., in his last will, dated 1774, left Locke's works to his son, "when he shall arrive to the age of fifteen years," adding, "May the spirit of liberty rest upon him!"[6] Thomas Jefferson in a letter to Dr. Benjamin Rush named Bacon, Newton, and Locke as "the three greatest men the world has ever produced. . . ."[7] Locke's influence is clear in the Declaration of Independence; so clear, in fact, that Richard H. Lee was led to charge that Jefferson had copied from Locke's *Two Treatises on Government.* Jefferson denied the charge of copying but added: "I did not consider it as any part of my charge to invent new ideas altogether and to offer no sentiment which had ever been expressed before."[8]

Alexis de Tocqueville was among the first to note the dangers accompanying individualism: its tendency toward incoherence and fragmentation, its aversion to government as an instrument for defining community need, its neglect of society as a whole. In 1840 he wrote, "Individualism . . . [at first] only saps the virtues of public life; but in the long run it attacks and destroys all others and is at length absorbed in downright selfishness."[9]

Communitarianism

Thomas Jefferson wanted to preserve the United States as an essentially rural society in which the individualist virtues would be safe. Although he mellowed somewhat in his later years, coming to welcome commerce and manufacturing, his Lockean thrust was indelibly inscribed in the Constitution's transcending concern for the protection of property rights and for limitations on the authority of government.

Alexander Hamilton, however, in the tradition of European mercantilism, postulated a far more communitarian view of government, seeing it as a tool for the design and development of the nation, especially for economic growth. Perhaps the first advocate of "industrial policy" in the United States, he proposed the allocation of state funds to those industries most likely to increase the capacity of the nation to grow and to export.[10] He wrote: "Capital is wayward and timid in lending itself to new undertakings, and the State ought to excite the confidence of capitalists, who are ever cautious and sagacious, by aiding them to overcome the obstacles that lie in the way of all experiments." Hamiltonian communitarianism was the justification for United States involvement in building railroads, canals, and highways, for erecting high tariff walls, and later for promoting land development, electric power generation, and rural electrification. Chalmers Johnson has noted: "On almost any given day in contemporary Tokyo, the Hamiltonian perspective is repeated back to us. Thus, Sadanori Yamanaka, head of the Ministry of International Trade and Industry in 1983, began a formal defense of his country's industrial policy with these words: 'One of the most important functions of the state is to facilitate economic development and to enhance the popular welfare.' "[11]

Around 1780 the business corporation emerged as a convenient device for satisfying a variety of community needs.

Between then and 1801, state legislatures chartered 317 corporations to carry out the building of bridges, roads, naval vessels, merchant fleets, and harbors. America was a young and vulnerable nation. Foreign powers threatened her interests; indeed, in 1812 the British burned Washington. In such circumstances there was little opposition to state intervention both to define community needs, fix priorities, and allocate capital for their fulfillment.

In the 1830s, corporations formed for profit to satisfy individual consumers were becoming distinguished from corporations chartered for community purposes. Businesses started to develop the Lockean ideology for their own purposes and profits. Business pressure and changing perceptions of community need brought about the loosening of state control over the corporation and the decline of the Hamiltonian view of government in national planning. Corporations were restive under Andrew Jackson's aggressive conception of presidential power and at the same time irritated by his unwillingness to help them.[12] Hamilton had been the friend of business, as business had been the instrument of the state; Jackson began to demonstrate that a strong conception of the state could well be the enemy of private, profit-seeking enterprise.

Ambivalence and the Corporation

By the mid-nineteenth century, industrial corporations were predominant in the American economy in a way they had not been at the founding of the Republic. The new breed of American businessmen almost uniformly accepted the premises of individualist ideology: Jefferson: who had hoped to preserve America as agricultural, became their hero; Hamilton was demonized. The national government was no longer taking the lead in promoting economic development, characteristic of the early years of the nineteenth century. John Quincy Adams lamented the change. A decade before, "the principle of internal improvement was swelling the tide of public prosperity," but now it was vanishing before the appeal to state's rights and laissez-faire. "I fell," cried the old statesman, "and with me fell, I fear never to rise again in my day, the system of internal improvement by means of national energies."[13]

By the 1850s, corporation law favored the centralization of decision making within the business organization. Active management was fixed in the board of directors as representative of the stockholder owners. A high value was placed on the continuity of management, regardless of changes in shareholders, and on providing a reliable frame for investment with limited investor commitment. The corporation was emerging as an ingenious vehicle of economic utility, capable of improvising and responding readily to opportunity.[14]

Predictably, however, the collective character of the corporation did not go unchallenged. Its threat to individualism was perceived early. William Gouge wrote in 1833:

> Against corporations of every kind, the objection may be brought that whatever power is given to them is so much taken from either the government or the people. As the object of charters is to give to members of companies powers which they would not possess in their individual capacity, the very existence of monied corporations is incompatible with equality of rights. . . . [15]

Gouge foresaw two continuing problems. First was the matter of power and its dispersion. How was corporate power to be allocated and contained? What was to be the relationship between corporate power and the state? The answer, such as it was, came in the form of the antitrust laws enacted toward the end of the nineteenth century. The control of corporate power was to emerge from the inexorable workings of competition in the marketplace—domestic, of course—that the state would keep free and open. These laws made a permanent part of American ideology the premise that if numerous small, self-interested individualistic corporate proprietors sought to satisfy individual consumers, the good community would result, power would be sufficiently dispersed, and the people as a nation would benefit. Regulation was enacted only to deal with those exceptional situations in which the decisions of the market were ineffective or inappropriate.

The second problem was the matter of individual rights. Would not great corporate concentrations suppress these rights? This question was answered in two ways. Corporations were to be regarded as artificial persons, as collective individuals, a basis of legitimacy that became increasingly tenuous over time, as the large publicly held corporations of America could not reasonably be construed as exhibiting any of the real attributes of individuals as Locke conceived them. Also, the right of corporate status was granted to virtually anyone for any purpose through simple administrative procedures, as in the standard incorporation acts of the 1880s. The notion of corporate status as a special privilege given to a few to serve an explicit community requirement was thus formally replaced by the notion of the corporation as a generally useful form through which to carry on virtually any economic activity.

The ideological confusion that arose around these two questions of corporate authority and individual rights in the nineteenth century remains troubling today. Nonetheless, the urge to grow and the general confidence in the pragmatic utility of the corporate form were so strong that the confusion has remained glossed over by common consent. Americans postponed "coming to grips with the creation of adequate legislative standards and adequate administrative means to deal with problems which the play of the market could not adequately handle."[16] They left unresolved the issues of power. They evaded more specific clarification of the public interest, and they delayed administrative designs to implement it. They were buttressed in this process by simple faith in the Lockean conception of individualism, particularly in property rights and the limited state, and also by sublime confidence that the impersonal competitive market would prevent abuse of corporate powers and thereby legitimize them.

The two questions scarcely troubled corporate managers. They saw their function largely as that of searching out and fostering consumer desires and then devising strategies by which resources could be allocated to satisfy the expected demands. Corporate structure and behavior have followed this strategy to the present, with considerable success and impact.

Thus, by the time of the Civil War, the corporation had burst its political and social bonds and taken advantage of its enormous flexibility. It became, by virtue of its usefulness, the dominant institutional force in American life. Until the 1930s, the corporation in the United States was held to be so unquestionably useful that the principal purposes of law became the enlargement of corporate ability to maneuver in any arena and the limitation of government's right to control its power.[17] As business grew, the idea of the limited state kept government small. In 1890, when railroads employed more than 100,000 people, the total military forces of the United States consisted of only 39,000 men. In 1928 more people worked for U.S. Steel or General Motors than for the government in Washington. States competed with one another in offering incorporation charters on liberal terms, granting, among other concessions, unprecedented insulation of managers from the interfering hands of their shareholder proprietors.[18]

The only real check on corporate power during this period came in the form of the Sherman Act of 1890. Reformers looked to government to protect the nation from manifest abuses by reviving and protecting the Lockean concept of competition. Big business was suspect because it restrained competition and thereby frustrated the invisible hand in the marketplace. In particular, it threatened individualistic proprietors, whose prosperity was the embodiment of the American Dream. At the same time, the Lockean emphasis on due process for the individual and on contractual relationships among buyers and sellers as well as on employers and employees, contributed to an adversarial and ultimately litigious society.

Ambivalence in Government

The experience of World War I showed the nation that it could achieve remarkable results through cooperative planning, organizing big business, and relating it to government so as to help fulfill the national interest. Under the leadership of Herbert Hoover as Secretary of Commerce in the 1920s, business was encouraged to organize into associations to collect and disseminate information, and to standardize work to promote efficiency and competitiveness. Secretary Hoover "looked at the economy as a kind of giant association, with himself sitting in the center as chief of the association bureau."[19] Hoover was searching for a way to align the authority of government with the competence of business to "reduce the irrationalities in the system that in his view were threatening progress."[20] His efforts soon confronted the Antitrust Division in the Justice Department, which feared that the statistics gathering that Hoover was urging would promote monopolies in industry. Small business in particular felt threatened by Hoover's "associationalism."

Hoover's initiatives blossomed during the New Deal of Franklin Roosevelt in the form of the National Recovery Act of 1933, under which a set of industrial associations was established to rescue the country from the ravages of depression. Liberated from the bonds of the antitrust laws, these associations would function as industrial "governments," in collaboration with organized labor, under the loose supervision of a new National Recovery Administration (NRA). The nation's experience with the NRA has useful lessons for the 1980s when similar types of collaboration are being undertaken or contemplated.

The NRA was the brainchild of Gerard Swope, president of General Electric, who felt that the proper coordination of production and consumption would provide jobs and increase purchasing power. Swope and others conceived of the NRA as a charter for a business commonwealth—a rational, cartelized business order, in which prices, profits, and wages would be assured, and markets planned, so as to avoid the waste of overcapacity, promote efficiency, and spur economic growth. A broad cross section of American leaders, including business and labor, supported the plan as a way to start an upward spiral out of the economic depths.[21]

In addition to its planning elements, the NRA was also perceived as a means to enable marketplace competition to work more effectively. From the beginning, therefore, it was rooted both in individualism and in communitarianism. Neither government, business, nor labor wanted to address the ideological confusion directly; all chose to see in it what they wanted to see.[22] Confused government deputies, many of whom had been recruited from the ranks of business, unguided by any clear definition of community need, and unaware of the ideological traps in their path, gave way before business pressure. Labor discovered itself poorly served and smelled "the advance guard of fascism."[23] Those antitrusters who had hoped for more competition found the marketplace becoming increasingly restricted by big corporations.

The NRA was thus a contradiction in terms from its beginning. "Its proponents wanted to permit agreements that would violate the Sherman Act, yet they could not admit that they would permit monopolies or monopolistic practices. . . . The incompatibility between the goals of the planners and those of the antitrusters was glossed over and the buck was passed to the administrators."[24] As a consequence, the goals of neither side were met. To compound the ideological problems, the plan simply did not work. Consumers complained of higher prices; unemployment was scarcely dented; small business felt abused by the large companies. The NRA was seen as a big-business racket.[25]

In May 1935, when the Supreme Court struck it down, the NRA died unlamented. There was a partnership, but business was unwilling to accept government as the senior member; government, for its part, was unprepared to insist. "It combined the worst features of both worlds," wrote Ellis W. Hawley, "an impairment of the efficiency of the competitive system without the compensating benefits of rationalized collective action."[26] Its failure, only two years after it had begun, was due primarily to ideological ambiguity: government had neither discerned nor resolved the ideological contradictions inherent in the Act.

The failure of the NRA exemplifies the difficulty of departing from an existing ideology without a credible substitute to sustain the transition. It is in some ways an extreme case, but in others quite typical. Those who initiate ideological departures—whether politicians or business leaders—frequently profess loyalty to the status quo to camouflage their movement away from it. Sometimes the camouflage is necessary and useful: during the administration of Franklin Roosevelt, many of the most significant departures from the Lockean tradition were made and solidified. But Roosevelt, like his successors, was essentially unmindful of the ideological implications of what he was doing. In the words of Louis Hartz, "Locke was bypassed so that problems could be solved, often in a most non-Lockean way."[27] The public had not been party to the implicit infusion of communitarianism; a transition had occurred in practice but the ideological consequences were ignored. After the great unifying efforts of World War II and the Cold

War, the United States was unprepared for the disappoint-
ments and creedal crises of the 1970s.

A review of the manifestations of communitarianism since
the 1930s gives some idea of how far we had strayed from
individualism. The depression persuaded Americans in general (and FDR in particular) that the old models of government,
business, and labor were deficient in practice. Because survival, justice, economy, and other values were not being acceptably implemented, the old individualism began to give way. At
General Motors, a bastion of the ideological status quo, the
rights of property were weakened when Michigan Governor
Frank Murphy refused to send in the National Guard to protect
the company's property against the new United Automobile
Workers during the sit-down strikes of 1936. The National
Labor Relations Act assured unions the right to exist, to organize, and to bargain. The company's legitimacy was also eroded
by the dispersion of ownership among many thousands of
shareholders. Alfred Sloan, hardly a communitarian, saw the
problem in 1927:

> There is a point beyond which diffusion of stock owner-
> ship must enfeeble the corporation by depriving it of virile
> interest in management upon the part of some one man
> or group of men to whom its success is a matter of
> personal and vital interest. And, conversely, at the same
> point the public interest becomes involved when the pub-
> lic can no longer locate some tangible personality within
> the ownership which it may hold responsible for the
> corporation's conduct.[28]

Marketplace competition began to demonstrate other failings. In the 1930s, it could not control the great oil companies,
whose worldwide capabilities, however distasteful ideologically, were seen as essential to the national interest. During
World War II the oil companies—partnerships among themselves and with government at the state, national, and international levels—were clearly essential to securing a place in the
Middle East, to holding market share and stabilizing prices, and
to assuring adequate flows of oil. The Justice Department's
predictable complaints about antitrust violations were put aside
to serve the community need.

Concurrently, the role of government was expanded to insure the welfare of the poor and the unemployed, to provide housing, to promote agriculture, to plan the war effort, and subsequently to generate a national consensus for the rebuilding of war-torn Europe and Japan. This was a massive agenda, in both relative and absolute terms. It was conceived and implemented with no explicit ideological change.

During the 1940s and 1950s a succession of communitarian enemies—Germany, Japan, and the USSR—provided Americans with "virtuous" purposes. But those very purposes— winning a war, containing an enemy, leading a large group of nations in a troubled world—added to and solidified the change, begun in the 1930s, in the domestic role of government. Government was becoming the source of America's national vision. It was becoming huge and pervasive, far removed from the traditional conception of what it ought to be. But besides ambivalence, there was inadvertence: government neglected the consequences of its new role. If government was to define and implement community needs at home and abroad, it should have simultaneously set priorities among those needs and acted coherently. Only one factor spared Americans from facing this reality: during the twenty years following World War II, the nation's economic strength was so vast and unchallenged that it could do essentially everything that it wanted, without counting the costs. There was little necessity to establish priorities and to work efficiently to achieve them.

The Time of Reckoning

The time of reckoning began in the late 1960s and continues in the 1980s. Two mutually aggravating elements were at work. First, the accustomed behavior of big government, big business, and big labor collided with hard economic reality; and second, those institutions had gradually fallen into ideological illegitimacy. A "creedal passion" period ensued.[29]

In retrospect, the economic realities seem straightforward. Government expenditures were escalating sharply to pay for both the Vietnam War and the Great Society antipoverty programs. Revenues were coming not from taxes but from borrowed or printed money. The results were twofold: inflation, and deterioration of investment by American business. The year 1969 marked the first trade deficit of the United States with Japan, and the nation fell behind in its competition with Germany as well. As inflation climbed, so did unemployment. By the early 1970s stagflation became a new phenomenon. The great American industrial machine, the source of unprecedented political and economic might, was running down. Government and consumers alike were spending wildly, and investing little. America's competitiveness, especially vis-à-vis Japan and its East Asian neighbors, was eroding.

In 1973 the rapid rise in the price of oil dictated by OPEC exacerbated the difficulties. Rather than facing the reality of increasingly expensive energy, the government sought to soften the blow. Its control of oil prices delayed the inevitable adjustment by the automobile industry and by the economy as a whole. The country was still feeling the consequences of that exercise in escapism as late as the 1980s.

Simultaneously, new perceptions of the environment were forcing Americans to realize that they were contaminating their life-support system. Air and water, like oil, were neither free nor inexpensive. In response to crisis and interest-group pressures, government regulation proliferated. This was a massive intervention in the free-enterprise system, but, because Americans were so adverse to the concept of planning, the intervention was fragmented.

By 1980 it was plain that America could not afford all that it was trying to do. Unfortunately, however, as soon as any effective solutions were proposed, the growing estrangement of its institutions effectively prevented the nation from coping. The Vietnam War, being neither a "good" war nor one the United States could win, served as the flash point for the smoldering resentment against big government.

Compound this with the general ineffectiveness of government economic policies (and the corruption of the Nixon White House), and the vigor with which Americans attacked their institutions was understandable. It was a holy war, waged in the name of the old religion. "The ideological challenge to American government . . . comes not from abroad but from home," wrote Samuel Huntington, "not from imported Marxist doctrines but from home-grown American idealism."[30]

As government was evil, so were business and labor. By virtue of its size and the nature of the stock market, business had departed from the notion implicit in property rights—that those who owned a corporation had the right and duty to set policy—and, despite the attempts of government to force it, shareholder democracy could not be made to return. Business had transgressed against the antitrust laws, and some—like Big Oil—had even conspired with government in doing so. Leviathans in limbo, America's corporations were attacked from all sides for polluting the environment, dehumanizing the individual, and corrupting the body politic at home and abroad. Their failures and transgressions had changed the game. Now, big was bad; small was beautiful. Battered and drained, reeling before the changing whims of government regulators, OPEC oil ministers, and the resolute onslaught of the Japanese, American business seemed to have lost its nerve.

Labor fared no better. Representing a decreasing share of the work force, and heedless of the impact of its demand for ever higher wages on the economy as a whole, the American labor movement was perceived as selfish, and in some quarters corrupt. Labor was not even managing to keep its members satisfied. Autoworkers and steelworkers, benefiting from the cost-of-living escalators built into their contracts after World War II, were being paid about twice the national average for manufacturing workers; even so, they were plainly not happy. More and more money was channeled through the contract apparatus, but that apparatus bought less and less productivity and competitiveness each year. Collective bargaining, that great American innovation, was increasingly suspect. For the first time since before World War II, there were cries to weaken the unions.

The backlash against all that had evolved since the 1930s reached crisis proportions during the last decade. Leaders of government, business, and labor reverted to the old hymns in the hope of regaining their lost legitimacy, but the result was discordant. One of the common themes running through the speeches of Presidents Nixon, Carter, and Reagan, especially in the early years of their respective administrations, was disdain for big government. Reagan's caution in 1982 to the National Association of Manufacturers was typical: "Feeding more dollars to government is like feeding a stray pup. It just follows you home and sits on your doorstep asking for more."[31] But a year earlier in his State of the Union message, Reagan had spoken of the need for this pup to provide "effective and coordinated management of the regulatory process." A year later, in the 1983 State of the Union address, he would assert that this versatile animal had to "take the lead in restoring the economy."

THE EMERGING IDEOLOGY OF THE 1980s

This brief review of the ideological history of the United States reveals that most Americans, today perhaps 70 percent, clearly prefer individualism in its ideal form. (Informal surveys conducted by the author among Harvard Business School students and business managers during the last 20 years confirm this figure.) At the same time, history shows a slow but steady movement toward communitarian practice on the part of government, business, labor organizations, and other institutions.

In the early 1980s, to be sure, some communitarian rights were diminished: housing for the poor, food stamps, aid to education, and the like. But the basic social safety net remained intact, despite record federal budget deficits. Furthermore, there were mixed purposes at work among those who cut funds. Some undoubtedly favored a return to individualistic practice: self-reliance, making one's own way, survival of the fittest. But others saw that many Great Society programs were having negative effects and were incompatible with the needs of the very communities purportedly being assisted. The problems of the poor in dilapidated urban neighborhoods were seen as being systemic, requiring a broad and holistic attack, not the ad hoc injection of funds. Police protection, job training, street repair, local organization and leadership had to function together for the torn fabric of urban communities to be woven together again. And holism in the form of the environmental movement was a permanent national commitment.

If rights of membership were curtailed, communitarian duties were emphasized both by government and by peer-group pressure in the workplace. The lazy were to be removed from the welfare rolls; and teamwork in the workplace brought pressure on the shiftless. In 1985, twenty-four states, including New York, required those on welfare to work.

Although President Reagan promised a reduction of government, power in Washington became more concentrated than ever in the Office of Management and Budget. The antitrust laws were loosened to expedite the cooperation and consolidation that were seen by the administration as consistent with the national interest, however imprecisely that interest was defined.

By the mid-1980s the fulfillment and self-respect of individuals in the United States had come to depend increasingly on how well communities were defined and designed; and upon the individuals' having a sense of identity, participation, usefulness, and control in the community, whether it was New York City or General Motors. In the real world of America in the 1980s, few could get their kicks à la John Wayne or Sylvester Stallone; if they tried, they would probably be in trouble. There was, of course, tension between American preferences in this regard and what was occurring, between myth and reality.

The causes of this transition to communitarian practice were various real-world phenomena. Individuals had come to depend on a complex web of relationships for income, health, work, and leisure. Increasingly they were being educated to understand those relationships and to join in their management. If they were denied the ability to do so, they were apt to feel alienated, resentful, or at least to lack motivation. In companies, productivity fell off, costs rose, and competition with communitarian nations could not be ignored. In the city, crime and poverty flourished; the social system deteriorated. Crisis in some form or other forced a change.

This practical drift in the direction of communitarianism was in no sense ideologically motivated: its aim was only to solve problems, seize opportunities, and perform more effectively. Even as the slow swing occurred, leaders in all walks of life propounded the virtues of traditional individualism: free enterprise, free trade, free markets, the limited state, and the rest. Indeed, when the ideological implications of the drift were perceived, the movement was apt to be retarded. For this reason, some argued that, just as in FDR's day, camouflage was desirable: change practice but keep in place a veil of ignorance to prevent the disturbing effects of the ideological fallout from disrupting that change. But it was impossible to make lasting and effective gains without a full awareness of both the realistic choices and the likely ideological consequences of any particular action. Obstacles to change had to be accurately perceived and measured before an effective way over or around them could be planned and managed.

THE CRISIS OF GLOBAL COMPETITION

In the past, communitarian implications of institutional change were forced by depressions, wars, ecological insights, demographic flows, market opportunities springing from economies of scale, technological innovation, and more. In the mid-1980s, the most powerful threat to individualism was unquestionably foreign competition. Focusing on this competition and its ideological implications provides an excellent opportunity for showing how an analysis of ideology illuminates the problems of industrial growth and decline, economic security and other social policies, labor-management relations, and the role of government in its relationships to business.

First, it is necessary to understand the phenomena. Even though U.S. competitiveness had been eroding for fifteen years, only in 1985 did Americans begin to recognize that there was a problem. Even then, its seriousness was underplayed because for many in high places in government, business, and academia, the remedy was worse than the disease. Ideology was at stake. It was easier for firms to leave the country and for the country to borrow at home and abroad to make up for competitive failure than it was to face reality and to change. In this way the effects of the crisis were blunted; its utility wasted.

The facts were stated simply in 1985 by a presidential commission under the leadership of John A. Young, the chairman of Hewlett-Packard:

Our ability to compete in world markets is eroding. Growth in U.S. productivity lags far behind that of our foreign competitors. Real hourly compensation of our workforce is no longer improving. U.S. leadership in world trade is declining. Finally, pretax rates of return on assets invested in manufacturing discourage investment in this vital core of our economy. . . .

Our world leadership is at stake, and so is our ability to provide for our people the standard of living and opportunities to which they aspire.[32]

In addition to these measures of failure, the merchandise trade deficit of the country had grown to $150 billion in 1985. The country was unable to offset the imbalance by selling services abroad, so the current account deficit in 1985 was over $100 billion. For the first time in fifty years the United States was a debtor country.

Japan, South Korea, Taiwan, Singapore, and Hong Kong had eroded America's manufacturing competitiveness in high-technology sectors as well as in the standard industrial ones—in machine tools and microelectronics as well as in steel and automobiles. These Asian competitors exported more to the United States in 1985 than did the rest of the world combined. (See *Table 5–1* for trade data on the United States and the other countries in this study.) The high-technology deficit with Japan alone exceeded $20 billion in 1985. Leading companies in the United States were slashing employment, and an ever-growing percentage of their products was being manufactured abroad.[33] The deterioration of American manufacturing, not just in mature industries but also at the very frontier of technology, was becoming ominously irreversible. Even cries for tariff protection would become hollow as the dependence of American producers and consumers on foreign products became greater than the discipline required to do without imports. It was easier to borrow and pay than to face reality.

The industry statistics are familiar. Employment in America's steel industry fell from 545,000 in 1977 to 351,000 in May 1984, with crippling effects throughout the nation.[34] At the technological end of the scale, the Japanese had captured 70 percent of the market for 64K random access memory chips and were expected to do as well on the new 256K RAM chips. By 1983 there were thirteen robots for every 10,000 employees

Table 5-1   U.S. Bilateral Trade, 1982–1984
(millions of dollars)

	U.S. Exports			U.S. Imports			Trade Balance		
	1982	1983	1984	1982	1983	1984	1982	1983	1984
Brazil	3,412	2,549	2,630	4,643	5,381	8,273	−1,231	−2,832	−5,643
France	7,019	5,941	6,012	5,815	6,308	8,516	1,204	−367	−2,504
Germany (FRG)	8,903	8,474	8,830	12,503	13,229	17,810	−3,600	−4,755	−8,980
Japan	20,668	21,600	23,173	39,931	43,559	60,371	−19,263	−21,959	−37,198
Korea	5,334	5,710	5,839	6,011	7,657	10,027	−677	−1,947	−4,188
Mexico	11,739	9,079	11,978	15,770	17,019	18,267	−4,031	−7,940	−6,289
Taiwan	4,153	4,401	4,822	9,587	12,110	16,088	−5,434	−7,709	−11,266
United Kingdom	10,397	10,466	12,038	13,541	12,900	15,044	−3,144	−2,434	−3,006

Source: U.S. Department of Commerce, International Trade Administration, *U.S. Foreign Trade Highlights: 1984,* (Washington: March 1985), 1–2.

in Japan, but only four per 10,000 in the United States. The American machine-tool industry had lost its entire export market, and imports had risen to 36 percent of the domestic market.[35]

The causes of U.S. competitive deterioration are many and varied: low rates of savings and investment; high costs of labor, the result often of adversarial labor relations; an overvalued dollar; high interest rates arising from a consumption-oriented, buy-now pay-later economic strategy; a short-term focus among managers who think more about quarterly dividends to shareholders than long-term market share; neglect of manufacturing innovation and efficiency; complacency; poor education; too many lawyers and not enough engineers. The problem is systemic. As my colleague Professor Bruce R. Scott has pointed out, the United States is being beaten by nations with more competitive systems, with national strategies aimed at earning a rising standard of living by gaining and retaining competitiveness through investment in the most profitable and fastest-growing global industries; by looking for long-run market share, not short-run profits, with government acting as a coach if not a quarterback; and by building and maintaining a broad social consensus that ascribes a high priority to competitiveness.[36] Other characteristics are employee relations and human resource management policies that insure high productivity, high quality, and competitive costs. Those strategies channel those winning nations' resources into the training, education, research, innovation, and organization required to acquire market share.

FOUR ELEMENTS OF A NEW PARADIGM

For the United States to regain its strength and avoid the deterioration of its standard of living and defense capability, a shift in practice is required. This shift in practice will require a concomitant change in ideology in the direction of communitarianism, a political, economic, and social paradigm that has occasionally flourished in American history, but that in 1985 was in disrepute.[37] The ideological shift should include changes in four elements: the place of the United States in the world economy; the role of government; the governance of the corporation, and the relations between managers and those whom they manage; and the rights and duties of membership in American society.

Free Trade and the Market

The old premise was that the place of nations in the world economy was properly determined by free trade among their individual firms in an open marketplacc. The relative position of each nation was determined by its "comparative advantage," that with which nature had endowed it. Portugal, the textbook example went, would properly grow grapes because God had blessed it with sunshine; England should raise sheep and make textiles. David Ricardo, the author of this "truth" was, of course, an Englishman not a Portuguese, and the Asian Five have shown that it is, in fact, not true at all. They had *created* their comparative advantage using quite different rules from those associated with ideas of free trade, free markets, and free enterprise.[38]

The old belief was that the national interest would be not only defined but fulfilled as a natural consequence of competition to satisfy consumer desires, government's role being essentially to keep markets open through the strict enforcement of the antitrust laws, occasionally administering a dose of regulation. The new premise was that community needs required explicit definition by the community, acting through government. The successful community was good at defining its needs, setting its priorities, and selecting the right mix of procedures for achieving them. The marketplace is surely one procedure the Asians use admirably (and the Soviets at great cost do not), but there are also other procedures, including partnership with government, and cooperation and consolidation among firms to achieve such community needs as international competitiveness, clean air and water, or, as the United States demonstrated, a landing on the moon.

In 1983 the federal government allowed ten electronics manufacturers to join together for cooperative research and product development. The resulting Microelectronics and Computer Technology Corporation (MCC), with ex-CIA Deputy Director

Bobby Inman as its first chief, was a direct response to the joint research ventures of the Japanese that had had such devastating effects upon American business. The ideological challenge represented by the new company was clearly reflected in the indignant cries of Lockean protest. "Your contemplated conduct is an unequivocal combination in violation of the antitrust laws of the United States," Joseph Alioto, prominent attorney and former San Francisco mayor, told the heads of the cooperating companies.[39] Indeed, he said, the mere fact that the companies had *discussed* cooperation was a violation of the law.

Whether the Justice Department will continue the communitarian drift implicit in its interpretation of antitrust law in the MCC case is in doubt.* It was only in 1981 that the Department had broken up AT&T, raising serious questions about the effects of that action on integrating a global communications system for national defense, on retaining Bell Laboratories as a preeminent creator of telecommunications inventions, and on maintaining the world's lowest-cost, highest-quality telephone service: community needs all of them. Peter Drucker suggested that in such cases the court might at least be advised by a panel of wise persons who would attempt to define the community need. The ideological implications of such a suggestion are obvious. If the marketplace does not decide community needs, who decides? An elitist group of unelected seers? The community through its government? Or perhaps, as in the MCC case, a group of business leaders headed by a trusted governmental representative?

Role of Government

Views about the role of government in the old paradigm contain two subelements that in the United States have come into

---

*In 1982 the Justice Department allowed some forty U.S. companies, including some of the largest—AT&T, IBM, General Motors, and Du Pont—to form the Semiconductor Research Corporation. The purpose of the consortium is to fund research and transfer the results of that research for industrial use in order to enhance the ability of the United States to compete more effectively worldwide in information technology.

conflict with one another. The first holds that government is a necessary evil. Its authority should be checked, balanced, and separated among the executive, the legislative, and the judiciary branches. As much power as possible should be dispersed, and government should not "plan," that is, think coherently about the community's needs. The second and quite different view holds that government should intervene when crisis or a collection of interest groups demands it.

The ambivalence resulting from the conflict is costly. The Congressional Budget Office estimated that in 1984 government allocated directly to business a total of $131.9 billion, but that other billions accrued to business indirectly: $140 billion spent by the Department of Defense for goods and services, and $110 billion paid to individuals through medical and housing subsidies.[40] Billions more were made available to consumers by allowing them to deduct from their taxes the interest on loans to purchase whatever they desired—a beach house, a yacht, a fur coat, or a Toyota.

The contradiction between the premises of the old paradigm and current practices demonstrates the need for a new paradigm. If the role of the government were more precisely and deliberately defined, government itself could be smaller. Bureaucracies had burgeoned as the result of lack of focus and comprehensiveness, the costly and ironic by-product of the notion of the "limited state." (In Japan about 10 percent of the gross national product is disposed of by government; in the United States it is close to 19 percent.) By focusing on long-term goals, the nation could better identify those issues that could be best addressed on local or regional levels, and those that required a federal approach.

The Young Commission and others have recommended that the federal government organize itself and join with private institutions to give competitiveness a high priority. Rather than subsidizing and protecting economic sectors that were already well insulated from competition, such as housing and real estate, an effective economic strategy for the future would encourage investment and efficiency in the frontier industries of the future. This would mean a simultaneous commitment to education and training for competitiveness as well as programs for those who were displaced; to data collection and analysis that would provide early warning of coming problems; and to the general integration of policies so that together they would support—not corrode—U.S. competitiveness. One does not have to be particularly insightful to realize that microelectronics, telecommunications, and biotechnology are going to be economically significant in the future and can be distinguished as frontiers for competition from fast-food chains and shopping centers that today benefit hugely from government policy.

In the mid-1980s many state governments—in Michigan, Tennessee, Kentucky, North Carolina, Ohio, Pennsylvania, and Massachusetts, for example—were designing strategies for competitiveness. The federal government, however, remained mired in ambivalence; three examples of its role are instructive. The policies of the U.S. government toward the declining basic *steel* industry exemplified the costs of responding to crisis with no coherent plan. The government's response to the ailing *textile* industry, on the other hand, showed how public policy could be used to enhance competitiveness. Finally, Washington helped make *Chrysler* competitive, but it may have failed to learn the lesson that that episode and others like it elsewhere can teach.

Steel. Whether under the guise of antidumping and countervailing-duty laws or trigger-price mechanisms, the United States for a decade tried to force other countries to accept its implicit policy of assuring high financial returns and high wages for the steel industry without government subsidies. Subsidization by governments, for whatever reason, was deemed "wrong" by the U.S. government, and it attempted to persuade other governments not to subsidize steel either. Its persistent attempts were unsuccessful, and the result was a decline in American market share. When the American steel industry failed to innovate, markets naturally went to more efficient producers willing to take lower returns. American steel either had to reduce its costs and profit expectations, accept a continuing decline in market share, or seek some form of protection.

In 1982 the U.S. government found itself once again obliged by law and by its commitment to free-trade principles to seek to prevent foreign governments—in this case, its European allies—from subsidizing their steel industries. The Europeans entered the bargaining under the threat that the United States would impose countervailing duties on our imports, but they were also angered by our disputing their right to help build the Soviet-European natural-gas pipeline. The Europeans therefore sought to negotiate guarantees of a certain share of the U.S. steel market. This represented a departure: the idea of market shares was clearly inconsistent with free-trade pronouncements. However, both the steel industry and the U.S. government found it appealing: the industry relished a more orderly marketplace, and the government was eager to prevent its political, diplomatic, and economic relations with Europe from being further soured. A deal was struck in October 1982. The Europeans agreed to reduce steel exports to the United States for the next three years to slightly over 5 percent of the market, down from 6 percent in 1982. Given this initial success, the United States sought similar deals with Japan, South Korea, Brazil, Mexico, and other steel exporters accused of subsidizing their steel industries. The issue was clear: if there were to be global quotas, the need for coherent thought and action—that is, planning—by the American government was unavoidable. Brazil and Mexico could repay their enormous debts to American banks only by earning the dollars to do so; and steel exports were one of the few ways open to them. Presumably they thereby acquired some priority, but the capacity of the U.S. government to assign it was limited by old structures and practice. Furthermore, the old ways prevented an adequate program of retraining, job creation, and placement to assure that unemployed American steelworkers could find useful places in the nation's economy.

Textiles and apparel. In the early 1980s the textile and apparel industry employed 1.9 million workers in 34,000 widely dispersed plants. For half a century it had suffered from severe competition from developing countries that benefited from low labor costs, easily transferable technology, relatively low capital requirements, small economies of scale, population growth, and substantial U.S. aid and cotton export subsidies. Between 1961 and 1972, U.S. imports of textiles and apparel products quadrupled, from 306 million to 1.2 billion pounds. The United

States responded by negotiating a series of multilateral trade agreements, culminating in 1974 in the Multi-Fiber Arrangement (MFA), a multinational framework to manage international trade in textiles. Stanley Nehmer and Mark Love argue that "by stabilizing world markets somewhat, the MFA has encouraged competitive responses by U.S. manufacturers through increased investment, innovation, and consolidation. Long-term structural adjustment has continued without the massive dislocation that would have otherwise occurred."[41] At the same time, they point out, developing countries' production and exports were allowed to grow significantly.

The idea of managed trade clearly runs counter to traditional American ideology. It is quite consistent, however, with both the practice and ideology of most other countries. It seems probable, therefore, that the United States will be forced into it on a more extensive scale. The success of a policy of managed trade depends upon the United States' having an overall strategy concerning our place in the world economy so that our needs are balanced in a comprehensive way against those of others.

Chrysler. Virtually all industrial countries have confronted the problem of huge corporations that are too big and too important politically and economically to be allowed to fail in the marketplace. Despite Britian's ideological proclivities, even the Thatcher government felt obliged to invest $2 billion into British Leyland in 1981 because the cost of bankruptcy would have been $7 billion in increased welfare.

Robert Reich argues in his study of bailouts[42] that the critical issues in such cases are how to shrink the sick company quickly while at the same time shifting its direction and organization so as to make it competitive and profitable; and how to do this with least cost in terms of unemployment and lost revenue to the company and the nation.

Reich analyzed four bailouts: AEG-Telefunken, A.G. in West Germany, British Leyland, Toyo Kogyo in Japan, and Chrysler. He found that there were two crucial determinants of rate of shrinkage and of efficient shifting: the availability to banks, companies, and government of comprehensive and accurate information about the company early in the game so that problems were known and were clear; and existing power and authority having the will and capacity to remove the old management, to change the company's organization, processes, and products, and to reduce its costs while increasing its profits. Toyo Kogyo was most successful; British Leyland least. Chrysler was in between.

Chrysler's first big loss came in 1970. Deeply in debt, it was rescued by the banks but no changes were made to improve its competitiveness. Nine years later the company owed $1 billion and needed more. It employed 140,000 people worldwide, with hundreds of thousands more working for its suppliers. In August 1979, the U.S. government came to the rescue with a loan guarantee of $1.5 billion, accompanied by demands for a complete restructuring of the company, new management, and $2 billion of financial concessions from employees, lenders, dealers, and affected state governments. Chrysler cut its employment from 110,000 to 60,000. Congress considered the deal cheap at the price. Bankruptcy, it estimated, would have cost some $15 billion: $11 billion in lower taxes and higher welfare and unemployment costs, a $1.1 billion drain on the Pension Benefit Guarantee Corporation, and a $3 billion increase in the trade deficit.[43]

At Toyo Kogyo the adjustment was faster and less costly. Redundant workers were trained as salesmen to sell door-to-door. The management, manufacturing processes, and product were changed more quickly. The banks and government moved faster to support and force the turnaround. Reich's crucial determinants—availability of information and capacity to change—were more in place in Japan than in the United States. Reich attributes Toyo Kogyo's success to the relationships among the Japanese company's banks, management, labor, and government.[44] In nations where these relationships were distant, intermittent, adversarial, and marked by suspicion if not mistrust, the bailout performance was poor. Where they were close, cooperative, supportive, and harmonious, performance was correspondingly better.

In short, the difference between good and poor bailout performance emerged from two quite different ideologies. U.S. relationships were shaped by a variant of the individualist ideology; Japan's by communitarianism.

The Chrysler case is viewed in the United States as a one-time crisis, an exception: the United States went communitarian in practice because it was compelled by the situation. But, just as the Chrysler change was slowed and made more costly by the structural effects of individualism, so the pull of the old ideology may well prevent banks, government, managers, and labor from establishing the new relationships upon which quick and reliable information about problem industries can be brought to bear to effect speedy adjustment for competitiveness.

Managers and Managed

The old premise held that the purpose of the corporation was to make whatever products, provide whatever services, adopt whatever methods, practice whatever behavior, and locate in whatever community would most enrich the corporation's owners or shareholders—provided only that its officers obeyed the laws and regulations of the various jurisdictions in which it was operating. The authority of management rested with a board of directors elected by the shareholders, and management's primary obligation was to satisfy their desires.[45]

As Alfred Sloan had anticipated almost sixty years ago, this premise that governance derived from the right of property was eroded by reality as shareholders of publicly owned firms became more numerous, dispersed, anonymous, and distant from the communities in which the firm operated. Thus, while in theory the purpose of the firm was to serve the interests of an involved constituency of shareholders who were presumably interested in the welfare of their community, in fact that constituency became increasingly remote and its commitment increasingly transitory. In these circumstances the divergence between the short-run interests of Wall Street and the longer-term interest of employees, suppliers, and communities was inevitable. Furthermore, the increasing mobility of capital and technology contributed to seeking worldwide sources for many products, increasing the vulnerability of employees, suppliers, and affected communities, all having long-run interests in the corporation. By virtue of the traditional premise, however, the latter groups were without representation in the governance of the corporation. Even those with a long-run interest found themselves with no formal mechanism for expressing their concerns.

In addition, the selection of management, although theoretically the responsibility of shareholders, had in fact become a function of management itself. Managers were thus a self-perpetuating oligarchy, increasingly important to the lives and fortunes of employees, suppliers, and communities, expected to serve a variety of ill-defined and often contradictory purposes, but subjected to stockholder control only in time of crisis. The old premise of corporate purpose and governance had eroded.

It did not seem likely that T. Boone Pickens and the other "corporate raiders," latter-day champions of the invisible hand, were going to be the means to competitive resurgence. The allocation of resources to takeover wars was not likely to improve U.S. performance against those who focused on investment for technological innovation.

Shareholder dominance. Richard Ellsworth has demonstrated that the "unquestioned dominance" of the goal of enriching the shareholders over the other goals of most businesses has seriously undermined American competitiveness in the world economy. It has resulted in a failure to invest in innovation for long-term growth because short-term returns would be inadequate. It has also meant that Americans had to finance their companies with far less debt than their foreign competitors, increasing their cost of capital and reducing their rate of growth.[46] Furthermore, the cost of debt in many countries, such as Japan, was lower than in the United States because of government policies aimed at competitiveness.

Ellsworth showed the effects of U.S. practice in *Tables 5–2* and *5–3.*

"The essence of the dilemma facing U.S. managers," wrote Ellsworth, "is that they are caught between the need to compete against foreign competitors who are willing to invest capital at lower returns and the need to provide returns to shareholders that adhere to the conventional norms of the U.S. capital market."

The problem, as it was for Gouge 150 years ago, was one of

Table 5–2 Estimated Weighted Average After-Tax Cost of Capital
(percent)

	1971	1976	1981
United States	10.0%	11.3%	16.6%
West Germany	6.9	6.6	9.5
Japan	7.3	8.5	9.2

Source: U.S. Department of Commerce, International Trade Administration,
"A Historical Comparison of the Cost of Financial Capital in France, The
Federal Republic of Germany, Japan and the United States," (Washington:
1983), 3.

purpose and ideology. "Whereas the ultimate purpose of German and Japanese companies is biased in favor of the interests
of the employees, lenders, and in the case of Japan, their
nation, most American companies define their goals almost
exclusively in terms of shareholders' interests."[47] Increasingly
those interests in the 1980s were leading U.S. companies to
leave the country for more hospitable climes. As in the bailout
examples, here too, national competitiveness requires a communitarian awareness of mutualities of interest among lenders,
managers, labor, and government.

Economic security. Plainly the time had come when management was expected to give due regard to the "investments" of
employees and of communities that were affected by its behavior, as well as of those who provided capital. If managers
expected employees to make a full commitment to productivity, those employees had to be assured employment security

Table 5–3 Comparison of Investment, Productivity, Growth,
and Capital Structure
(1971–1980)

	Net Fixed Investment as % of GDP	Growth Rate in Output per Hour in Manufacturing	Real Growth Rate in Industrial Production	Average Equity as % of Total Assets
United States	6.6%	2.5%	3.3%	50.1%
Germany	11.8	4.9	2.2	28.1
Japan	19.5	7.4	4.6	20.0

Sources: Economic Report of the President (1983), 81; the OECD; the U.S.
Department of Commerce.

in return. Indeed, to reach full potential, employees would expect and need participation in a wide variety of decisions that affected their work lives. Employees, in turn, had to accept the responsibility to keep the company competitive.

America's Asian competitors had shown that employment security, carrying with it a reciprocal commitment to hard work, was a more competitive way in which to provide people with economic security than was income security, where there was no such reciprocal commitment to work. Until recently, however, U.S. managers had assumed little responsibility for employment security. They had felt empowered to hire and fire workers as market conditions and the satisfaction of share-holders might require. While a number of companies granted employment security to their "permanent" employees, this informal, largely unnoticed development had left formal respon-sibility for economic security almost wholly with the federal government.

As in almost all of the other older industrial democracies, the U.S. government met its responsibility by providing income security, typically requiring no work in return. Such an approach maintained consumption but did little for produc-tion; and it imposed the "overhead cost" of economic security on society as a whole. To increase productivity and to serve the national economy, therefore, business should be required to take greater responsibility for employment security while government takes correspondingly less. To those who cling to traditional ideas of managerial authority, this reasoning will come as a shock.

Labor and management. The union's fundamental mission, according to the old ideology, was to bargain with manage-ment to acquire a larger share of corporate revenues for its members and to preserve and promote their safety, health, and general welfare. Little consideration was to be given to the competitiveness of the firm.

The new premise augmented the old mission by an overrid-ing concern for the health of the firm, which must be compet-itive or there would be no welfare, no wages, no jobs, and no members. The union's task was thus as much to help design and govern a corporate consensus as to bargain an adversarial contract. The form of union participation in governance varied widely and could extend from the shop floor to the board of directors. Since all workers must be committed to the corporate consensus, some form of effective two-way communication with employees was essential to allow appropriate employee participation in the consensual process and appropriate sharing of gains derived from competitiveness among all of the corporate constituencies.

In a number of industries the pressures of foreign as well as domestic competition have forced change. The Japanese challenge impelled the automobile industry toward greater involvement of employees in what had previously been the prerogatives of management. Speaking of the 1982 agreement between the automobile industry and the United Automobile Workers, Peter Pestillo, Ford's vice president of labor relations, said: "We made a great effort . . . to work toward greater participation by the work force in the business process. I think that's the wave of the future. We used a word deep in the agreement that's simply called 'governance.' "[48] At Eastern Airlines, competition from consensually organized People Express likewise forced changes in governance. In 1984 four employee representatives were placed on the board of directors, and union participation was required in corporate decisions ranging from finance to aircraft maintenance. Similar changes were under way throughout American business, in nonunion as well as union settings. The involvement of employees in decision making and problem solving eased the introduction of new technology at AT&T, and allowed for competitive pricing at Intel. Similar involvement at Bethlehem Steel improved quality while lowering costs.

In a number of cases consensualism has entailed employee ownership, sometimes of a minority of shares as at Eastern, but occasionally of the whole company as at Weirton Steel. In these instances the survival of the company was deemed essential to maintain both employment and the health of the surrounding community.

The ways of consensus, however, did not come easily. The hierarchies and assumptions rooted in the old idea of contract lingered to cause difficulties. Irving Bluestone, one of the chief architects of consensual quality-of-work-life programs at Gen-

eral Motors, where he was vice president of the United Automobile Workers in the 1970s, spoke of the tensions the new
ways caused among traditional management. He specifically
mentioned George Morris, vice president of industrial relations:

> I think George felt that any encroachment upon manage-
> rial prerogatives was an erosion of his authority, and that
> management must retain for itself all possible control over
> the work place.[49]

Middle managers and supervisors wondered about their authority too. Said one: "I'm like one of those lizards that is always
changing color, except that I don't have any control over what
color I am. When the workers want me, I've always got to be
there. When they don't, I have to tread lightly."[50]

Unions were similarly uneasy. Trained in the arts of conflict
and bargaining, many of their leaders wondered what the role
of a union could be in a consensual setting. Would their members not suffer from the erosion of the carefully constructed
protection of the contract? Could there in fact be cooperation
between managers and managed without conflict? As union
strength and membership declined, union leaders feared the
deterioration of the American labor movement as a whole.
Who then would speak for workers in the larger community?
What would be the implications for democratic government?

Early in 1986, the path-breaking governance procedures
adopted by Eastern Air Lines were in jeopardy; the company
faced acquisition by rival Texas Air. An important cause of the
breakdown was the inability of both managers and unions to
change their ideological mind-sets to keep pace with the new
practice. Old assumptions about roles and relationships prevented both sides from achieving the goal they shared: a strong
and competitive airline.

Rights and Duties

The traditional view of the rights and duties of membership in
American society derived from the notion that the community
was little more than the ever-shifting groupings of the individ-

uals in it. Self-fulfillment derived from an essentially lonely struggle in which the fit thrived and the rest either died or became the objects of charity. This idea has been substantially softened over the years, especially since the 1930s, by public demand that the nation recognize certain rights as belonging to its citizens: rights to income, education, health, employment, and more. These rights required providing a "safety net" to save the "truly needy" from disaster. The old premise of individualism, however, restrained the community from imposing many duties of membership, preferring to leave these to each citizen's upbringing, religion, and conscience.

The new premise was that just as the community assures rights to its members, so it must require duties. A community's performance will deteriorate if the former were more extensive than the latter. The assignment of duties by the community must be fair: if the poor and the weak are expected to work hard and well, so must the rich and the strong. If the wages of assembly-line workers are to relate to productivity, so must those of the chief executive officer. If welfare for the poor was to be cut, so must subsidies to the affluent. If America needed a well-trained elite to innovate and produce for the future, its educational system must permit access to all. Most fundamentally, each generation has a duty to pay for what it consumes and not to saddle its children with the debt for what it enjoys today.

CONCLUSION

Tension in American society is shaped by an improper fit between its prevailing ideology and a changing world. Individualism has marked the nation's history and has been its strength, providing its institutions with the flexibility required for growth and adaptation to changing circumstances. Whatever waste may have resulted from its imperfections was covered by the nation's vast resources and self-sufficiency. By the 1980s, however, two critical changes had occurred: the United States had become dependent on the rest of the world for funds, markets, products, and resources; and other national systems, especially Japan and its Asian neighbors, were proving themselves to be more competitive.

At the same time that the United States confronted the crisis of competitiveness, other crises arose that the nation's institutions were ill-equipped to deal with. These crises included urban disintegration; projected shortages of electric power in the 1990s; environmental contamination; and poverty and ignorance among a growing underclass that had become increasingly cut off from mainstream America. The pragmatic pursuit of remedies to these problems was forcing a change in the roles and relationships of government, business, labor, and other institutions. The change had profound ideological implications, representing a transition from the historically preferred individualism to a communitarianism that had been suspect since the days of Alexander Hamilton.

We may speculate that crisis in each of these areas will increase as long as the transition is retarded or carelessly made, slowed by ambivalence, or troubled by inadvertence. The form the crisis will take is reasonably clear: slow growth or even recession as the nation's manufacturing base continues to erode, unemployment and bitter division between those who continue to "make it" and the increasing numbers who do not, increased antagonism toward the competitors, a diminished economic pie with intensifying conflict about its distribution, a decline in the standard of living and defense capability, financial failures, and a continued deterioration of the country's infrastructure.

It may be hoped that leaders of government, business, and labor will acknowledge the fundamental law of evolution— adapt or perish—and strive to minimize these crises by using each one to ease the transition to a more effective system. Here leaders will be greatly assisted by the nation's traditional strengths: openness to change and experimentation, entrepreneurial zeal, a sense of fresh possibility, and respect for innovation. But even these may wither if unaccompanied by a full appreciation of the new challenges America faces.

The task is to seek out in America's traditions and experience those communitarian capabilities that are present but too little used. This requires recognition that individual fulfillment and self-respect depend upon the careful design of communities, whether they are cities or factories; that justice demands the emerging hierarchy be made compatible with the idea of equality; that consensus is often a more effective idea around which to mobilize individual capabilities than the contract, especially its adversarial form; that economy as well as justice require the definition of rights and duties of membership in a way that is compatible with both the needs of the community and individuals. It also requires recognition that community needs be explicitly defined and priorities realistically set; that government, whether at the local, state, or national level, has a primary role in making such a definition together with other elements of society; that implementation of the needs should be made by the most efficient instrument, whether it is the marketplace, regulation by the state, or business in partnership with government; that if it is partnership, care needs to be taken so that its criteria are legitimate and its structure consistent with democratic traditions; and finally that those charged with the work of science and education learn to think holistically, to discover and to teach the systematic interconnections of specialized events and actions. Success in all this depends upon a wise combination of pragmatism and ideological sensitivity.

6

JAPAN

Adaptive Communitarianism

Ezra F. Vogel

Foreigners looking at Japan from afar might easily assume that
Japanese ideology has been in existence for centuries without
major changes. Japanese feudalism did continue much later
than Western feudalism, and the transition from feudalism to
modern corporatism went quickly, without intervening centuries dominated by individualistic ideology and independent
businessmen. However, Japan has been buffeted by many
changes since the coming of Admiral Perry in 1853: by the
threat of domination by colonial powers, by rapid modernization and the rise of new social classes, by new currents of
thought and technology from the West, by militarist domination in World War II, by defeat and occupation, by growing
individualism and democracy, and by increasing involvement
in the international community. The changes the Japanese
confront in the real world and in their practices and ideology
have been far more profound than most Westerners imagine.
Yet the Japanese have been remarkably successful in adapting

141

to these changes while maintaining a strong commitment to an ideology that is quite plainly communitarian.

I shall try to convey a sense of Japanese ideology as dynamic by describing circumstances in which its elements originally came together as well as the subsequent changes and continuities.

THE CONSOLIDATION OF FEUDALISTIC COMMUNITARIAN IDEOLOGY

In 1600, after decades of war between clans, one clan leader, Ieyasu Tokugawa, emerged victorious. Tokugawa's key problem was how to provide a structure that would enable him to maintain leverage over the other clans without stretching his authority beyond its capabilities. The new national structure that he established provided a more unified leadership over the clan fiefdoms than existed in feudal Europe, though far less unified than in the European monarchies. The Tokugawa structure remained until 1868. During these 268 years, the Tokugawa clan directly ruled almost one third of Japan and maintained hegemony over the other two hundred-odd feudal clans.

Tokugawa leaders required the *samurai* ("warrior class") everywhere to locate in castle towns apart from the land. They alone could wear swords and continue military training, but they were to turn their attention to civilian study. A later official history written during the early nineteenth century said of Ieyasu Tokugawa, "He conquered the nation on horseback, but being an enlightened and wise man, realized early that the land could not be governed from a horse. He has always respected and believed in the way of the sages. He wisely decided that in order to govern the land and follow the path proper to man, he must pursue the path of learning. Therefore, from the beginning he encouraged learning."

Ideology was at the heart of this study. Tokugawa leaders believed that loyalty and service, a sense of responsibility, and a respect for discipline, training, and craftsmanship were necessary to provide a stable basis for political order. Many of these elements could be found in previous Japanese teachings, but Tokugawa made them more systematic and arranged for their more thorough dissemination. Ieyasu and his successors drew most heavily on a form of neo-Confucianism previously borrowed from China's great scholar, Chu Hsi, whose philosophy provided an excellent basis for a central state. The most fundamental virtue was loyalty: of friend to friend, of wife to husband, of child to parent, of brother to brother, but, above all, of subject to lord.

Everyone was to be taught these basic virtues and encouraged to develop them through his own occupation in his appropriate social station, but the *samurai* were expected to study them much more intensively. They began the study of Confucian classics in their youth and continued throughout their lifetime. *Bushido,* "the way of the warrior," was a highly disciplined approach to study that incorporated the basic ideology not only in content but in a strongly authoritarian subordination of the student to his teachers.

The ideology had as its core belief the importance of maintaining a social order that would benefit society as a whole. Issues of individual morality were subordinate. In what became a famous case, the philosopher Sorai Ogyu (1666–1728) was asked to offer his advice on how to judge a poor peasant who, driven to poverty, became a monk, with the name of "Donyu." He had decided to move to Edo (the ancient name for Tokyo) with his mother, but on the way he abandoned her. Sorai's advice was that although Donyu's action was wrong personally, being a very unfilial thing to do, it was of little import to the state. What mattered to the state was maintaining order and dealing with the basic problems of poverty that had caused someone to engage in unfilial activity. Unlike Christians, Japanese did not believe in a transcendent being or value system that could serve as a legitimate basis for challenging the power of the state.

The system of political rule and its underlying ideology provided impressive stability for 268 years. Although merchants remained at the bottom of the official hierarchy, the society permitted a very lively development of commerce, especially in the Osaka area. Business skills became sophisticated, complex business networks grew, and in some areas a group of wealthy merchants emerged. As with Jews in medieval Europe, merchants often became wealthier and had more leverage over others who were officially in higher positions. Since the growing power of merchants was viewed as a threat to feudal stability, Tokugawa leaders and *daimyo* ("feudal lords") made great efforts to keep merchants under control and to keep the love of wealth and pleasures from affecting the *samurai*.

This long period during which the basic ideology persisted and was diffused throughout the society provided a strong basis for consensus. The leaders who undertook the modernization of Japan, beginning in the latter part of the nineteenth century, used it as their starting point.

THE MEIJI RESTORATION: COMMUNITARIAN NATIONALISM AND MODERNIZATION

During the Tokugawa period, Japan was isolated from other countries. It did not yet have a European type of nationalism that arose from close contacts across borders, an awareness of national differences, and a perception of outside threat. This spirit and the accompanying willingness of people to exert themselves on behalf of the nation began to develop in Japan in the 1830s, as leading *samurai* closely watched British activity in East Asia. Nationalism burst out in the 1840s with the shocking British victory over the great power of China and the sudden arrival of Commodore Perry's "black ships" in 1853. Until the coming of Admiral Perry, Japan had been self-sufficient and wanted no part in international trade. President Millard Fillmore in November 1852 wrote a letter for Admiral Perry to deliver to the Japanese emperor, stating, "We know that the ancient laws of your imperial majesty's government do not allow foreign trade, except with the Chinese and the Dutch, but as the state of the world changes . . . it seems to be wise, from time to time, to make new laws . . . (Americans) think that if your imperial majesty went so far to change the ancient laws as to allow a free trade between the two countries, it would be extremely beneficial."

Tension began to develop among leaders in the clans as well as in Edo, particularly in some of the outlying clans closest to Korea and China. Tokugawa leaders were unable to resist the outside powers' demands for Japan to open its doors to the West. Some young *samurai* in the largest and most exposed clans opposed these concessions and rallied behind the emperor, who had been relegated to a largely ceremonial role during the Tokugawa Period. In 1868, the Tokugawa Clan was overthrown in a peaceful surrender to those young *samurai* from the outer clans, on behalf of the emperor. They became a new force to achieve national unity, resist the foreigners, and set up a strong modern state under the banner of the young Emperor Meiji who just then succeeded to the throne.

The New Nationalism

During the Tokugawa Period, the main loyalty was to the clan. There was virtually no mobility of people from one clan to another, nor from one caste (samurai, farmer, artisan, or merchant) to another. Under Emperor Meiji, some of the younger *samurai* from the stronger clans who had been loyal to their own fiefs were willing to give up the familiar structure and ideas they considered sacred to rally the nation against the outside threat.

The clans, which had been far stronger than American states before the American Revolution, were abolished within several years. They were replaced by a new system of prefectural government having administrative boundaries far different from those of the original clans and without inspiring the loyalty previously enjoyed by clans. The formal class system was abolished. *Samurai* took the lead in eliminating their own class privileges, albeit with a modest pension later turned into bonds. To be sure, even in the newly open class system, most high officials were former *samurai* but anyone could now seek a government position. People could move more freely from one part of the country to another.

During the Tokugawa, the requirement that *samurai* spend alternate years in Edo had paved the way for a common understanding that could solidify modern nationalism, but switching *samurai* loyalty from the clan to the nation was a significant transition. Local social ties, especially in the villages, remained very strong, but they were abandoned when people moved to cities and into modern organizations that would help strengthen the nation.

Rights and Duties

During the Tokugawa period, land had been owned by the clan, not by the tillers or even the local tax collectors. However, the rights to land use were generally passed down through the *ie*, the "House" or family line. By the middle of the Tokugawa, the loyalty of farm laborers had begun to wane. The philosopher Sorai specifically cautioned against contractual use of labor, urging a system that would encourage lifelong commitment of farmers to the fief to assure superior loyalty.

In practice, the head of the household in rural areas was not considered the owner of the property but rather the current custodian or trustee of the House. These rights of use were passed down through the generations from the senior head of the household to one of his sons, usually the first. If the first son were not able, or if the House had no sons, the family would adopt a son. If the House lacked a son and had a suitable daughter, then the daughter's husband would be the heir. If none of these was available, they could adopt a relative or even someone not previously related, usually from a large family where the young man had no chance of being an heir to his House. However selected, the heir then was responsible for passing on the rights to the next generation. By the later part of the Tokugawa, land was ordinarily passed on to only one child because land was limited; other children were expected to marry out. Since the population was stable during the Tokugawa period, roughly the number of Houses remained the same. Daughters entered the House of their husbands, and sons who did not inherit their own House either remained single or became the heir of another House.

When the domains were abolished in the early Meiji period, a program of land reform and land registration passed land ownership to the tillers who had previously enjoyed only the rights of use. Land was considered not personal property but property of the House. The current head of the House had considerable power over House members, but he was also responsible for looking after relatives and for maintaining prosperity so that the land could be passed on to the next generation.

During the Tokugawa period, small business families, of artisans as well as merchants, had been much like rural families. Although little capital or possessions had been accumulated, the location, the specialty, and the skills were generally passed down from generation to generation as younger people were taught the ways of the House. Any property that had been accumulated would of course also be passed down through the generations.

When the Meiji Period opened new opportunities for modern business, few traditional merchants had the capital, the know-how, the entrepreneurial spirit, the boldness, and the information to take advantage of them. Most former *samurai* had little entrepreneurial skill. However, by the end of the Tokugawa a small number had become economic administrators for their domain; they had the necessary entrepreneurial and management skills even though they did not have the personal property and capital to develop their own businesses. Government-supported regional banks, established in the 1870s, gave special help to sectors considered important for national development. Former *samurai* were more likely to gain governmental approval than were entrepreneurs from the merchant class who might be considered too willing to pursue their own personal interests. Many loans were government approved and sponsored and were used to carry on government-led efforts to acquire technology and know-how from abroad.

The very first large industries were developed in the 1870s. Some began as government corporations, but in 1881 they were sold at a relatively low cost to private companies. Although the government had ended its support of these companies to meet a financial crisis, another principle underlay its move: some basic industries might require government help to start or government models to teach them new ways, but they would prosper better and grow under private enterprise. Thus the decision to let some companies go private was made for communitarian reasons, an ideological basis very different from that for private property in the United States and Europe. The purchasers of these companies knew from the beginning that their success depended in part on the initial assistance given them by government. Even if they came from the merchant class rather than the *samurai* class, they did not feel that their success sprang entirely from their own efforts or that they had property rights on which outsiders could make no claim.

The greatest private financier of the Meiji Period was Eichi Shibusawa. A commoner son adopted into a *samurai* family, he worked briefly in the Ministry of Finance but quit to help modernize the private sector according to ethical principles adapted from traditional *samurai* values. To develop capital quickly, he promoted the joint stock company, and he played a great role in financing young companies. In 1890, when a chemical fertilizer plant was in difficulty with continuous losses, many shareholders wanted to scrap it. Shibusawa said, "This enterprise should not be looked upon from the angle of profit-making alone but for the good of the country. If the majority of shareholders decide to sell it, I shall take over its affairs myself by buying up all the shares that are left."

From the beginning of Meiji the large companies in key sectors had the view that, while it was permissible to make money and while in a certain sense they had the rights of private ownership, they were bounded by and responsible to the government and national interest. Some individuals, particularly from the merchant class, did build modern industries with very little support from government banks. However, the dominant view was that large companies created with government assistance were not privately owned but were operated for national purposes. The company existed for those working in the company rather than for the bankers and stockholders.

In the political arena during Meiji, the leaders were slow to extend new powers to ordinary citizens. People had duties but few rights. Citizens selected to serve the emperor in high government positions were beyond the influence of ordinary citizens, "above the clouds." Some elite opposition advocated strengthening "people's rights" and creating a parliamentary system, but when the constitution was finally promulgated in 1889, it was a "gift" from the emperor, not something created by voting or even legitimized as representing the will of the people. As in traditional Confucian thought, the advocates of

greater "people's rights" were regarded as selfish people looking after their own interests rather than attending to the higher
and more worthy cause of serving the nation as a whole.

The Market and Community Need

Just as during the Tokugawa the artisan ranked above the
merchant, so during the Meiji Period industry enjoyed higher
prestige than commerce. During the Tokugawa, the major
purpose of the state was to maintain order; the ideas of progress
and growth had not really taken hold. In the Meiji Period, the
purpose of industry was to strengthen the nation and increase
its well-being, and progress toward these goals could be measured. In the view of Meiji leaders, industry built wealth and
power for the nation and therefore met community needs.
Commerce met only the lowlier private desires. Creative merchants sometimes expanded their markets to meet consumer
desires in the marketplace, and some of them became quite
well-to-do, but they did not enjoy the same community respect
as those who were developing mining, public works, and
industry for the good of the nation. Because most of the industrial leaders came from the *samurai* class, it is not surprising
that they were prepared to think about the public good and
that they worked easily with government officials who shared
the same values, attitudes, and class background.

International trade was on a minor scale in early Meiji. The
main concern was acquiring industrial know-how to enrich
the nation. Imports of industrial goods in the early 1900s were
paid for by coal rather than by industrial products. Although it
is now common both at home and abroad to stress Japanese
dependence on energy imports, in the early twentieth century
Japan was an energy exporter.

After the economic boom of World War I, the great growth
of private income enabled the consumer market to expand
vigorously. The state had prospered, and Japan had earlier
acquired colonies—Taiwan in 1895 and Korea in 1910—that
could bring in more raw materials and food. As in England,
industrial goods could be produced on a larger scale because
they could be sold in the colonies. The resulting rise of living
standards reduced the necessity for sacrifice and permitted

some relaxation in the rush to modernize, but industrial and national development still had priority over commerce and consumerism.

The Unlimited State

The Meiji government was far from democratic. Leaders wanted a system that would select and cultivate a small but capable elite, totally dedicated to serving the nation. They found such people in the *samurai* class, and they were not concerned that everyone did not have equal access to opportunities for acquiring high levels of education or wealth. They wanted to insulate the elite who served national interests from possible pressures of commoners who could not be equally concerned or knowledgeable about national interests.

In line with the traditional neo-Confucian value placed on learning, early leaders of Meiji searched throughout the world for the best ideas and the most modern technology to stimulate and modernize their nation so that they might avoid being colonized by foreigners. Their first major mission abroad, the Iwakura Mission (1871–73), included senior officials from all major departments of government who traveled for more than eighteen months. They were pleasantly surprised to find themselves welcomed throughout the world and given open access to leaders in every walk of life. The Iwakura Mission, a huge success in opening access to new technology and new systems of organization, became the inspiration for later study tours, delegations, and extended study in every important area of economic, political, and military activity. Japanese leaders then began a systematic and careful introduction of new systems in all fields: government, administration, business organization, banking, military, education, local government, agriculture, and commerce.

Although the dominant view was that bureaucrats should be isolated from the public pressures of interest groups, the Emperor Meiji from the beginning accepted the notion that there should be a forum for public expression of opinion. In 1884 the Diet was established. Both the upper house, composed of former noblemen, and the lower house, composed of elected officials, were given the freedom to express the views of the public. Diet members gradually clamored for more rights, basing their argument in part on the existence of democratic assemblies in other modern countries. The Diet had the right to increase government budgets. Its refusal to vote such increases in some years created constraints on the bureaucrats who were forced to fulfill their duties within the budget level of the previous year. Otherwise, relations between the government officials and the public (including the politicians) were commonly expressed by the phrase *kanson minpi,* "respect the officials, look down on the people": the officials had the power and prestige, and the public had no legitimate basis on which to criticize them. Officials were selected on the basis of strict competitive examinations. In the early years only a very few were chosen, usually from *samurai* backgrounds. Thus, even other *samurai,* let alone commoners, were reluctant to criticize them. The public went as subjects and supplicants when they approached officials, not as citizens demanding their rights.

Education was to provide universal literacy so that everyone could play his role in society, but it was also a means for channeling the most talented to the top, where, as bureaucrats, they could work for the good of the nation. Meiji leaders moved rapidly to enhance public education. By the turn of the century, virtually all children of school age attended elementary school. Uniform national textbooks provided standardized information for all students. Special technical schools provided opportunities for people to acquire skills needed for newly growing industries, and for improving agriculture, fishing, mining, and forestry. Schools also provided a moral basis for the society. The most talented students from the entire country were selected to attend one of the eight regional numbered high schools. As in elite English schools, students there not only acquired common training but developed a sense of community and a common social perspective. The most talented of these high school graduates were admitted to one of the leading national universities, and the most talented graduates of these universities were destined to be bureaucrats. The government's education policies supported the idea of a meritocratic hierarchy rather than of egalitarianism.

Holism and Generalists over Specialists

Among artisans in the Tokugawa Period, the worker's responsibility to his master was not limited to the technical performance of the work itself. It included a broader responsibility to the master's family. The master was similarly responsible for the personal life of his worker. Apprentices and young workers acquired skills and rose slowly up the hierarchy. Great pride was taken in craftsmanship, for it was understood that skills were acquired only slowly and laboriously. The very complexity of the skills helped retard the rise of younger people so as not to threaten the social hierarchy. These feudal relationships between workers and their masters continued long after World War II, especially in small enterprises associated with traditional crafts.

Late in the nineteenth century, when modern industry was introduced, innovation was so rapid that traditional crafts lagged behind. Even schools could not always keep up with the latest changes, and large enterprises commonly offered systematic training to impart skills as quickly as possible. To insure that the employees remained with the company, repaying with their labor for the years of training they received, companies rapidly increased salary after training. Increases continued step-by-step with seniority. Salary was based not upon performance using a particular skill but on seniority, and therefore workers were happy to accept new assignments and learn new skills. Although workers expected to profit from acquiring new skills, the idea of training and self-improvement had an added aura of traditional Confucian respect for learning and self-cultivation. Workers also realized that the world around them was modernizing, and they wanted to acquire the latest skills so that their company and they themselves could keep up with changes that would enhance their competitive position with other companies and other employees. Companies could therefore move quickly to adapt to technological change; featherbedding rarely blocked technical modernization. Until well into the 1960s those employees in the modern sector received far more salary than those in the traditional sectors, and they were responsive to their leaders' wishes even if they were less prepared to accept the personal obligations that artisans in the traditional sectors acknowledged.

The highest positions in companies and in the government bureaucracy went to generalists not to specialists. The ablest young people were selected for advancement at the time they entered the company or bureaucracy. At the university such persons may have studied law, economics, or engineering. Within the bureaucracy there were three major levels of career track, and a person was assigned to one of them on the basis of his entrance exam. Once in the company, the person was given training and the opportunities to acquire a broad solid background to enable him to follow developments in Japan and around the world. The trainee performed a variety of jobs and learned a great deal about each of them, but the goal was broad preparation for leadership. Those on the elite track were given the leisure to think about the big issues without being constrained by questions of details. By the time they reached the higher levels of the company they would have an understanding of all the basic issues. With their broad training, they could then provide the perspective to guide their respective ministries and companies through rounds of progressive modernization. In every Japanese organization, the leading people are still concerned with the health of the organization as a whole.

When the Japanese began learning from the West, they took institutions that they thought would benefit the nation as a whole. They eagerly brought in modern factories, corporations, banks, universities, army, and navy. They tried to avoid lawyers of the Western sort, who created greater divisiveness in society and tended to pull it apart. They avoided excessive concern with individual rights and due process, both of which they believed would make it difficult for organizations to look out for the overall order.

At the beginning of Meiji, there were enormous differences of culture. People had such strong regional accents that many people in Japan were unintelligible to each other. When universal education was introduced, the same textbooks were used throughout the nation to provide a common base of culture for everyone. Standard pronunciation was stressed in schools and radio broadcasts so that people of all social stations in all localities would speak the same way. Foreigners occasionally talk of the advantage of homogeneity in Japan. The homogeneity did not occur naturally: it was forged by national policy.

It is easy to idealize the Japanese consensus. But its roots were firmly laid by Meiji, when consensus was imposed by leaders. At the national level, decisions of the government were not to be questioned for they were made by servants of the sacred emperor; at the local level, respected senior citizens made the decisions. Revolutionary sentiments and populist movements from the lower ranks—labor, farmers, and ordinary citizens—have existed, but they have not been powerful. Marxists might explain this as a result of oppression. Philosophers might explain it as the result of Confucianism. A social scientist might explain it as a result of a certain kind of benevolent concern by persons in authority for the welfare of those lower down, especially in a stable feudal society. Whatever the explanation, benevolent persons in authority are also willing to isolate and punish whoever might challenge the basic social order.

EXTREME COMMUNITARIANISM AND THE "SECOND OPENING" OF JAPAN

In the 1920s many of the Western ideas of individualism began to circulate widely in Japan. The press became freer and more varied. The burgeoning cities and the growing white-collar classes provided a basis for challenging the more feudalistic ideas grounded in the countryside. After 1930, with rising unemployment, unrest began among laborers and farmers. But after the Manchurian Incident in 1931, and especially after the outbreak of the China War in 1937, war mobilization was wrapped in the flag and Imperial decrees. Controls became tighter, sacrifices became greater. The rights of free speech and publication were increasingly curtailed, and thought-police gained new powers. Low-priority industries received fewer goods, and the interests of the individual were further curbed. Soft authoritarianism became hard authoritarianism, an extreme form of communitarianism that demanded sacrifice and ultimately led to defeat.

The American-led Occupation (1945–52) occasioned a reexamination of every aspect of Japanese society. This "second opening" of Japan had more impact on the average person than the "first opening" with the arrival of Admiral Perry in early Meiji, for more people had direct contact with the world outside Japan, especially after the consumer revolution began. Under American leadership, new efforts were made to democratize government and education, to deconcentrate industry, to strengthen labor unions, and to decentralize government power. Although some initiatives came from foreigners, much of the real work was done by Japanese working within the Occupation. Even the Japanese public basically accepted the thrust of the Occupation. Filled with revulsion for the wartime secret police, the millions of deaths, the sacrifices, the military who had dragged the country into the war with propaganda that proved to be false, the Japanese public was broadly receptive to many of the changes introduced by the Occupation. Furthermore, as Edwin O. Reischauer and others have argued, many of the trends introduced during the Allied Occupation were a continuation of trends introduced by the Japanese themselves in the 1920s, before the aberrations of ultra-nationalism in the 1930s.

After 1952, when the Japanese regained control of their own government and could once again engage in foreign relations, the Japanese could have eliminated all changes introduced by the Occupation. Some companies split by the Occupation were recombined, and some officials once purged were welcomed back to companies and government. Antitrust efforts faded and labor militancy became less effective. Yet the main lines of reform introduced by the Occupation were continued under Japanese rule. Although democratization and individualism have taken firm root, communitarian concern for family, company, community, and nation have continued to be strong. Leaders not only maintained their communitarian ideology but worked to provide the conditions that would reinforce it.

IDEOLOGICAL COMPONENTS OF THE 1980s

Communitarianism with Growing Individualism

All groups and individuals in the society acknowledge—even take for granted—the desirability of working together for national purposes. Since World War II, the preeminent concern has been reviving the country, bringing the fruits of a high standard of living to all citizens and giving the Japanese a place of honor in the world. Japanese work well together because they were trained as children to enjoy the benefits of cooperation, because the view persists that people are subjects of the nation rather than citizens with inalienable rights, because there are rewards for those who cooperate and benefits are withheld from those who do not, and because they believe that the fate of everyone living on the Japanese islands is closely bound together. There is no moral basis for resisting the group, but the Japanese are not machines who respond automatically to calls for cooperation. Like people elsewhere, they have personal interests that they pursue, but social norms give greater rewards for cooperation.

Individualism is still not a positive value. It would be a grave mistake to assume that Japanese will acquire that ideology, as if individualism were a more advanced stage of development. There is a growing belief that the existing system should accommodate the special needs of people in various situations, especially the young and the widowed. Even then, part of the reason for helping the less fortunate is to increase more people's commitment to the system as a whole, to make it more effective for everyone.

Hierarchy. The Japanese accept the sorting of talent on the basis of exams and interviews when people enter the university, a company, or the bureaucracy. They recognize that people who do not then become regular employees of the bureaucracy or large firms will never again have the opportunity. People in small companies obviously have great opportunities to rise later, and it is even possible for some to leave large companies and become more successful elsewhere. In large companies and in the bureaucracy, minor differences in position among those in the same age group also become very important foci for competition. But within broad limits, the Japanese accept the legitimacy of different tracks with different hierarchical positions beginning at a young age.

At the same time, a person is evaluated not just in how high his status is but how well he plays his particular role. People in all stations commonly take pride in their work. They are eager to improve their performance, and they seek new opportunities to upgrade their skills. Society is sufficiently stable that others know how well they are performing their assigned function and respect them accordingly.

Consensus. Employees at all levels in the bureaucracy and in a company are encouraged to find ways to assist their organization in performing its job better and to inform others of these ideas. Employees are expected to work hard and to make some sacrifices when it is in the company's interest. In turn, management will look after the interests of employees, help them grow and develop, and give them a substantial share of the benefits of the company's success.

In a very important sense, the purpose of the company is to serve the interests of its employees rather than those of its stockholders. It is understood that the long-term interest of the company may require it to go into debt for some years, and that employees will be laid off or fired only after every other reasonable measure has been taken. When no alternative is available, a company will release people over a long period of time, making great efforts to assist each of those of work age to find new employment. Workers do not share in management. Management is often frank in sharing basic information about a company, but in the end the decisions are in the hands of management. This is considered necessary for timely and effective responses, and it is generally accepted that management is looking out for the interests of workers.

When problems arise, Japanese are quick to form ad hoc organizations that will draw on information from around the world to create flexible and rapid solutions. Opportunities are provided for everyone in the society. Those who cooperate are rewarded. Those who do not cooperate or work with others, and people with no employment are not confident of their ability to win a satisfactory livelihood. Deviants are ordinarily dealt with quickly and harshly.

Although loyalty to family, village, neighborhood, community, and to a variety of special-interest groups is encouraged, it is understood that in times of great change an employee's loyalties to these groups may be subordinated or reorganized to accord with the needs of his place of work and with those of the nation as a whole.

Duties with Increasing Rights

Broadly speaking, the individual had duties but no rights before World War II. In the postwar period, the individual's assertion of rights is still equated by many with selfishness, but many employees no longer believe that they have responsibilities to their superiors that extend beyond regular work hours. Employees ordinarily expect that they will not work more than forty or forty-five hours a week, that they will have more than a few vacation days each year, and that the company cannot call upon them in their free time except under the most unusual circumstances. Superiors in the company are expected to continue to look after the welfare of the employees. These mutual obligations are not contractual or legalistic but social, and they are subject to a certain degree of flexibility that people assume will not be abused. Company leaders are committed to their employees, and employees are committed to the long-term success of the company and of their friends in the company. People in various sections of a company are expected to have a good sense of the purposes of the whole company, to identify with and act in accord with those purposes, and to take initiatives that will help bring them about.

While Japanese ideology still strongly supports the importance of craftsmanship and continuing training to perfect a worker's skills, there is not a sharp dividing line between people of different specialties. Companies may reorganize radically every few years to accommodate to rapid changes in the world, and people are assigned to different jobs as the need arises. But pay systems for regular employees are based not so much on specific skills or specific assignments as on general abilities and on loyalty and service to the company. Therefore, employees are not worried about reorganizations, believing they will benefit from the growth that the changes herald. Workers expect that they will receive bonuses in accordance with company profits and that the company will assist them if they are ill or in need. However, if workers do not perform their jobs properly, it is understood that the company can easily get rid of them. The social pressures are strong on those who do not exert themselves on the behalf of their enterprise and their co-workers.

Social security and welfare are tied to employment. It is not assumed that every human being is automatically entitled to certain benefits, although each is entitled to opportunities to work. The benefits of security and welfare come to a person because he is willing to work and accept his obligations to society. Unemployment has remained low. Bureaucrats have fought to protect agriculture and other declining sectors from imports to preserve employment opportunities.

The Market Bounded by Community Needs

Certain leaders are expected to define what is good for the country and then to find ways that their own organizations can help in that effort. Nonetheless, each enterprise is expected to pursue vigorously its own interest. Enterprises are to remain competitive, to expand or maintain large shares of the market in certain key product lines, and to find ways to use the skills within the company to take advantage of areas that offer a promising future. It is accepted as natural that units in the bureaucracy struggle to preserve their authority within their jurisdictions and to expand their jurisdictions in areas important for the future.

Just as the Tokugawa leaders acknowledged that strong clans had to be given considerable leeway to manage their own affairs, so contemporary Japanese government officials acknowledge that local government and especially private enterprises must have sufficient leeway to run their own organizations without interference or surprises from government. Businesses are allowed a fair share of the market so long as they operate within certain bounds.

Japanese believe that competition in world markets is a powerful driving force and they want to use it to the fullest. However, the market can work hardships on individuals and companies that are still operating in the nation's long-term interest. The most knowledgeable people in the relevant fields are constantly discussing how to assist organizations to make necessary adjustments to changes in world markets with the greatest speed consistent with solving the human adjustment problems. Government and sectoral leaders try to assist enterprises in understanding trends and in obtaining access to low-cost capital, technology, and human talent to hasten and strengthen appropriate competition.

The public acknowledges that the government should assist sectors adversely affected by economic changes beyond their control. Sectoral and governmental leaders try to anticipate such developments, seeking out new areas or promising parts of familiar areas where companies can still compete effectively. When copper cables for telephone wire were in the early stages of becoming obsolete, companies were assisted in learning fiber optic technology so that good use could be made of the talent and organization they had already developed. In coal mining, however, where economic circumstances beyond anyone's control render a company incapable of adapting, other companies are assisted so that they can absorb the displaced personnel over a period of several years.

It is believed that major sectors will prosper best by having several strong companies competing vigorously with each other, but not in a vague "free market." The market is guided by sector leaders in various companies who cooperate with government officials to encourage the use of the most important technologies, rapid reorganization to cope with changing international markets, and substantial investment in areas considered strategically important for the future. This is a far cry from the antitrust notion that the U.S. Occupation sought to introduce.

Companies are considered responsible for meeting and adapting to the requirements of the surrounding community. They are praised for providing recreational and educational facilities that are beneficial to the employees and others in the communities in which they live. Since 1970, companies have been held responsible for the effects of pollution. Government and business associations work together in trying to promote research and new technology to speed the development of pollution control equipment, reduce pollution, and spread the expense of installing controls among the polluters.

At the local level new mechanisms enable community representatives to present the needs of their community to relevant business and government bodies. Leaders of protest movements are generally co-opted to work within government and business organizations. If the protest group is considered too uncompromising, an effort is made to isolate it, reduce its base of power, and limit its room for maneuvering.

Government Guidance

The role of the government is not to maintain a level playing field, but to provide the climate necessary to preserve social order, encourage business to perform well in every sector, and benefit the entire nation. Government helps define community need and mobilizes the consensus necessary to implement it.

Since 1944 when the bombing of Japanese ships cut Japan off from imports, the Japanese have been acutely aware of their dependence on international trade. Japan's military domination of Taiwan, Korea, and Manchuria had previously permitted the necessary imports, but after 1945 it could import only by using foreign currency derived from exports. Making Japan's exports competitive in world markets, therefore, became the top government priority. Government leaders had no difficulty persuading people in all arenas to work for this priority.

The key government person in each sector is less like a general giving orders than like a symphony conductor working with each player to bring out his best performance while keeping in mind the necessity of guiding the whole toward the desired result. Groups with different interests are constantly meeting to explore possible common ground for mutually beneficial activity. Bureaucrats therefore work closely with many different groups of leaders in a given private sector, goading them to consider issues, collect relevant information, and push toward a consensus without imposing a particular solution. They stand ready to implement a sectoral consensus about what is desirable in the long run. Officials have administrative means for keeping companies from colluding in cartel-like arrangements that are not in the public interest, but the constant sharing of information between government and business and the mood surrounding sectoral discussions has the effect of persuading the sector toward better performance for the company, for the sector, and for the nation as a whole. Short-range profit taking is not a part of the game plan.

Government officials in a particular sector are held responsible for overall developments in their area. This sense of accountability serves as a powerful motive for them to further the interests of the sector for which they are responsible. Japanese ministries constantly poll the public on policy-related issues in their sphere. They are guided by public opinion, but they also consider it their responsibility to guide opinion to greater awareness of the public interest.

Bureaucrats work to insulate themselves from the particular interests of companies and local communities, which usually turn to politicians to represent their interests. Politicians have limited leeway, within the framework of broad national interests, for helping special-interest groups. Nevertheless bureaucrats retain greater moral authority and more de facto power than politicians, for they are seen as representing national rather than selfish interests. Bureaucrats try to articulate issues so that everyone will participate. They try to provide fair shares for all enterprises and communities that cooperate. Japanese companies and communities do not necessarily yield easily to requests for consensus, but bureaucrats endeavor to find ground rules for dividing up benefits in ways that all groups believe to be fair and that give them a stake in the success of the system. Companies benefit by cooperating with the sector as a whole. Labor cooperates because wage adjustments every year are based upon the success of the company.

Holism

Labor and management, government and business leaders, and leaders of competing companies in the same sector work together for common purposes much more than in most Western countries. Great efforts are made to cultivate strong informal ties and to create a climate of human warmth and understanding that will make it easy to find new flexible ways to solve problems. In the Japanese view, many Westerners are excessively rigid, conservative, unimaginative, legalistic, and egotistic when they deal with common problems.

GROWING AND DECLINING INDUSTRIES

By World War II, the determined drive that began with the Iwakura Mission in 1871 to build modern industry by learning from the West had achieved considerable success. The textile industry was highly developed and Nippon Steel was a world-class steel producer. At the beginning of the war, Japanese Zero fighter planes were far superior to American fighter planes, and the *Yamato* and *Musashi* were the world's most advanced battleships. Communications had been modernized, especially in Manchuria. Although there was not yet a modern automobile industry, Nissan and Toyota were producing trucks in substantial numbers. Mitsubishi, Mitsui, Sumitomo, Hitachi, Toshiba, NEC, and Kawasaki were well-established large corporations. By World War II, the Japanese population was entirely literate, and specialists in science and engineering were rapidly approaching or achieving world levels of excellence. The population that emerged from World War II was highly disciplined, and institutions were in place for industry to cooperate with the government.

In the late 1940s Japan lacked the equipment and the capital to produce modern industrial goods. Within days after the end of the war Japanese business and government leaders began meeting to discuss how they should work together to revive the nation. The old Industrial Club had somehow escaped bombing, and former business leaders and government representatives began assembling there to plot strategy for their various sectors and for business as a whole. When senior business leaders were jailed for cooperating with the militarists in bringing about World War II, their former underlings continued in their place. When the old *zaibatsu* ("financial cliques") were disbanded, former associates kept in touch. New associations were established to help bring back modern industry. *Keizai Doyukai* (the Committee on Economic Development) was uncannily successful in selecting promising young people in every major area, virtually all of whom dominated their fields in later years.

By 1952 when the Occupation ended and the Japanese took control over their own fate, some of the basic industries had already been rebuilt. Production was not yet at prewar levels, but it was well started, helped along considerably when purchases and repairs were ordered by the Allied Forces during the Korean War.

By that time, Japanese government and business leaders had already achieved a high level of consensus about how to develop their industries. They were determined to prevent foreign control of their economy. With minor exceptions considered absolutely essential, they did not allow foreign companies to establish factories. The government, with full business support and cooperation, accepted some limited foreign capital, but only when it let them retain control of activities. They strictly controlled foreign currency to bring in critical equipment and technology needed to modernize their own equipment. They imported only when models and building tools were necessary for their own manufacturing, for rebuilding industry was assigned higher priority. They sent people abroad to study and find the most appropriate technology, and when necessary they bought the patents and licensing agreements, always at the cheapest possible price.

They tried to produce all the basic minimal goods the society needed, including simple housing to replace that destroyed by bombing. But they concentrated their capital, their foreign currency, and their modern technology in areas where they could produce for export. They knew that a domestic economy would continue for decades behind the export economy, but they chose to modernize in sectors necessary for export. They found ways to encourage the accumulation of capital. They began by exporting textiles and low-grade electronics products requiring only small investment where low wages gave them the competitive advantage. Since the nation could not prosper only by exporting such low-priced goods, they began to lay the foundation for heavy industry, concentrating in strategic areas: steel, basic for all machinery industries, and shipbuilding, where they felt they had the expertise and could quickly become world leaders.

Before the war, the labor movement was kept under tight control by traditionalism, strong authoritarian leadership combined with a measure of benevolence, and an excess labor supply. After the war the Occupation encouraged a democratic labor movement, and pent-up dissatisfactions of laborers working long hours with low pay fueled a militant labor movement. Strikes were frequent during the 1950s, culminating in the great Miike Coal Mine strike in 1960.

In the 1950s, business leaders realized that modernization required the cooperation of labor. *Nikkeiren* (the Federation of Employers), a national organization of company leaders, tried to work out a modus vivendi with labor leaders to meet the needs of both. Real union power was at the enterprise level, and here managers worked closely with labor to gain their cooperation. Labor's key concern was "rationalization," the national effort to increase productivity, for unions feared it would cost them jobs. In 1955 leaders established the Japan Productivity Center to guide the rationalization program nationally. The Center was designed to be a neutral place where business, academics, labor, and appropriate liaison with government officials would study together how to raise productivity. The Productivity Center and other similar organizations were crucial in building an understanding among labor leaders about what was necessary to meet foreign competition and in forging understandings with business leaders that would reduce workers' anxieties about their future.

Top officials in the Ministry of International Trade and Industry (MITI), *Keidanren* (Federation of Economic Organizations), *Nikkeiren,* and the Industrial Structure Council (the advisory group to MITI) focused on the needs of the economy as a whole. The workaday units in MITI, *Keidanren,* and elsewhere focused on particular sectors but remained in constant contact with higher-level leaders to coordinate sectoral plans with overall plans. Higher leaders constantly refined their agendas about which sectors were at any one time best able to use substantial support so that the nation could be pushed to new levels of competitive advantage. The Economic Planning Agency, formed in 1955, played a fundamental role in this coordination, bringing together forecasts in each sector to consider their implications for other sectors.

Each industrial sector (whether steel, ships, computers, or petrochemicals) spawned a network of associations bringing together MITI officials, academics, labor, media people, and business. Some associations brought together all companies in the sector; others brought together only the major companies in the sector; still others dealt only with finance, manpower, training, or public relations. There were regular associations and ad hoc groups, working meetings and social gatherings. The Industrial Structure Council, *Nikkeiren, Keidanren,* and major trading companies had subgroups concerned with a particular sector. Each sector had a press club. This network of associations was the crucible for working through issues concerning sectoral growth. MITI and other government officials enunciated policy, but only after the ideas had been vented in the appropriate sectoral networks. The basic issue that preoccupied all the associations in a sector was how to make Japanese companies competitive in international markets. The associations became vehicles for raising awareness, collecting information, sifting and refining the information, and reducing external uncertainties.

In the 1950s, electronics and watches were seen as areas of growing value to the economy, but the firms themselves were considered capable of handling the required levels of funding, organization, and technology. The government closely monitored developments and offered institutional support and a business-friendly climate, but the main issues of growth were left to the businesses. On the other hand, steel and shipbuilding were considered important growth areas that required considerable government assistance in technology, know-how, and funding. The officials responsible for these sectors became gadflies in the network of associations. They called attention to the stakes, the foreign competition, the need for a vision, and the need for concerted action. They were also implementers, using the leverage of government power if necessary to keep reluctant companies in line and to get the necessary cooperation with other sectors.

Their means were remarkably ad hoc and flexible. When cooperation between the companies was hard to achieve, they enlisted the Development Bank in setting up a program of financing that was so attractive that the companies could not refuse. When a small company was not strong enough to make good use of a foreign license it wanted to acquire, MITI made sure that the approval went rather to a stronger Japanese company that could make better use of it. MITI would even work out arrangements whereby the company that obtained the technology by licensing was rewarded for sharing it with all other relevant Japanese companies. When the sector needed critical information, MITI contacted trading companies, or reporters, or Japanese students or scholars abroad, or foreign experts. They followed foreign competition in incredible detail.

When key products required mass production to be competitive, MITI encouraged mergers or product segmentation or found ways to guarantee that products would have a market in order to encourage the firms to move more rapidly into production. They found ways to insure that ample low-cost capital was available, and they helped devise tax and other incentives. They found ways to learn about the relevant research being conducted in key parts of the world and to encourage key engineering applications. When foreign products threatened to smother the development of Japanese products or to take away significant market share, they found ways to make competitively priced products so that there would be little market opportunity for foreign products. They put the actors in touch with others who might speed up the development of products and markets that might otherwise fall between two stools. In short, in the urgency of meeting foreign competition, the network of sectoral associations gave tremendous support to companies that were themselves working hard to meet foreign competition and even other Japanese competition as well.

The same network of associations operates in the case of declining sectors. The effort is always to modernize portions of an industry, even helping to locate financing, so that the sector does not decline absolutely but only relative to other sectors that are growing rapidly. High technology in Japan is not considered a sector by itself but a means for increasing productivity so that sectors such as steel and shipbuilding can remain competitive, despite high costs of labor or energy resources. New technologies are made to put in place as rapidly as possible, like computer-controlled manufacturing, robots, lasers, and sensors. In textiles, an effort was made to speed the transition from cotton to synthetics first, and later to newer materials like ultrasuede but also to higher fashions so that Japan's higher labor costs can be met. In steel, companies are helped to move into new composite materials so that, if steel itself is partly replaced, the personnel in these companies can have continuing employment opportunities.

When the market is saturated, cartels are formed (as in textiles, steel, and shipbuilding), to work out acceptable formulas for reducing overall production. It is common for the government to subsidize the destruction of a certain percentage of a company's productive facilities, usually the outmoded ones, so that only the most modern and competitive facilities will remain. This prevents successful organizations from disbanding teams of personnel, and it avoids serious dislocations. If necessary, the government offers incentives for unsuccessful companies to merge so that as many competent personnel as possible from the old companies can be absorbed. In case of bailouts, constant government surveillance makes it possible to identify problems early. The controlling banks, trading companies, parent or affiliated companies, or the central government will send some of their own staff into the ailing company to provide the know-how, firm backbone, or special aid necessary for developing a plan to reconstruct the company. If a merger is necessary, the private and public sectors cooperate to relocate and retrain personnel displaced by the closing of noncompetitive facilities.

Many of these strategies simply involve frequent discussions that clarify opportunities, define the market situation with greater information so as to reduce risks, and divide the market so as to reduce competition. The Japanese government and quasi-government institutions give far less direct aid than most foreigners imagine, but subsidies and tax incentives are available when a sector needs to be restructured or when important activities that companies could not do themselves need to be made possible.

When a sector becomes uncompetitive internationally, as in aluminum, foreign imports may gain significant shares of the market. More often, foreign imports are restrained so that they capture only a very small portion of the domestic market. Since the mid-1960s, Japan has responded to pressures from trading partners by reducing import duties and by resorting to less formal trade association practices to preserve the domestic industry. By and large Japan's "declining" industries—textiles, steel, and shipbuilding—have maintained fairly high levels of production and market share.

SUCCESSES AND PROBLEMS

In the 1980s, Japan compares favorably with other nations by almost any measure—the economy, the health of the population, educational levels, pride in work, or commitment to company and fellow workers. Explanations given for Japanese success are legion, but certainly one key ingredient is the adaptability of Japanese ideology to changing external realities.

During the course of modernization, *samurai* gave up their own class privileges, clans went along with their own abolition, tightly knit communities accepted amalgamation into larger units, landlords gracefully yielded property during land reform in exchange for little more than token payments. The Japanese have changed loyalties from clan to nation, from village to town, from family to firm. Yet a basic communitarian ideology that acknowledges the importance of cooperating for the collective good has remained firm throughout.

Japan's relative success, now known by leaders around the world, should not disguise the tremendous internal struggles and rivalries and even ideological conflicts. Ever since the Meiji Period when some Japanese citizens first traveled abroad and returned to demand greater individual freedom and rights, the Japanese have disagreed with each other about how much to move from feudalism to individualism, how to balance rights and duties, and how to balance national and sectional interests. Such conflicts have occurred at every level of society.

At the national level one of the most basic struggles is between the politicians, who nurture their power by responding to entrenched and increasingly wealthy interest groups that represent sectors and localities, and bureaucrats, who see their responsibility as assuring that the nation as a whole responds to the demands of world markets of the future. At the local level there are constant struggles between companies and communities involving *rigai kankei* ("real issues of interest"). There are struggles between employees who want more benefits and privileges, and managers who expect more effort from workers. There are jurisdictional struggles between bureaucrats who believe that their particular approach is better for the nation than rival portions of the bureaucracy. Yet, compared to other contemporary societies, the society works relatively smoothly with considerable success.

The goal toward which Japanese communitarianism is directed is still economic success, and here the Japanese are unparalleled. They are automating manufacturing more rapidly than any other nation. The unprecedented accumulation of assets by Japanese companies, together with its efforts to achieve superiority in the service sector, give Japan the potential of dominating service industries. Japanese companies are becoming so competitive that it is not clear whether other countries can protect their own industries while maintaining open markets. Japanese vulnerability to charges of erecting nontariff barriers makes it easier for other countries to increase their protectionism.

Japan's biggest problem is coping with pressures from other countries. The interests of certain domestic groups are threatened by these pressures, and the capacity of the network of communities to broker the kinds of consensus that have served Japan so well is being unhinged. The very success of Japan in international trade leads other countries to be passionately concerned with issues of reciprocity. Japanese groups achieve a consensus by agreeing that all will unite against pressures from foreigners. When the choice is between yielding to Japanese pressure groups or to foreign pressure groups, Japanese politicians give priority to maintaining their domestic base of support. Internationalists within Japan who, by virtue of excellent contacts with foreigners, have provided a buffer that enables Japanese society to retain its basic internal cohesion, ordinarily lose out to nationalists. However, the continuing dissatisfaction of foreigners who demand a more thorough going opening of markets remains a threat to common procedures of consensus building. Leaders at the highest level recognize in theory the need for greater openness, but bureaucrats and sectoral leaders are constantly finding ways to look after their own interests, regardless of platitudes enunciated at higher levels. Having evolved their own style and organizations that are now operating with considerable success, the Japanese are reluctant to open their doors further. They fear that their own brokering institutions would be deprived of the sanctions that keep Japanese organizations responsive to the national consensus.

Aside from the ongoing difficulty of responding to foreign pressures, Japanese ideology appears to have served the nation well.

SELECTED BIBLIOGRAPHY

Bellah, Robert N. *Tokugawa Religion.* New York: Free Press, 1957.

Craig, Albert M., and Donald H. Shively, eds. *Personality in Japanese History.* Berkeley: University of California Press, 1970.

Dore, R. P., ed. *Aspects of Social Change in Modern Japan.* Princeton: Princeton University Press, 1967.

Duus, Peter. *The Rise of Modern Japan.* Boston: Houghton Mifflin, 1974.

Jansen, Marius, ed. *Changing Japanese Attitudes Toward Modernization.* Princeton: Princeton University Press, 1965.

Marshall, Byron K. *Capitalism and Nationalism in Prewar Japan.* Stanford: Stanford University Press, 1967.

Maruyama, Masao. *Studies in the Intellectual History of Tokugawa.* Tokyo: University of Tokyo Press, 1974.

—— *Thought and Behavior in Modern Japanese Politics.* Oxford: Oxford University Press, 1963.

Reischauer, Edwin O. *Japan: The Story of a Nation.* New York: Alfred A. Knopf, 1970.

Shively, Donald H., ed. *Tradition and Modernization in Japanese Culture.* Princeton: Princeton University Press, 1971.

Tsunoda, Ryusaku, ed. *Sources of Japanese Tradition.* New York: Columbia University Press, 1958.

Vogel, Ezra F. *Japan as Number One.* Cambridge, Mass.: Harvard University Press, 1979.

Ward, Robert E., ed. *Political Development in Modern Japan.* Princeton: Princeton University Press, 1968.

7

STATISM AND FAMILISM
ON TAIWAN

Edwin A. Winckler

Some years ago I attended a conference at which a young
Chinese-American scholar aptly contrasted American, Japanese, and Chinese "national character." In the language of this
volume, what he said was:

> Americans' primary values are individualistic and under-
> neath, most of their secondary values are individualistic
> as well. The primary values of Japanese are communitarian
> and, underneath, so are most of their secondary values.
> However, the primary values of Chinese are communitarian
> but, underneath, most of their secondary values are highly
> individualistic.

Dozens of literary, academic, and journalistic accounts identify
this same conflict in Chinese ideology between a genuine
commitment to public conformity and an ingenious pursuit of
private interest.

From this perspective, Taiwanese appear triply conflicted.* First, the typically Chinese tension between communitarianism and individualism is exacerbated in their case. Until 1895 the island of Taiwan was a southeastern frontier of the Chinese empire where the veneer of communitarianism was particularly thin and the imperatives of individualism particularly strong. Second, the communitarian side of Taiwanese ideology was reinforced by contacts with communitarian Japanese. Japan ruled Taiwan as a colony from 1895 to 1945 and, after 1945, resumed active trade and investment. Third, since 1945, the individualist side of Taiwanese ideology has been reinforced under Nationalist Chinese rule by direct interaction with individualist Americans. The United States has influenced Taiwan indirectly through American involvement in prewar China and postwar Japan, and directly through forty years of extensive postwar American involvement in Taiwan's own development. Postwar swings between communitarianism and individualism on the Communist mainland have also had some impact. Taiwan continues to develop separately from the rest of China, however, because the Nationalist government on Taiwan continues to reject any overtures from the Communist government on the mainland for direct political, economic, or even social or cultural relations.

These historical tensions convey the gist of Taiwan's position on the dimensions of ideology explored in this volume: Taiwan's indigenous heritage, external contacts, and present situation all contain both communitarianism and individualism, partly complementing and partly contradicting each other. However, like any country, Taiwan occupies a somewhat distinctive place on these dimensions. The custodian of communitarianism on Taiwan is the state, a mildly authoritarian and partly alien state that claims to represent the interests of Taiwanese society but has pursued its own objectives as well, primarily survival against Chinese communism. The manifestation of individualism on Taiwan is the family, still the dominant form of business

---

*In this paper "Taiwanese" refers to Chinese who came to Taiwan from Southeast China before 1945, and "mainlander" refers to Chinese who came to Taiwan from all parts of China after 1945.

organization, to which most individual interests remain firmly subordinated. Consequently, the version of communitarian ideology that is most relevant to Taiwan is statism, and the most relevant version of individualism is familism.

Statism asserts the independence of the state from domestic social forces. The Nationalist party that rules Taiwan bases its claim to autonomy primarily on nationalism. This is an awkward stance, because the state has lost the nation (China) to which its nationalism refers, and it has imposed itself on another society (Taiwan) with its own aspirations to nationhood. Nevertheless, the Nationalist party continues to regard itself as having an ideological mission of national defense and even national salvation that supersedes the immediate interests of Taiwanese society. The economic development policies of the Nationalist state on Taiwan are the upshot of another struggle among the various bureaus of the Nationalist state itself over how to minimize foreign dependence and maximize domestic autonomy.

Familism guides what is still the most important mode of political-economic organization on Taiwan: the economically corporate, occupationally diversified, spatially dispersed Chinese family. The extended family pools resources, spreads risk, and maximizes returns across male-related branches and male-related generations. It performs many of the functions of investment, production, and employment assumed by Western corporations, and many of the security, welfare, and retirement functions assumed by Western states. Depending on the political-economic environment, the family can reallocate resources between economic and political entrepreneurship, and between offensive and defensive strategies. By forming networks and stabilizing them through formal organizations, elite families can eventually form an economic class. If the state is occupied by an alien force, they may even form a shadow government as well.

Thus the postwar transfer of the Nationalist state to Taiwan adds a final further fillip to the ideological tension between statism and familism. Despite much convergence of interests since 1945, the state remains largely mainlander-Nationalist, the families mostly islander-Taiwanese. Meanwhile both statism and familism have come under increasing pressure from the growing internationalization of economic activity and the accelerating pace of economic change.

PAST

The past relationships between mainlander statism and Taiwanese familism have ranged from traditional commonality as part of imperial China, to prewar divergence under Japanese rule, to the postwar convergence that continues today.

Imperial Chinese Taiwan (1600–1895)

Imperial China was for centuries the largest market in the world, with probably the lowest ratio of bureaucratic control to market activity. The state assumed responsibility for maintaining external security, internal order, and religious orthodoxy. However, families operated the economy, rural and urban.

Within this empire, Taiwan remained a maritime frontier of pirates, strongmen, uprisings, and aborigines. Colonization began about the same time as that of North America and proceeded proportionately. Because of its coastal location, Taiwan received some of the earliest and strongest foreign influence in all China, and it began some of the earliest and most adaptive responses. In 1860 harbors in north and south became treaty ports open to foreigners. The Ch'ing state responded to Western military contact and commercial penetration by modernizing Taiwan's administration and improving its communications. Families seized opportunities for exports of tea and camphor and for the crude processing of sugar and rice. By the end of the nineteenth century Taiwan was already externally connected to much of East Asia and internally adapted to further development.

Confucianism, the ideological legacy of traditional China for modern Taiwan, charged state officials with heavy responsibilities for managing society. Nevertheless, even more than on the mainland, on Taiwan the family remained the basic unit of economic and political survival.

Colonial Japanese Taiwan (1895–1945)

Taiwan's first major encounter with Westernization was rule by Japan. Taiwan was Japan's first colony, and Japan wanted to prove itself the equal of Western powers. By the 1920s, as part of its own drive for upward mobility within the world economy, Japan had equipped Taiwan to export semitropical agricultural products to Japan and to import light industrial products from Japan. A Taiwanese elite of commercialized landlords and radicalized intelligentsia demanded better terms of trade and greater political participation. Taiwanese peasant and labor movements demanded greater freedom and higher compensation. Both elites and masses were soon suppressed.

In the 1930s, responding to an economic nationalism that accompanied worldwide recession, Japan tied Taiwan still closer to itself. In preparation for war, Japan began installing some heavy industry on Taiwan (hydropower, aluminum, chemicals). In the early 1940s Japan even began to transfer some of its light industries to Taiwan.

What was the ideological legacy of Japanese colonialism for postwar Taiwan? The state had proved itself a demanding but rewarding leader. The family had proved itself a versatile and adaptive follower. Taiwanese had learned to look to Japan as both model and market. Japanese had monopolized the modern sector, but Taiwanese had observed modern production technologies and managerial techniques, modern bureaucratic administration, and political representation.

Nationalist Chinese Taiwan (1945–present)

Mainland China had its own century of external encounters with Westerners—and of internal economic and political development. Gradually a modernizing Nationalist state emerged. However, in the 1940s the American defeat of Japan precipitated dependence on Americans, and internal defeat by Communists precipitated flight to Taiwan.

On Taiwan, the Nationalist government ran the infrastructure and industry inherited from the Japanese. Economic austerity took priority over economic welfare, political security over political participation. Nevertheless, the state achieved much support for these institutional arrangements among the then majority rural population, in part by land reform, which gave at least some land to most families.

A policy struggle ensued between those within the Nationalist state who gave priority to short-term defense and those who gave priority to long-term development. Americans played a crucial role in enabling the latter to establish three points: the economy should gradually open to world trade, the private sector should have a major role in industrial development, and Taiwanese should participate in the private sector. These objectives were gradually achieved by 1965. Support was consolidated among the island's increasingly urbanized population by the great expansion of industrial and commercial opportunities, to which even rural families had access. The Nationalist government increasingly shifted the rationale for its rule from patriotism to prosperity.

By 1985 new adversities had further strengthened the sense of community between mainlanders and Taiwanese and further merged the diverse ideological currents traced above. Dual external political shocks (Communist China's admission to the United Nations in 1971, and its recognition by the United States in 1979) undermined the diplomatic status of the Nationalist regime, but underlined the absence of a viable alternative. Dual external economic shocks (brief recessions following oil crises in 1973–74 and 1979–80) reminded Taiwanese families that prosperity remained problematic and reinforced their rationale for cooperating with the Nationalist state. Chiang Ching-Kuo adopted a more populist profile than his father, promoting elite Taiwanese and courting the Taiwanese public. To be sure, the would-be opposition, even moderates, was still denied party organization and media access, while radicals resided in jail. Nevertheless, voters gave Nationalist candidates 70 percent majorities in most elections.

What then has been the ideological legacy of the first two generations of Nationalist rule for the third? For the state, the official Nationalist answer remains Sunism, the early synthesis of Chinese and Western ideals formulated by Sun Yat-sen. Sunism set some useful parameters: participation in international diplomacy, pursuit of international trade, priority to nationalized infrastructure, attention to mass welfare, and democracy. However, Sunism also left much room for differences in emphasis: how much foreign involvement, how large a public sector, how much welfare, and how much democracy how soon? Since 1945 some parts of the official Nationalist ideology have declined in relevance (mainland-focused patriotism) while others have taken on new life (Taiwan-focused developmentalism). For the family, the ideological legacy remains familism. Nationalist state and Taiwanese families have converged on basic values—developmental authoritarianism and entrepreneurial familism.

PRESENT

The current impact of statism and familism on Taiwan's development involves the current content of ideology, the constraints that ideology places on major institutions, and the consequences of ideology for basic development processes.

Content of Ideology

Dynamics: contract versus consensus. Relations among large-scale public and private organizations are mostly consensual; relations between large-scale organizations and small-scale family firms are mostly contractual. Relations between employers and employees within firms are largely contractual, except within the smallest firms composed entirely of family members, and even here implicit contracts govern obligations within the family.

In relations involving government agencies and big business, the ideal of consensus has predominated. First, the conviction among leaders of conflicting bureaus that they should work together has facilitated the professionalism, caution, and stability that have been much of the state's contribution to Taiwan's economic development. Unfortunately, however, the consensus between bureaus has often simply protected their respective interests and caused statism frequently to degenerate into mere "bureauism." Second, despite poor lateral communications, consensual outcomes have predominated also in relations between policymakers and public enterprises. Government corporations have always received a large share of public investment and have greatly contributed to Taiwan's economic independence and policy stability. However, by the 1980s their poor return on investment had brought budget cuts, management reforms, and even the prospective denationalization or discontinuation of some public enterprise. Third, major private firms, both mainlander and Taiwanese, also have been part of the Nationalist political-economic establishment. Though the role allotted Taiwanese firms in the 1950s was small, it has grown large. Despite some remaining social distance, collaboration between the Nationalist state and Taiwanese bourgeoisie has become increasingly effective.

In contrast, relations between the large-scale establishment and small family firms have been governed mostly by contractual opportunities. As in other "dualistic" economies, large firms conserve their resources while small firms bear the costs of adjustment to fluctuations in the level, and changes in the composition, of economic activity. Second, there is little in the state's ideological heritage that would require it to go beyond equality of opportunity to equality of outcomes. In the state's view, expanding education to help families seize these opportunities is enough. Third, there is little in the family's ideology that would lead it to demand more than equality of opportunity. The family expects to rely on itself for its livelihood, and it agrees that, aside from hard work, the key investment for getting ahead is more family-financed education.

The state: minimal versus activist.   The state on Taiwan is important largely the way the Japanese state is important: defining national economic objectives, providing public economic infrastructure, regulating foreign economic transactions, and orchestrating domestic economic competition. The Nationalist state owns even more basic industry, controlling inputs to private production, than does the Japanese state. However, the Nationalist state has a less intimate relationship with the Taiwanese business class than the Japanese state has with Japanese businessmen.

The Nationalist state's main economic role has been to establish many of the parameters of the economy, without attempting to implement any grand economic design. Much of the system's success has resulted from its obdurate conservatism about the current balance of external payments and internal budgets. A partial exception proves the rule. In the 1970s the state dramatized public construction of modern infrastructure and heavy industrial projects, the vanguard of "capital deepening," to upgrade both military independence and export products. However, these were housekeeping projects that planners regarded as already overdue, rather than the kind of bold plunge into heavy industry that Korea was then making. By the 1980s Taiwan's public projects had achieved modest, mixed results; South Korea had achieved some spectacular successes but at the cost of foreign payments problems.

The state has also indicated priorities both between and within sectors. The state has offered concessionary loans and other favorable treatment to certain sectors and then waited to see what projects foreign or domestic private investors would propose. Nevertheless, it remains unclear exactly how much impact the state's priorities have actually had on domestic private investment, most of which is self-financed. The state continues to have difficulty inducing domestic entrepreneurship in target industries and discouraging investment in what it regards as declining industries, such as textiles and footwear, and in redundant luxury services or speculative luxury development.

The state has also sometimes decided that specific projects were needed and then directly commissioned either public enterprises or private entrepreneurs to provide them. In the fifties and sixties, production bottlenecks were relatively easy to spot, particularly for the foreign engineering consultants and experienced Chinese engineers doing the planning. In the seventies and eighties, the high cost of heavy industry has encouraged triangular collaboration among the Nationalist state and domestic and foreign private firms. Nevertheless, as the economy grew larger and more complex, public planners could dictate only a declining proportion of private projects. In the future, the state plans to concentrate less on particular target sectors and more on improving the overall efficiency of the economic system.

Individuals: rights and duties. On Taiwan today duties to the state still outweigh rights, but in practice the individual is only moderately affected by either. The imperial Chinese assumption that the family owes unlimited duties to the state remains in the background as a principle. Duties and how to perform them remain better articulated than rights and how to obtain them. However, like most contemporary governments, the Nationalist state has written Western notions of individual citizenship into its constitution. Though many political rights remain suspended indefinitely, the fact that they have been conceded in principle has provided the most viable strategy for demanding change: quietly encouraging the state to live up to its own constitutional ideals. Moreover, there are practical reasons why individual duties to the state are not so unconditional. The government demands political conformity but grants economic opportunity in exchange.

Within the family, too, both in principle and in practice, the emphasis remains on the duties rather than the rights of individuals. The traditional family system emphasizes duties, particularly between generations. Children owe a heavy debt to their parents for supporting them when young. In return they should support their parents when old and produce male children to continue the family line. On contemporary Taiwan, the family rights and duties of individuals have been somewhat "modernized," but not much. The nuclear branches of families, although smaller and more dispersed, continue to pool resources between households and across generations. Adult males still should defer to their parents' wishes. The family attempts to reabsorb unemployed members and redeploy their labor while supporting them, so long as it can afford to do so. The duties of women are particularly onerous. Young women work until they marry, to repay their obligations to their father's family, and to accumulate resources for serving their husband's family. Whence the cheap and docile labor most sought by foreign firms.

Property: interests versus controls. The right to own property is probably as dear to Chinese as to Americans. On balance, the use of property remains even less regulated on Taiwan than in the United States. However, an ideological consensus in favor of more regulation may be emerging faster on Taiwan than in the United States.

The Nationalist state has made untrammeled family use of small-scale private property the cornerstone of both its political legitimacy and its development strategy. It took previous concentrations of public property for itself and redistributed small amounts of private property to as much of the population as possible. At the same time, the Nationalist state deplored the negative economic effects of private property, particularly speculation in money, commodities, land, and other assets. Today Sunism still provides ample ideological rationale for state control of additional recent negative effects such as pollution and congestion. Nevertheless the Nationalist state avoided regulating the use of private property as much and as long as possible. It did not want to alarm foreign investors but, in response to domestic concern, has raised token standards of occupational safety and pollution control. It did not want to inhibit domestic development but, in response to foreign concern, it has cracked down on piracy and counterfeiting by small family firms. It did not want to create domestic political protest, but it has even regulated large domestic manufacturers when domestic concern has outweighed domestic support for their activities.

Family ideology of property use provides little encouragement for state regulation. Family property is a sacred trust to be passed on to descendants not only intact but also expanded. Firm and family finances are fused, the family leaving funds in the firm as much as possible but drawing on the firm as needed. Some small family firms still show remarkable indifference to product quality. Too many still find their competitive advantage through shortcuts in design or materials, despite the risk of losing markets. Moreover, until recently the population continued to display little awareness of the danger of modern industrial materials and the interdependence of a modern urban ecosystem. Consequently, familism accorded little legitimacy to state interventions such as urban planning, industrial zoning, or waste regulation.

Technology: specialization versus holism. By now the relationship between specialization and holism in the ideology of state and family on contemporary Taiwan is not very different from that in the United States. Although this poses some impediment to environmental regulation, it mostly encourages an adaptive relationship between education and occupation, and between science and industry.

As regards the environment, until recently most of the population on Taiwan still assumed they had an "open" rural ecosystem, in which the activities of individual farms have little effect on each other or on the environment as a whole. This optimism has carried over not only into business but also into government, whose early response to environmental deterioration in the most developed metropolitan regions was to disperse the problem into the less developed intermetropolitan regions rather than to control it. Though some bureaus of the state began to study these problems almost as soon as industrial growth began, the rest of the state, and the population at large, supported state regulation of such deterioration only where further growth was either physically impossible, prohibitively costly, or unacceptably obnoxious. However, because tiny island Taiwan is manifestly a "closed" ecosystem approaching its limits, both public and private learning is rapidly accelerating, and the state is emphasizing nonpolluting high-tech industries in the next phase of development.

As regards education, since 1945 the Nationalist state has extended compulsory education on Taiwan from primary through middle school, and it has expanded higher educational capacity. Families have eagerly seized the opportunities provided. However, both the traditional Chinese and the modern Western systems on which Nationalist public education has been modeled emphasize general, humanistic education over the technical, vocational education in which Taiwan has experienced chronic shortages. These limitations have been greatly overcome by traditional apprenticeship, extracurricular schooling, technical high schools, technical institutes, and study abroad. The joint result of state policy and family strategy is that the population is more educated than that of other newly industrialized countries, though not as educated as that in most earlier-industrialized countries. Consequently, the question remains of how to reform the educational system to meet the needs of further high-tech development.

As regards science and technology, by 1945, exposure to the West and Japan had established the preeminence of technological development both within the coastal Nationalist elite and among islander Taiwanese. Between 1945 and 1965, engineers often outranked economists among top makers of development policy. Experienced professional leadership and strong engineering talent staffed many public enterprises. At least some private enterprises had the technology necessary for most light industrial processes. Between 1965 and 1985 practical science assumed high priority among both elites and masses. The atmosphere in the 1980s seems closer to the preoccupation with high-tech education in Japan than to the swing away from engineering careers in the United States. As a result, Taiwan has a stronger engineering corps than most newly industrialized countries, though still not as strong as the most advanced earlier-industrialized countries. Nevertheless, some older managers remain more willing to buy new equipment than to pay for new technological or managerial expertise.

Table 7-1, parts A and B, summarizes the interplay of these five ideological components in both statism and familism throughout the three main periods of Taiwan's history.

Constraints of Ideology

Government and business are both quite strong on Taiwan, facing relatively weak constraints from present ideology, both statist and familist. Organized labor, however, is quite weak, facing strong constraints from both government and business.

Government. From the government's perspective the major ideological constraint on economic policymaking is the familist organization of most of the economy. The government's own tacit commitment to citizen economic rights ranks a weak second. On balance, government faces more choice than constraint.

Small family firms are well adapted to developing light industries in which efficient and flexible operations are important and can be achieved on a small scale. The family is not well adapted to developing heavy industries with large capital requirements, indivisible technologies, and slow returns. The small family firm may be quite good at some high-tech industries in which efficiency and flexibility are important and can be achieved at small scale. However, family firms are not good

Table 7–1

IDEOLOGICAL COMPONENTS[a]		A.*Traditional Baseline* Imperial Chinese
Contractual Opportunities vs.	STATISM	Personalistically factionalized bureaus monopolize large-scale traditional opportunities
Consensual Outcomes	FAMILISM	Economically corporate families contractually pursue small-scale opportunities; quite equal outcomes
Limited State vs.	STATISM	In principle, state claims unlimited rights of ownership and regulation
Active State	FAMILISM	In practice, state limited to maintaining order and collecting taxes
Property Rights vs.	STATISM	Few rights, some duties from family membership in suprafamilial communities
Membership Rights	FAMILISM	Most rights and duties from family membership; little individual autonomy
Consumer Competition vs.	STATISM	State favors interests of bureaucratic/gentry elite; high inequality but some mobility
Community Need	FAMILISM	Some customary locality control of family property use; little locality redistribution
Scientific Specialization vs.	STATISM	Some early state diffusion of agricultural technology; increasing environmental imbalance
Environmental Holism	FAMILISM	Locality economic specialization, family occupational diversification, customary environmental adaptation

[a]In order of importance for Taiwan.

(cont.)

Table 7–1 (continued)
B. *Modern Transformation*

Colonial Japanese	Nationalist Chinese
Colonial bureaus run system, limited Taiwanese participation in large-scale modern sector	Nationalist bureaus run system; unanticipated Taiwanese prominence in large-scale modern sector
Most Taiwanese families confined to commercialized traditional sector	Taiwanese families transfer most assets into small-scale modern sector
State directly runs both economic and political development	State controls inputs to economy but induces private enterprise; opposition party forbidden
Both economic and political behavior highly regulated	Mostly indirect control of economic behavior but much direct control of political behavior
Some rights but more duties from only partial citizenship in colonial state	Some duties but more rights from almost full citizenship in Nationalist state
Most rights and duties from family membership; little individual autonomy	Most rights and duties still from family membership; limited individual autonomy
State favors interests of Japanese colonial elite, but somewhat benefits everyone	State favors interests of political-economic establishment, but greatly benefits everyone
Some modern state control of family property use as result of political compliance	Still little modern state control of family property use in exchange for political compliance
Limited state sponsorship of primary mass technical education; temporary environmental fix	Extensive state sponsorship of mass technical education; increasing environmental strain
Limited family diversification into modern occupations; limited educational mobility	Extensive family diversification among modern occupations; much educational mobility

at some of the commercial services the government would like to improve, such as trading and banking, because of their informal accounting practices and personalistic business methods. The family firm, so far the building block of Taiwan's private sector, may prove the stumbling block to some types of further development.

A second, lesser constraint on the government is its own commitment to a variety of political and economic rights. In an authoritarian regime such ideals provide one of the few levers that citizens can use to press demands. The political rights that have yet to be realized in practice—freedom of press and party organization, election of other than local executives and representatives—are clearly defined but unlikely to be granted in the foreseeable future. The economic rights that might be attained—higher minimum wage, severance pay, and retirement benefits—are less clearly defined but more likely to increase.

The basic constraint is more political than legal, however. A regime committed to both economic nationalism and popular prosperity, and whose current legitimacy rests largely on successful development, must avoid the appearance of auctioning its population as cheap labor for domestic or foreign corporations, and it must maintain the appearance of protecting both domestic capitalists and worker-consumers from global recession. Nevertheless, the government retains much leeway, so long as it appears to be trying to do something, since most of the population understands that many of the relevant economic forces are beyond the government's control.

Business. From the perspective of business, the major ideological constraint is statism. The major manifestation of this constraint is the continued dependence of the private sector on many kinds of state support. On balance, business on Taiwan faces both some constraint and some choice.

The Nationalist state's lack of international legitimacy also limits business. Nationalist carriers cannot obtain landing rights in many countries; Taiwan citizens cannot obtain visas to enter many of the countries with which they are trying to do business. Both government and business have been energetic in finding ingenious ways around these constraints, but neither has a solution, and the costs remain considerable.

The state's ambivalence toward private capital affects the very nature of capitalism itself on Taiwan. The Nationalist state broke up private concentrations of capital, annexing the banking system and encouraging the accumulation of capital by as much of the population as possible. The state also took measures to prevent the reappearance of large-scale private finance, such as forbidding private insurance companies from owning industries. Nevertheless, government banks lend mostly to large firms, public and private. This leaves middle- and small-scale private firms largely on their own, off the state's budget but also somewhat out of the state's control.

In the mid-1970s, to promote the further accumulation and concentration of capital for industrial "deepening," the state relaxed restrictions on the formation of financial-industrial conglomerates. The result, however, was just what the government had feared: financial empire-building, unproductive speculation, and failure of some of the largest and ostensibly most respectable groups. The Nationalist state can live with an industrial bourgeoisie, but can it live with a Taiwanese bourgeoisie that combines the speculative instincts of commercial capitalism with the monopolistic aspirations of financial capitalism? These are interests over which, for its own survival, the Nationalist state cannot but exercise control.

Labor. Statism and familism pose equal and great constraints on the development of an activist labor movement on Taiwan. Organized labor faces many more constraints than choices. However, from the mid-sixties to the mid-eighties, this lack of worker organizations was largely offset by the fact that the demand for most kinds of labor consistently exceeded the supply, forcing employers to raise wages and improve working conditions, and enabling employees to change to better jobs. In the mid-eighties, global recession and factory automation have begun to raise unemployment above its long-time 2 percent, reducing the market leverage of individual workers.

The state not only forbids activist labor organization, it also has preempted such organization by installing its own passive unions in major plants. These unions are largely restricted to the promotion of good management-labor relations. Strikes are illegal. The state itself nominates political candidates to represent these captive unions in corporatist seats within the national legislature. Recently some parts of the state have begun to speak up for labor interests. In 1984, over the objections of capitalists, the national legislature passed an oft-postponed Labor Standards Law requiring employers to finance severance pay and pension funds for all employees. Exactly how the law will be implemented and what its effect on workers will be remain to be seen. The state continues to be uncertain how to promote workers' welfare without discouraging investment and imposing costs that neither business nor government can afford.

The small scale and familial ideology of most firms poses less deliberate but equally great constraints on labor activism. Historically, consciousness of belonging to a working class has been weak on Taiwan, particularly because of rapid postwar upward mobility. Most families consider themselves middle class and plan to start their own firms. Few families have provided wage labor to any industry for several generations. Most families have diversified not only across industries but also between blue-collar and white-collar wage work, and between wage work and self-employment. Workers in family firms do not become labor activists because they are relatives and friends of the owners, ideologically committed to their own firm and organizationally separated from others. Workers in large factories do not become labor activists because they regard themselves as agents of their entrepreneurial families rather than as members of a working class.

Consequences of Ideology

Statism and familism have contributed to the effectiveness, efficiency, and equity of development on Taiwan.

Strategic effectiveness is the capacity to maximize long-run political independence and economic advantage.

Taiwan's economy has alternated in almost textbook fashion between first creating industries to meet domestic needs and later adapting them to export promotion. It has advanced from consumer nondurables through consumer durables to producer durables, and from less to more sophisticated products within each of these categories. Moreover, the Nationalist state has been able to choose sectors and projects for both defense and development. Nevertheless, Taiwan has not effected transitions between products as rapidly as the state hoped. So far there has been little progress from imitation to innovation in either defense or development.

Between 1945 and 1965 the state's strategic problem was to persuade inexperienced and uncertain businessmen to produce labor-intensive light industrial products first for the domestic and then for the foreign market. The state motivated import-substitution by guaranteeing early entrants import protection and monopoly profits in Taiwan's domestic market. Fortunately for the state, foreign markets themselves motivated exports by affording Taiwan high returns as an early participant in the exceptional expansion of world trade.

Between 1965 and 1985 the state thought the strategic problem was to identify more capital-intensive sectors into which Taiwan could shift. But the government's heavy-industrial candidates—ships, trucks, cars, steel, chemicals, and petrochemicals—achieved only mixed success. To a greater extent than the state had expected, the economy continued to run on upgraded light industrial products.

Between 1985 and 2005 the strategic problem will be to identify viable roles for Taiwan in skill-intensive, high-technology, and modern service industries, mastering new processes and even innovating some new products. Again the government proposes to open Taiwan still further to global markets, and again it is facilitating adjustment by organizing infrastructure and disseminating information. Again, however, the state's major contribution is likely to be in setting parameters, not in selecting projects.

What, then, has been the impact of ideology on strategic effectiveness on Taiwan? So far the internal convergence between statism and familism appears to have enabled Taiwan to adapt well to external circumstances. However, it remains unclear what share of the credit should go to statism (whose long-run defense preoccupations promoted transitions to new products) and how much to familism (whose short-run profit preoccupations motivated the upgrading of old products). In any case, this symbiosis succeeded under exceptional conditions: Japanese and American interest, an early and fresh start, and postwar global economic boom. If world growth remains slow or if Taiwan becomes more isolated, the future interaction of statism and familism, even if more internally harmonious, could become less externally adaptive.

Allocative efficiency is the capacity to make good use of resources in producing goods for defense and development.

The private sector of Taiwan's economy is, by most accounts, highly efficient. Manufacturers on Taiwan can now deliver the goods, not only at low production cost but also reliably and on time, to changeable and rising product specifications. The state itself deplores the allocative inefficiency of Taiwan's public sector, though it regards some of this inefficiency as necessary for national defense. Overall, it remains a mixed performance for a mixed economy.

Between 1945 and 1965, Taiwan made great progress toward aligning domestic prices with world prices. Competitive advantage was defined as maximizing returns from cheap unskilled labor in low-tech manufacturing. The state recruited manufacturers, the family provided the labor. Production functions were highly divisible for different scales, and highly adaptable to different mixes, of production. The domestic market was large enough to support initial production of consumer nondurables; export markets were a bonus that followed.

Between 1965 and 1985, Taiwan departed somewhat from world prices as the state cushioned the impact on established industry of increases in oil and other prices. Competitive advantage was defined as increasing the capital intensity of plant and the skill level of labor in mid-tech manufacturing processes. The state recruited foreign capital, the family educated domestic labor. Particularly for producer goods, production functions were indivisible and inflexible, requiring large scales of production with expensive equipment. Both domestic and foreign markets were necessary for economical production. The domestic market became overburdened with products and by-products. Neither foreign partners nor foreign markets were always forthcoming.

Between 1985 and 2005, some pressure will remain for departure from world prices, but pressure for realignment will

increase. Competitive advantage will be defined as increasing
the technology intensity and labor skills not only of manufacturing processes but also of product design and supporting
services. The state will be increasingly active in recruiting the
technology, and the family will increasingly adapt by larger
educational investment in a smaller labor force. The domestic
market will become large enough and sophisticated enough to
support the initial production of many high-tech products,
though from the outset they will be conceived for export.

Again, the evolving interaction between statism and familism
has been largely adaptive, the state engineering a competitive
environment and the family mobilizing a competitive response.
Both face dilemmas, however, particularly in their attitudes
toward scale. Statism requires large scale for deepening the
technology of both defense and development. But since the
state fears economic concentration in the efficient private sector, it pursues economic concentration through the inefficient
public sector. Familism prefers small scale, resisting state-
promoted mergers into nonfamily firms. Intense competition
between small family firms keeps Taiwan's economy lean and
adaptive, but it also keeps profits thin, horizons short, and
innovation weak.

Distributive equity is the capacity to provide citizens with
basic needs for political membership and economic survival.

Taiwan has combined rapid economic growth with increasing economic equality, a widely noted exception to the general
experience that distribution gets worse before it gets better in
the course of development. "Basic needs" have long since been
met. Not only current income but also asset ownership has
been widely dispersed, at least until recently. By redistributing
rural assets through land reform before 1965, and by creating
urban employment through export promotion after 1965,
Nationalist policy has greatly contributed to such equal outcomes. However, Taiwan's exceptional distributive performance has occurred under exceptional circumstances—the
broad distribution of assets in a mature rice-farming economy,
the prior history of diversification away from agriculture, the
arrival of an autonomous state, the availability of entrepreneurial families, and the small geographic and demographic scale
of Taiwan. In the future, concentration of ownership in larger

firms and transition from family employment to wage work may somewhat impair this equality. Finally, despite much political progress, mass participation remains both indirect and circumscribed.

The years between 1945 and 1965 saw an actual increase in the equality of Taiwan's already flat distribution of income. The Japanese had confiscated any Taiwanese industrial assets during the war; Nationalist hyperinflation leveled Taiwanese finance after the war; and Nationalist reform further equalized land ownership within the then rural majority of the population. Meanwhile Taiwanese attempts at autonomous political participation were largely suppressed.

Between 1965 and 1985, Taiwan maintained its exceptionally equal distribution of income, unlike most rapidly developing countries. Like the population, the leveling mechanisms shifted from the rural to the urban economy. Labor transferred from less productive, less equalizing agricultural employment to more productive, more equalizing industrial employment. Wages rose in all sectors as employers bid for increasingly scarce labor. Meanwhile, generational succession within the Nationalist leadership inaugurated a transition from "hard" to "soft" authoritarianism, encouraging more autonomous Taiwanese political participation.

The period from 1985 to 2005 may finally see some worsening of the relative distribution of income, though at a high absolute level. If assets concentrate in larger and fewer firms, some concentration of income may follow. If differentiation between white- and blue-collar employment continues, wage differentials may widen and family occupational mixes diverge. Presumably the demand for more political participation will continue to rise, but whether Taiwan will progress from "soft" authoritarianism to representative democracy remains problematic.

Again, the interaction of statism and familism has been largely benign in its impact on distributional equity on Taiwan. The state's normative economic ideology and pragmatic political interest have fostered a broad distribution of property assets and employment opportunities. The family has provided high rates of capital mobilization, thus contributing to broad distribution of ownership, and high rates of labor mobilization, thus contributing to broad distribution of income. Nevertheless, both statism and familism have added countertendencies toward disequalization. For example, the state has favored essential industrialists, and the family has exploited inessential women.

FUTURE

The future impact of statism and familism on Taiwan's development will derive from Taiwan's major future problems, will differ from one sector to another, and will depend on how both statism and familism respond to the growing internationalization of economic activity and the accelerating pace of economic change.

Future Problems

Taiwan's three basic problems are maintaining external defense, export earnings, and internal economic security and political stability.

Inventories of American economic problems do not usually start with military security. The Nationalist state, however, must consider defense needs in planning industrial structure. Since the United States terminated its mutual defense treaty, Taiwan is increasingly on its own in defending itself from any attempt at takeover by the People's Republic of China. Therefore, Taiwan's first imperative is to maintain de facto relations with its trading partners, particularly for the purchase or co-production of arms that it cannot produce for itself. A second imperative is to make its domestic industrial base capable of producing as much advanced military equipment as possible, and to enable Taiwan to survive in war as long as possible, on as few additional imports as possible. A third imperative, for both defense and trade, is to maintain whatever international diplomatic status it can while fending off both threats and blandishments from the People's Republic of China.

Assuming that Taiwan can maintain the political-military framework for continuing international trade, the next block of problems concerns maintaining export earnings. Here, argu-

ably, the basic problem is product timing: producing goods and
services with promising markets, while continuing to advance
Taiwan from being a late recipient of worn-out technologies,
toward becoming an early innovator of the most promising
new ones. This will require continuing to upgrade both technological and managerial capacity, the former for high-tech
goods and the latter for supporting services. A second basic
problem is maintaining market access in an increasingly protectionist world. This requires artfully dodging the quotas that
trading partners try to impose while increasing the capacity of
its own trading companies to promote exports. Finally, assuming access to a market, product competitiveness becomes an
issue. In newer mid-tech and high-tech product lines Taiwan
is likely to remain highly competitive, but in older low-tech
products Taiwan must either further raise the productivity of
its labor force or remain ahead of new low-wage competitors
in product quality. Overall, Taiwan would like to reduce its
dependence on Japan and the United States for equipment and
materials (about half of Taiwan's imports) and to reduce its
dependence on the United States for markets (about half of
Taiwan's exports). Unfortunately, upgrading production processes and product mixes may increase both dependencies,
because the new inputs tend to come from Japan and the
United States, and the new output tends to go to the United
States. A persistent deficit in trade with Japan is the main
reason Taiwan maintains surpluses in its trade with the United
States.

Military security and export earnings are preconditions for
domestic stability. Mass economic security depends basically
on export earnings. However, government and business can
contribute domestically by further upgrading the labor force
through education and investment, maintaining low inflation
rates and other financial parameters, and by improving welfare and retirement programs. Assuming full employment, a
second problem of increasing concern to all citizens is quality
of life. In particular, congestion and pollution are becoming so
bad that even stoical Chinese no longer regard combating them
as a luxury. The last, and unfortunately probably the least,
component of domestic stability is political atmosphere. If the
Nationalist government can maintain a creditable performance

on most of the problems listed above, probably it will continue to receive majority public support. However, since partial disenfranchisement under Nationalist political institutions does rankle the Taiwanese public, and since basic political reform seems unlikely and even unwise, the establishment must continue its skillful efforts at political window dressing. It must appoint still more Taiwanese loyal to Nationalist policies to government positions; it must run still more attractive Taiwanese candidates loyal to the Nationalist party for legislative assemblies; and it must maximize cooperation with the moderate opposition and minimize confrontations with radical dissidents.

Strategic Sectors

Taiwan's problem is to achieve a continuingly viable mix of light, heavy, and high-tech industries that meets the needs of both defense and development. The relative roles of statism and familism in solving this problem, and the particular ideological tenets involved, differ from industry to industry. In labor-intensive and skill-intensive industries, both statism and familism are highly compatible with sectoral requirements, contributing to good economic performance. However, in capital-intensive industries and financial-technological institutions, statism and familism contain ideological tenets that significantly impair economic performance.

Financial-technological institutions. Elements of both statism and familism impair the performance of financial and technological institutions. The state's preoccupation with military security skews its industrial investment criteria, and its preoccupation with political stability inhibits reform of economic institutions. The family's preoccupation with quick profits distorts its industrial investment criteria too, and its preoccupation with hiding its assets from the state through phony accounting procedures undermines confidence in Taiwan's business practices. The recent performance of all these institutions has been poor. Capital markets and company management have not been working to transform savings into technology. Declining investment has inhibited technological change, allowing wage increases to outrun productivity gains. To understand this, let us first consider statism and familism as they affect financial-technological performance, then describe the most conspicuous recent example of failure.

The Nationalist state's approach to both economics and politics since 1949 can be summed up by the conservative formula: "progress amidst stability." Balanced trade, balanced budgets, low interest rates, and low inflation have been placed ahead of rapid growth or institutional transformation. Successful though this approach has been (producing rapid growth as an unexpected by-product), by the mid-1980s it may have become too much of a good thing. A ballooning export surplus is threatening domestic price stability and annoying foreign trading partners. Low interest rates in formal banks have discouraged deposits and directed loans only to the safest companies, particularly government corporations. Lack of protection for patent rights has encouraged small firms to steal technology, thus discouraging large firms from developing technology.

Most of Taiwan's private firms therefore remain chronically undercapitalized, overindebted, and underaudited, driven into high-interest informal money markets to finance long-term development through short-term loans. They have relied on quick profits from proven technologies, and they have neglected basic research and development. In the 1960s and 1970s, increasing revenues from expanding exports concealed these institutional weaknesses; in the 1980s, slowing exports and declining revenues in some industries revealed them. What is worse, Taiwan's family firms are disillusioned with old investments (labor-intensive light industry) but are still wary of new ones (expensive heavy industry and uncertain high-tech industry). Unfortunately, there are no simple answers to their questions about how their relatively small firms can compete with Japanese or Korean conglomerates, or in what industries they should make such investment as they can afford. All this makes for a weak base for management of either declining or rising industries, by either government or business.

Recently one of the country's largest family conglomerates went bankrupt as a result of inadequate government supervision and irresponsible family management. The founder's second son had inherited a thriving credit cooperative and a declining plastics firm; he had milked the former to sustain the latter, among other financial manipulations. Meanwhile he built a fancy hotel to increase his public prestige, and he began a political career in the ruling Nationalist party. Although aware of his mounting debt, government regulators did nothing. Eventually the process collapsed, ruining the conglomerates of both the second son and his older brother, endangering the conglomerates run by their two uncles, forcing the resignation of high government officials, and shaking confidence in both government and business. Most observers agree that the unsound business practices involved—illegal loans, high debt, speculative investments, phony books—are not the exception but rather the rule for family firms on Taiwan, albeit not on such a scale or to such an extent.

This and similar scandals have intensified discussions about reforming Taiwan's banking system and other financial-technological institutions such as the tax system and stock market. The government is raising interest payments on deposits to attract money from the informal money markets, and lowering interest charges on loans to encourage businesses to shift their borrowing to formal banks. However, it remains to be seen whether the government will allow banks enough autonomy to meet the business needs currently met by informal money markets (about 30 percent of business loans). Moreover, there is serious question not only whether the government failed to enforce existing regulations against particular corporations but also whether the government could succeed in challenging the modus operandi of the entire business class with which it is allied.

Labor-intensive industries. In light industry, neither statism nor familism seriously impairs economic performance. The state wants exports, and families want profits. Of course, the labor-intensiveness of Taiwan's light industry is under competitive pressure as new countries undercut Taiwan's rising wages. For more than a decade the state has urged family firms to upgrade or abandon light industries, but for the same decade family firms have continued to find more opportunities than the state expected. If the state had intervened more directly it might have prevented overexpansion within these industries.

It might, however, have forfeited export returns that have proved vital to Taiwan's prosperity. However, in the mid-1980s businessmen have become less eager to invest in labor-intensive light industry, mostly because of global oversupply, but also because of rising labor costs, including newly mandatory severance pay and pension funds. In any case, the total value of exports of textiles, garments, footwear, and other consumer nondurables has continued to expand. The more progressive firms have lowered labor costs and raised product quality by installing more sophisticated equipment and improving worker training. Faced with quotas, exporters have maintained rising revenues by substituting better products with higher unit values. However, such efforts have their limits: regardless of quality, if prices rise too high, some foreign buyers will simply go elsewhere.

Footwear provides a telling example of the domestic interaction among government, business, and labor. At the peak of Taiwan's first spurt of export growth just before the first oil crisis, Taiwan had more than three hundred footwear manufacturers. The 1974–75 recession reduced this number, but by the second oil crisis it had grown to more than five hundred. The 1980–81 recession again caused a decline, but by 1984 the number had risen to one thousand. Meanwhile, between 1980 and 1983 the average value of exports per manufacturer fell 23 percent, and the average price per pair of shoes remained roughly the same. Directive state? Corporate strategy? Prosperous labor? No, rather laissez-faire, cutthroat competition and self-exploitation.

Capital-intensive industries. The state dominates heavy industry, and state political objectives conflict significantly with purely economic criteria. The state wants Taiwan to become as self-reliant as possible, industrially and militarily, even though Taiwan cannot make many heavy industries competitive internationally. Taiwan has not broken through to become a major exporter of either consumer or producer durables but it has deepened its industrial base.

On the one hand, the state has inaugurated measures to improve the economic viability of state heavy industries (electricity, oil, steel, ships) and to shift future development of heavy industry toward the private sector (chemicals, cars, machinery, equipment). The state has decided not only to reform the management of state-owned firms but even to shut down those (copper and aluminum) that cannot cover their costs. The government's approach to future private heavy industries now emphasizes specialization in profitable components of world-wide production processes (auto parts, precision equipment, specialty chemicals) rather than trying to export whole finished heavy industrial products (cars, ships, weapons).

On the other hand, the government continues to refuse to sell state-owned heavy industries to the private sector, and it continues to promote new heavy industry deemed vital to national security. At best, the Nationalist state owns basic industries to steer the economy and to be able to subsidize private firms when desirable. At worst, it owns basic industries to dominate the polity and to be able to retaliate against private firms when necessary.

Cars provide a recent example of groping toward a viable strategy for heavy industry in the future. Since 1981, Ford has collaborated with a major mainlander-run textile company to manufacture small cars for sale to Taiwan and southeast Asia. Long negotiations between Toyota and state-run China Steel to set up a large auto plant collapsed when the Japanese could not guarantee to sell enough cars abroad and would not agree to transfer enough technology to Taiwan. In exchange for part ownership, Nissan has agreed to show another mainlander-run automobile company how to manufacture a competitive small car. Though it remains unclear how many whole cars Taiwan can export, developing the automobile industry will help upgrade Taiwan's machinery sector and increase the kinds of automobile components Taiwan can produce.

The public—whether as employees, consumers, or citizens—has little direct influence on investment in heavy industry. However, existing heavy industry already strains Taiwan's environment, and groups are organizing to say so. For example, the new Nationalist mayor of Kaohsiung City, Taiwan's principal center of heavy industry, has demanded that the many state enterprises there cut back their pollution. People are asking whether such a small island can safely accommodate the ten more nuclear power plants that the Taiwan Power Company plans to build by the end of the century.

Skill-intensive industries. In high-tech industries, state and family play complementary roles. Neither statism nor familism needs to impair economic performance. The state wants new industries, and families want new investments. Nevertheless, uncertainties about "which ones" and "how much" still inhibit private investors. Some high-tech firms provide collegial relations and competitive rewards to secure the loyalty and motivate the performance of professional managers and technical staff. Manufacturing high-tech products requires significant amounts of skilled labor, and labor relations on production lines resemble those in progressive light industries. However, rising labor costs, including future pension payments, are not yet a significant problem for these profitable new industries.

The government has defined the leading sectors as electronics and information. It has provided special support (priority loans, research grants, training fellowships) to encourage domestic firms, and it has offered special inducements (priority approval, industrial parks, research institutes) to attract foreign firms. These policies have produced some results. Taiwan companies (Multitech, Mitac) have made original progress in such areas as processing of Chinese language materials. American companies (IBM, DEC, Hewlett-Packard, AT&T) continue to produce circuits, terminals, monitors, and switches on Taiwan, while the largest Taiwanese electronics company (Tatung) has begun producing such items in the United States itself.

Nevertheless, Taiwan remains restricted from marketing its own completed high-tech products. For example, IBM, Microsoft, and others are suing many of the Taiwan companies whose finished personal computers violated their patent rights. Moreover, even in producing components, Taiwan firms have not been very aggressive in seizing technological initiatives. For example, unlike the South Korean conglomerates, they did not attempt to mass produce the current largest memory chip (256K). Taiwan's small firms still decline to invest in research and development (0.7 percent of GNP on Taiwan versus 2.4 percent in the United States and 2.1 percent in Japan). Finally,

Taiwan still lacks the engineers to achieve significant break-throughs in the most advanced technologies.

The Nationalist government summarizes its future strategy as: "liberalization, internationalization, systematization." *Liberalization* means that Taiwan must open its hitherto heavily protected domestic market to foreign products, both to appease foreign trading partners by evening trade balances, and to stimulate domestic firms through foreign competition. *Internationalization* means that Taiwan must itself reach abroad to cooperate with multinational corporations, and to market and even manufacture its own products abroad. *Systematization* means that both state bureaus and family firms must reform, both to withstand the foreign influences that liberalization entails and to provide the organization that internationalization requires. Debate continues over how fast these measures should proceed, and whether systematization must precede or follow liberalization and internationalization or can result from them. Nevertheless, the future direction of state policy seems clear, and the prospects seem bright for increasingly close cooperation among managers of all kinds—foreign and domestic, public and private, large and small.

Family systems do not have conscious strategies, but the trends are individualization, cosmopolitanization, and professionalization. As Westerners increasingly recognize the competitive strength of Eastern communitarianism, Easterners increasingly recognize the attractiveness of Western individualism. At least on Taiwan, however, a more individualistic life-style has not yet changed the family obligations that have made parents educate their children, children support their parents, and everyone work hard, save money, and start businesses. Meanwhile, ordinary people on Taiwan have become increasingly cosmopolitan, quickly aware of events and trends around the globe. Finally, the Taiwanese family is gradually improving the professionalism of its management of family firms and emphasizing economically viable professions in educating its children, partly in anticipation of tougher economic times ahead. Cosmopolitanization and professionalization may make the Chinese on Taiwan more competitive managers or more demanding workers, but on balance it makes them more rewarding partners as well.

Appendix Table 1.   Major Economic Indicators, 1955-1985

	1955	1960	1965	1970	1975	1980	1985
A. EXTERNAL							
Total Trade (billion US$)	0.3	0.5	1.0	3.0	11.3	39.5	50.8
Trade Balance, (billion US$)		−0.3	−0.3	−0.6	−0.0	+3.8	+18.1
Foreign Capital/Capital Formation		40.0%	14.9%	5.0%	2.6%	−6.0%	N.A.
Exports/GNP	8.3%	11.3%	18.7%	29.7%	39.5%	53.0%	54.5%
Imports/GNP	12.6%	18.9%	21.8%	29.8%	42.8%	54.2%	41.9%
Manufactures/Exports	7.6%	28.2%	42.6%	76.7%	81.3%	88.2%	
B. NATIONAL							
GNP (billion 1981 NT$)	189	261	411	654	996	1,646	2,244
GNP Growth Rate	4.9%	6.7%	9.5%	9.8%	8.8%	10.3%	6.4%
Total Savings/NI	4.9%	7.6%	16.5%	23.8%	25.3%	32.7%	29.0%
Total Savings/GNP	9.0%	12.7%	19.6%	25.5%	25.9%	33.0%	31.6%
Primary Sector/GDP (mostly agriculture)	34.6%	35.1%	29.3%	19.4%	16.2%	10.4%	6.4%
Secondary Sector/GDP (mostly manufacturing)	23.4%	26.7%	21.5%	39.1%	44.0%	50.5%	49.7%
Tertiary Sector/GDP (all services)	42.0%	38.2%	30.3%	41.5%	40.0%	39.1%	44.3%

(cont.)

C. SECTORAL

Government Revenue/GNP	24.6%	23.8%	20.1%	22.7%	23.4%	24.3%	22.0%
Government Firms/Industry	51.1%	47.9%	41.3%	27.7%	18.8%	18.7%	N.A.
Government Savings	5.1%	4.0%	2.4%	3.5%	7.0%	8.0%	4.3%
Foodstuffs/Manufacturing Value-added	53.3%	35.9%	20.8%	13.4%	11.2%	8.6%	N.A.
Textiles/Manufacturing Value-added	5.3%	10.7%	10.9%	19.2%	17.0%	15.4%	N.A.
Machinery-Electrical-Transportation/MVA	2.1%	8.4%	16.5%	22.2%	25.9%	30.1%	N.A.

D. INDIVIDUAL

GNP/capita (thousand 1981 NT$)	19.9	23.4	31.7	44.9	62.2	93.3	117.3
Income distribution (top fifth/bottom fifth)			5.3[54]	4.6	4.4[74]	4.2[79]	4.4[84]
Non-governmental savings/GDP	9.6%	13.1%	18.5%	22.3%	20.0%	25.5%	27.2%
Population (million persons)	9.1	10.8	12.6	14.7	16.2	17.8	19.3
Literacy	62.1%	72.9%	76.9%	85.3%	87.1%	89.7%	91.2%
Social insurance/employed persons	N.A.	N.A.	23%[66]	28%[71]	35%	45%	66.3%

Sources: *Taiwan Statistical Data Book*, various years, Kuo-shu Liang and Ching-ing Hou Liang in *Industry of Free China* 64, 1 (January 1984). Quality of life research institute *First social report on the Republic of China*. Taipei: Ming Der Foundation, 1985.

BIBLIOGRAPHY

Ahern, Emily, and Hill Gates, eds. *The Anthropology of Chinese Society on Taiwan.* Stanford: Stanford University Press, 1981.

Balassa, Bela. *The Newly Industrializing Countries in the World Economy.* New York: Pergamon Press, 1981.

Barclay, George W. *Colonial Development and Population on Taiwan.* Princeton: Princeton University Press, 1954.

China Credit Information Service. *Business Groups in Taiwan.* (biannual)

China Information Office. *Republic of China: A Reference Book.* Taipei: Government Information Office, 1983.

Clough, Ralph. *Island China.* Cambridge, Mass.: Harvard University Press, 1978.

Cohen, Myron. *House United, House Divided: The Chinese Family in Taiwan.* New York: Columbia University Press, 1976.

Commonwealth Magazine. Taipei.

Fei, John C. H., Gustav Ranis, and Shirley Kuo. *Growth with Equity: The Taiwan Case.* New York: Oxford University Press, 1979.

Galenson, Walter, ed. *Economic Growth and Structural Change in Taiwan.* Ithaca: Cornell University Press, 1979.

Ho, Samuel P. S. *Economic Development of Taiwan.* New Haven: Yale University Press, 1978.

Hofheinz, Roy, and Kent Calder. *The Eastasia Edge.* New York: Basic Books, 1982.

Jacoby, Neil H. *U.S. Aid to Taiwan.* New York: Praeger, 1966.

Knapp, Ronald, ed. *China's Island Frontier.* Honolulu: University Press of Hawaii, 1980.

Kung, Lydia. *Women Factory Workers on Taiwan.* Ann Arbor: MMI, 1983.

Kuo, Shirley W. Y. *The Taiwan Economy in Transition.* Boulder: Westview Press, 1983.

Kuo, Shirley W. Y., Gustav Ranis, and John C. H. Fei. *The Taiwan Success Story.* Boulder: Westview Press, 1981.

Li, K. T. *The Experience of Economic Growth on Taiwan.* Taipei: MeiYa, 1976.

Myers, Ramon H., and Mark R. Peattie, eds. *The Japanese Colonial Empire, 1895–1945.* Princeton: Princeton University Press, 1984.

Silin, Robert H. *Leadership and Values: The Organization of Large-scale Taiwanese Enterprises.* Cambridge, Mass.: Harvard University Press, 1976.

Wolf, Margery. *The House of Lim.* New York: Appleton, Century, Crofts, 1968.

—— *Women and the Family in Rural Taiwan.* Stanford: Stanford University Press, 1972.

8

KOREA

Vincent S. R. Brandt

Korea's dominant ideological tradition during the premodern period (before 1900) was strongly communitarian, with emphasis on the subordination of individual interests to those of the group and an authority structure of ranked status and power. It would probably be a mistake to overemphasize the authoritarian aspects of traditional ideology. While inherent in the Confucian world view, these elements have been given a disciplined formal rigidity by the influences of Japanese colonialism and post–Korean War domestic militarism that was not characteristic of the premodern period. In the Korean ideological tradition no attempts were ever made to deify the ruler or to make his power absolute. The demands of the state did not necessarily have priority over individual moral imperatives, particularly with regard to family issues. Good government was the institutional expression of ethical principles, and in ideal Confucian terms if the ruler or high official did not behave in a moral manner, the ultimate goal, social harmony, could not be attained. These principles are very much alive today, and the issue of virtuous conduct in high places is a constant contemporary preoccupation. There is a universal right to benevolent rule inherent in the Korean ideological tradition, and the duties that are required of individuals are contingent on the proper fulfillment of that right. Each individual in an institutional context knows that he is expected to serve his superior loyally and faithfully. But he also is inclined to judge his superior's behavior on moral grounds, and he is highly sensitive to the issue of whether he himself is being treated fairly.

An informal spontaneous tradition of individual self-expression and heroic challenge to authority has been a force for volatility and instability since ancient times. Christian missionary doctrine and later the wholesale introduction of American political and social thought after 1945 have legitimized and systematized this formerly subversive, individualistic element within the ideological tradition. Thus, the potential exists for a kind of rebellious egalitarianism based on the appeal to a higher, more persuasive morality than that of the established hierarchical order. Much of the tension in contemporary Korean society can be attributed to the fact that mainstream communitarianism has been pulled in sharply contrasting directions. Militaristic authoritarianism, popular desires for greater individual freedom and self-expression, and a deep-rooted longing for benevolently righteous rule by virtuous leaders coexist without integration or any established consensus.

Most Koreans today regard their present system, which might be labeled "militaristic-technocratic authoritarianism," as a useful, perhaps even necessary but nevertheless ideologically aberrant stage in national development. Although the foreign observer is likely to claim that contemporary Koreans have deeply internalized a whole set of communitarian values, and that strongly communitarian institutions shape and control their lives, the Korean perspective tends to be quite different. Most members of the educated, urban middle class see themselves as strongly individualistic but constrained by an illegitimate and, to a greater or lesser degree, distasteful political regime.

The country is deeply divided ideologically between adherents of paternalistic communitarianism and those who long for more individual freedom under a democratic representative government. Not only do different sectors of society support or oppose the government in varying degrees, but any given individual is likely to be pulled in both directions. The current situation can be described as one of uneasy ambivalence in which different ideological tendencies co-exist in a state of constant tension. Until now popular acquiescence in repressive authoritarian rule has been the result of concern with the threat to security from the North and recognition of the important role played by the "hard state" in bringing about economic development. People have been kept in line by governmental persuasion, the threat and occasional use of coercive force, and worry over what might happen to their newly achieved prosperity if there were serious social disturbances.

The business community has by and large avoided taking sides. Without a long or respected entrepreneurial and industrial tradition, businessmen have tended to be pragmatic opportunists, adapting readily to whatever policies promoted profits. On the one hand, there has been frenetic competition within parameters set by the authorities; on the other hand, the largest and most favored firms have collaborated closely with the government, following instructions and receiving substantial benefits in the form of loans, tax breaks, and other incentives. In the area of economic policy a rather dramatic shift in course is now under way, with less governmental intervention in corporate decision making and greater reliance on market mechanisms for regulation. The most advanced and productive sectors of industry are now operating pretty much on their own, and increasingly they tend to resist bureaucratic interference. Favored treatment is gradually being withdrawn from the large conglomerates, while small and medium industries are being encouraged in the interest of promoting competition and innovation. The banking system is being liberalized. Implementation of these measures has begun, and the economy is now in a difficult period of transition.

Thus, Korea's strong communitarian traditions are being challenged all along the line, and tensions are correspondingly great. Government control of business is much more tenuous than in the years of rapid growth when profits depended on preferential loans. Large corporations, while not adopting an adversarial stance against government, are nevertheless insisting on their rights to operate pretty much as they please. The imposed popular consensus is breaking down, and demands for political change based on individualistic ideological principles are becoming more insistent. Society itself, now nearly three fourths urban, comprises mainly small, nuclear family units, within which a much more individualistic younger generation has grown up. Communitarian traditions of collectivist group orientation and hierarchical authority are still strong, but they are being frequently questioned and even directly opposed.

TRADITIONAL IDEOLOGY

Throughout the more than five hundred years of the Yi Dynasty (1392–1910), Korea was in a tributary relation with China "as younger brother to elder brother." Neo-Confucian orthodoxy was the dominant ideology, not only of the educated elite but increasingly, as the centuries passed, of the common people as well. From the beginning of the fifteenth century the Yi Dynasty rulers and their advisors imposed Confucianism with relentless insistence, as a blueprint governing every aspect of moral, social, political, and economic life for a utopian society.

This dominant ideology was close to the communitarian end of our continuum. Confucianism as a family- and lineage-centered belief system, a secular religion, carried the message that social harmony was possible only within a hierarchically arranged order, in which each individual's relative status, role, and behavior were clearly spelled out. Loyalty and devotion to superiors and the subordination of individual to collective interests were values that had absolute moral priority. Virtue, defined in terms of mastery of the Confucian literary classics, was the only legitimate qualification for high office. Theoretically the well-being of the poor, the weak, and the powerless was protected by the wisdom, benevolence, human-heartedness, and righteousness of virtuous officials.

Virtue in high places was believed to have a mystical efficacy in promoting good behavior and industry among the ordinary people, and in preventing conflict and disorder. At a higher and still more mystical level of abstraction, there was a belief that only if the state were regulated and ordered in accordance with Confucian principle it would be in the kind of harmony with cosmic forces that could prevent invasion, famine, or plague. The whole system, then, was directed at achieving a harmonious, prosperous, and peaceful society here and now on earth, and the main instrument—the embodiment of moral principle—was good government.

From the standpoint of formal ideology the consensus was virtually universal. Children were indoctrinated from birth by a family system that was the embodiment of Confucian principles. Later experiences with other members of their own lineage and with neighbors, landlords, and tax collectors all served to drive home the principles of hierarchy and of submission by the individual to the community. When things went wrong and there was evident injustice, it was the fault of imperfect men, not of the ideological blueprint.

Traditional communitarian loyalties were expressed mainly in terms of kinship or territorial groups at the local level. Among people of high rank engaged in the struggle for power, political factions became another focus for identity, allegiance, and conflict; the pattern persists today. The shift in orientation from a preoccupation with parochial and particularistic loyalties to a sense of participation in the entire national community has been a very gradual process that is still by no means complete.

Neo-Confucian metaphysics extended beyond society, culture, and the state to establish links with the entire cosmos. Society was regarded as an organic whole, not as a collection of separate individuals. Ideologically, the purpose was to encompass everything in a single harmonious system. This cultural orientation toward communal holism was applicable not just to the state but also, and probably more fundamentally for the actual functioning of society, to the family, village, school, political faction, or work group, endowing each of them with great cohesion and capacity for collective effort. Thus, the community in East Asia was formally legitimized as an expression of the moral order. The implications of this tradition for modern industrial and bureaucratic organization are obvious. For the individual, it was the community—usually the family and lineage in traditional Korea—that represented both the context within which fulfillment was achieved and whatever guarantees existed for personal safety, subsistence, and welfare.

Actually, there was also a great deal of "give" in the system. Tolerance, understanding, and the fact that those in authority made exceptions for, or extended special favors to, relatives and other members of their personal networks enabled most individuals to maneuver informally while paying lip service to the strict rules of propriety.

In the course of the Yi Dynasty's five hundred years, a growing population—including ever-larger numbers of low-ranking, rural and provincial quasi-aristocrats, for whom labor or involvement in any kind of commercial or productive activity was intensely degrading—competed more and more ferociously for whatever official positions and resources were available. Public office provided the only legitimately sanctioned route to power and wealth. Other avenues of achievement and upward mobility were severely restricted by the prejudice against commerce and industry and by the heavy exactions on agricultural production. With the number of examination passers kept very small relative to the size of the gentry, much of the energy and aspirations of the lower-ranking members of this class, along with those of ambitious commoners, were directed at acquiring influence, status, and wealth through the manipulation of personal relations, or by other informal means.

While never legitimized by formal values, strong egocentric behavior was frequent enough in the context of traditional society so that a kind of informal "underground" ideology of individualism can be postulated. Possibly rooted in the dim past of tribal egalitarianism, a pattern of unrestrained self-expression and cocky self-confidence on the part of many Koreans has been remarked on ever since foreign observers first reported their impressions in the mid-nineteenth century. Foreigners have also commented frequently on the lively and noisy quality of social life: the fact that there was a high incidence of laughter and quarreling and a love of drink, song, and dance. No matter how low a man's socioeconomic status might be, or how great the odds against his success, Koreans have frequently dared to dream fantastically exalted and ambitious dreams, and have then risked everything trying to achieve them, often with disastrous results. Respect for authority has co-existed with constant challenges to it. Spontaneous emotional self-expression and heroic ambition have existed somehow together with an extreme concern for appearances and acute sensitivity to position in the hierarchical order. People "know their place," but they refuse to stay in it.

The individual had little recourse from the tyranny of the consensus. He could often freely state his position, but once he had done so he was expected to give in and join cheerfully with the prevailing view. For men of strong will and convictions there was no way to change things except to challenge the existing leadership, either by leaving the community (or group) or by establishing a faction of their own within it. In other words, while normal respectability requires conformity to Confucian values of restraint, dignity, and propriety and an acceptance of the forms of deference to rank, at a different level there is likely also to be restless discontent, challenges to authority, and dreams of glory.

The fact that there was a standoff, a kind of equilibrium between aristocrats and ruler, was probably responsible in part for the relative lack of internal political conflict that permitted the dynasty to stagger on for such a long time. It also resulted, however, in an administrative paralysis that made it impossible for the government in the last half of the nineteenth century to take decisive action when challenged by domestic rebellion, the depredations of imperialist powers, and a series of disastrous internal economic crises. The military had been denigrated and neglected to the point where Korea was nearly defenseless against outside enemies. Commerce and industry were despised as occupations unfit for men of virtue, and all kinds of regulations and restrictions were imposed on both artisans and merchants, which had the effect of keeping their activities at low and primitive levels.

BREAKDOWN, CHANGE, AND CONTINUITY

By the second half of the nineteenth century, the traditional Confucian system was on the verge of complete breakdown.

After hundreds of years of isolation as a "hermit kingdom" dependent on China for protection, Korea was completely unprepared for the challenges from outside, to which it was now exposed as a result of China's weakness and the opening up of the country through treaties with foreign powers, beginning with Japan in 1876.

Lack of strong direction at the top, refusal among the elite to accept ideological or institutional change, corruption and inefficiency in the administrative bureaucracy, and an extreme shortage of governmental financial resources jointly contributed to the ignominious eclipse of the Yi Dynasty. The governing elite continued to spout traditional ideology, and the forms of institutions were maintained until the end. One brief exception occurred between 1865 and 1874, when the Taewongun, regent for King Kojong, successfully challenged the power of the aristocracy to increase the authority and resources of the crown. The situation returned to "normal" when Kojong came of age.

Two major efforts at ideological and institutional change were made by Koreans in the closing years of the dynasty, in response to the obvious inadequacy of decayed traditional institutions. Both failed. The first was a series of large-scale peasant rebellions inspired by a religious revitalization movement (*Tonghak*) that was nationalist and egalitarian in nature. This series of bloody uprisings was finally put down only with the help of Japanese expeditionary forces. The other attempt at fundamental change was led by a group of young aristocrats with progressive ideas who had considerable influence in the government during a brief period from 1896 to 1898. Their reform movement had no real popular base, however, and it was eventually suppressed by reactionary political elements whose position had been threatened.

After defeating its rivals for hegemony in Korea—first China in 1894 and then Russia in 1904—Japan moved quickly to take over actual control of the country in 1905; this move was followed by formal annexation in 1910.

In looking back at the traditional period, it seems evident that the prestige and pervasiveness of the dominant Confucian doctrine was so great as to provide enormous resistance to change, even when survival of the society was in question. The period of approximately thirty years between the emergence of Korea from tributary status in 1876 and its domination by Japan in 1905 was not long enough for Koreans to adapt their traditional values and institutions to the internal and external pressures for change, and to develop new ideological orientations. As things have turned out, this has all been done for them by outsiders. Korea, both North and South, can still be regarded as engaged in a long and agonizing search for a new, intrinsically Korean, ideological synthesis.

A radically different ideological element, Protestant Christianity, took root during the last two decades of the nineteenth century as a result of determined missionary activity. Protestantism in particular carried with it a very strong element of American (and Western European) individualism, but this was successfully adapted to the communal context of Korean family life and the tightly knit Christian congregations.

The coming of the Japanese as colonial rulers in 1905 brought both a new intensity and a new dimension to communitarian ideology in Korea. Native traditions of hierarchy, loyalty, and bureaucratic authoritarianism were strongly reinforced through education, propaganda, and the actual functioning of Japanese colonial institutions. On the other hand, Japanese militarism, with its glorification of physical courage and violence and its emphasis on discipline, precision, efficiency, and the conscientious fulfillment of assigned duties, represented a new and different set of value priorities.

But the most important ideological influence was probably not the result of conscious efforts by the colonial administration to promote Japanese ideals, institutions, and rules of behavior. Rather, the dramatic change brought about by industrialization, urbanization, and other aspects of colonial development policy had a far more profound effect on the values and behavior patterns of ordinary Koreans. The large expansion in primary school education, a radically different curriculum, new kinds of occupational experience, changed living conditions, and exposure to new technologies in relatively modern institutional settings combined to tear people loose from their previous ways of thinking and acting. Large-scale population movements intensified the effects of this social mobilization process, particularly after 1932 when the pace of industrialization picked up rapidly to accompany Japan's preparation for war. Even greater upheavals followed the outbreak of actual hostilities. Popular education became much less a moral goal in itself and was directed specifically at training youth for practical—usually technical—activities. Millions of people were forced to adapt to continuous rapid change in an environment where education, technology, and productive effort were associated with detailed planning and strict supervision.

The colonial experience also intensified Korean patriotism. Japanese assumptions of superiority and the accompanying discrimination and exploitation created not only indignation and hostility among Koreans but also a determination to catch up with Japan to prove they were not inferior. Many observers have cited this motivation as an important psychological factor in subsequent economic development.

Koreans today tend to stress the political harshness and exploitative aspects of colonial rule, insisting that nothing positive can be attributed to the experience. From an outsider's perspective, it seems that while great suffering resulted, Japan's presence helped stimulate during a relatively short time social and ideological processes that had taken place over a period of a hundred years or more in the advanced industrial countries. In ideological terms a large proportion of the subjugated population was wrenched out of a traditional environment and thrust (however brutally) into a new context of modernization. The Koreans themselves had almost nothing to do with shaping this modernization process, which was imposed from outside and from the top down in an extremely rigorous manner. Hierarchically ordered authoritarianism, far more comprehensive than in the past, had a direct and far-reaching impact on the life of each individual. Opportunities for Koreans, while strictly limited, depended on merit as demonstrated by achievement in Japanese institutions. Community need was defined in terms of service to the economic interests of greater Japan. Although hated and consciously rejected, the Japanese model continued to be influential, both ideologically and in terms of social structure and behavior in the years following liberation in 1945.

The American occupation force entered South Korea in 1945, unprepared for the deep political divisions that existed in the immediate post-liberation period. Koreans, however, were bitterly disappointed, even outraged, by the division of the country at the 38th parallel and by the fact that they were not granted full independence. The Americans, who had come with vague notions of fostering democratic political institutions after a period of benevolent tutelage during which their primary mission would be to maintain order, became deeply concerned with violent leftist agitation in South Korea. Confronted with the beginnings of Soviet implacability in the North, American officials increasingly gave their support to rightist politicians. Eventually they helped Syngman Rhee win what amounted to a small-scale civil war in the South, and in 1948 he was established as the head of a new government with a democratic facade. Once again, Koreans had been deprived of the opportunity to work out their own institutions in accordance with shared values and aspirations.

With the suppression of the left and with increasing American economic and political support, the country turned enthusiastically to the United States for inspiration. Ideals of individualism, equality, free enterprise, and democratic political institutions were incorporated into Korean political culture, becoming enshrined in primary school textbooks, the constitution, and the popular vocabulary.

Christianity also flourished during the post-liberation years, gaining millions of adherents and reinforcing the individualistic influences from America. During this period it was common for Koreans to denounce their Confucian heritage, blaming it for the weakness and backwardness that had led to the country's colonization by Japan. Individualism as an abstract ideal was much admired, both as the underlying principle of American efficiency and wealth, and because it offered people of energy and ability—particularly the young—a liberating alternative to the heavy constraints of hierarchical order.

Two other sociological phenomena of the Rhee period deserve to be noted: the boom in education, and the growth of the military establishment. Education has been almost universally perceived by Koreans both as a means of strengthening the country and as a path to upward mobility for the individual. The national obsession with education, affecting people from every socioeconomic level, is obviously rooted in Confucian values, and since liberation in 1945 a large percentage of available resources, both public and private, has been invested in the expansion of schools.

During the Korean War (1950–53), the Republic of Korea (ROK) army was expanded over sixfold, to more than six hundred thousand men, out of a total population of about twenty million. In addition to regular military combat training, Korean officers in large numbers attended American staff schools in South Korea and in the United States where they studied military organization, administration, logistics, and planning. After the war, the program was further expanded and intensified in an effort to make the Korean military more self-sufficient. By the late 1950s, the ROK military had more highly trained management skills, much greater discipline, and higher morale than the government bureaucracy or any other group in Korean society. Its approach was one of pragmatic problem solving, of achieving established objectives as quickly as possible by whatever means were available. Individual promotion depended on successfully carrying out assigned duties. All this represented a radical change from previous organizational behavior.

Nevertheless, many traditional values remained deeply rooted and widespread. In everyday interaction, individualism tended to be labeled as selfishness, and social pressures for the subordination of the individual's interests to those of the group continued to be strong. Notions of elitism, status, and paternalistic authority retained their importance for structuring institutions as well as for regulating interpersonal relations. Personal connections with relatives, school classmates, people from the same native place, or other close friends continued to be critical for access to jobs, loans, or government favors. Individual objectives, whether economic, political, or social, were achieved as much through the manipulation of personal networks as through energy and ability.

Just as success during the colonial period carried the opprobrium of presumed collaboration with the Japanese, success during the 1950s and afterward has implied, from the popular perspective, ill-gotten gains. It has been a truism that the greater an individual's wealth, the more certainly it was acquired through official collaboration involving bribes, kickbacks, and other kinds of secret favors. This feeling of ideological ambivalence regarding the acquisition of personal wealth is still widely held.

Increasingly, after the Korean War, the Rhee government's legitimacy eroded. To many Koreans the inefficiency, the corruption, and the preoccupation with political intrigue were reversions to the worst aspects of late Yi Dynasty rule.

When Rhee was overthrown in April 1960 after a massive student uprising, it seemed that at last South Koreans would be able to realize their widely shared ambition of establishing a stable, enlightened government based on genuine democratic institutions. The following year, however, was a period of growing disillusionment. Weak leadership, intense internal political division, demands for punishment for the abuses of the Rhee era, and constant popular agitation on the part of labor and other groups produced chaotic instability and governmental paralysis. The result of this "democratic period" (1960–61) was a collective loss of confidence (that persists to some extent to the present) in the ability of Koreans to govern themselves effectively through democratic means. The principle of unrestrained competition among free individuals or among groups seeking private advantage was to some degree discredited as a basis for political and economic institutions.

ECONOMIC DEVELOPMENT UNDER MILITARY LEADERSHIP

Sustained economic development did not get under way until after General Park Chung Hee came to power in the 1961 military coup. Reliable evidence regarding the state of public opinion does not exist, but it seems likely that there was more relief than consternation when the previous government was overthrown. Park was accepted as a reformer by a substantial portion of the population, to whom it appeared evident that only a strong man in charge of a united, disciplined administration could deliver the country from its precarious situation. The haunting doubt about whether Koreans could govern themselves, combined with domestic economic stagnation and the realization that North Korea was rapidly industrializing, had created a crisis of confidence.

Like Japan, Korea had suffered tremendously from a destructive war. It was a latecomer to industrialization, it was crowded, and it was without natural resources. The Korean population, also like that of Japan, was motivated by a strong work ethic and a thirst for education. In both countries, national mobilization for development was met by an energetic popular response.

President Park imposed on the country a developmental strategy of modernization through planned growth and combined it with a determination to maintain a strong military posture against the danger of renewed attack from the North. The success of this effort, which was increasingly apparent after 1965, was probably due as much to the sustained pressure for results from the top and the relative efficiency of a revitalized bureaucracy as it was to the wisdom of the economic policies that were adopted. Both aspects were crucial. South Korea had become a "hard state," in which plans were effectively carried out in accordance with military standards of discipline and achievement that had been transferred to the administrative bureaucracy. As production and the value of exports continued to rise along with employment and wages, popular confidence and optimism rose too. The Park regime acquired a certain measure of acceptance and legitimacy on the basis of demonstrated performance. This performance not only continued in the 1970s, it improved.

The period of extremely rapid growth in South Korea between 1962 and 1979 has been intensively studied by economists, and the story is well known. During these years annual GNP growth averaged over 9 percent. The value of exports (in current prices) climbed from $62 million to over $15 billion seventeen years later, and per capita GNP rose from $87 to $1500. By 1985 the figures were $30 billion for exports and about $2,000 for per capita GNP. The degree of structural change in the economy was also great: agriculture, forestry, and fishing were responsible for 43.3 percent of GNP in 1962 but only about 18 percent in 1981, while the share contributed by mining and manufacturing rose from 11 percent to 36 percent during the same period. In 1962 the first of five five-year plans was drawn up by the Economic Planning Board, a newly created agency having substantial power and influence, headed by the deputy prime minister. In subsequent years the planning process became more complex and sophisticated, as experience and skills were acquired. Most available resources were allocated according to the five-year plans or as a result of policy decisions by high-level bureaucrats. In general, direction was pragmatic, flexible, and heavy-handed. There was close collaboration between government and business, and creative, export-oriented entrepreneurship was encouraged and rewarded. But by and large businessmen did as they were told.

After a somewhat uncertain initial period of continued import substitution and the improvement of domestic infrastructure financed largely by foreign loans, economic policy after 1966 shifted to an emphasis on export-led growth.

A system of establishing export targets for each firm, with significant rewards for successful achievement, has promoted continuous, close collaboration between businessmen and the bureaucracy. Strong incentives were provided to exporters: subsidies (usually in the form of loans), tax breaks, a devalued exchange rate, tariff exemptions for raw material imports, and cheap sources of energy. Successful exporters not only made large profits, they were awarded presidential medals at elaborate ceremonies. The monthly trade promotion meetings were usually attended by the president himself, his economic ministers, high-ranking bureaucrats, and the presidents of large firms. The products of Korea's labor-intensive light industries, such as textiles, clothing, shoes, plywood, wigs, and (later) electronics, proved to be extremely competitive in world markets.

With high debt-equity ratios in private companies and a desperate shortage of capital, businessmen were (and are) extremely dependent on bank loans. The government's control of the banking system has enabled it to intervene to whatever extent it considered necessary in carrying out industrial policy. Its export success and growth enabled Korean industry to attract large amounts of foreign capital, but this too was allocated under strict government control through preferential loans to favored firms in favored industries.

Businessmen and government officials have also collaborated closely in dealing with labor problems. The government has provided "guidance," which in recent years has established limits to wage increases, although in the 1970s firms were sometimes encouraged to raise wages for political reasons. Whenever necessary, or when requested by private firms, the government has also intervened, using force if necessary, to head off serious labor disputes and prevent strikes.

The policy of channeling preferential loans to favored businessmen with close ties to the governing elite and a proven track record contributed to the rapid growth during the 1960s and 1970s of large conglomerate corporations, the *chaebol*. A *chaebol* may comprise a wide variety of companies engaged in manufacturing, transportation, mining, construction, service, or agriculture—all under the centralized supervision of the founding entrepreneur. The inner core—the men who actually run the *chaebol*—comprise a small group sharing close personal ties that have developed over a long period. Even though many of the first generation founders have died or retired, control of the conglomerates has remained in their families.

Chaebol have grown at a disproportionate rate compared to the rest of the economy. The top thirty conglomerates accounted for about one third of total sales in 1984. It is generally agreed that this industrial concentration has been accompanied by a substantial degree of monopolistic and oligopolistic control of domestic markets. As early as 1974, efforts were made by the government to control and restrict their growth, but the *chaebol* have continued to prosper as the favored instruments of development policy, both in innovating new products and in mass producing for export. They have consistently been able to attract more highly qualified personnel, acquire more advanced technology, build larger and more modern plants, invest more in research and development, and pay better wages than other firms. Under highly paternalistic leadership they represent the most advanced and productive sector of Korean industry.

Despite the current widespread criticism of *chaebol* their important contribution to Korean economic development must be recognized. With the advice and support of the administration they have undertaken the tough jobs, starting new industries and importing more advanced technology. They achieved economies of scale and penetrated export markets at a critical stage in the nation's export-led growth. In general they have been consistently at the forefront of the processes of dynamic industrialization and cosmopolitanization in South Korea.

After 1975 the Korean government (reportedly at President Park's personal insistence) made extremely large investments in heavy industry and chemicals. Confidence engendered by previous economic success, the belief that Korea's competitive edge in light industry was being challenged by other developing countries, and, probably most important, the desire to develop a larger defense industry were responsible for the shift in industrial policy during the late 1970s. The Nixon doctrine, U.S. disengagement from Vietnam, and finally President Carter's attempt to withdraw U.S. troops contributed to the desire of the Korean military for less dependence on American weapons. But the investments in heavy industry were so large that officials found it impossible to follow the flexible, trial-and-error system that had worked so well previously for making gradual corrections in economic policy.

By 1979 the deleterious effects of the shift in emphasis from exports to heavy industry were evident: large over-capacity, particularly in the relatively inefficient machinery industry; serious distortions throughout the economy; rapid increases in the external debt; inflation rising to 35 percent in 1979; and a sharp decline in the export growth rate. *Chaebol* dominance of Korean industry was further enhanced. The 1979 oil price increase and political and economic disruption following President Park's assassination in October 1979 exacerbated the situation.

In 1980 real GNP actually declined by 5.2 percent. The new government of former general Chun Doo Hwan intervened massively in an effort to correct the problems of structural imbalance in industry. Consolidation in some industries was accomplished by forced mergers; in others, by the wholesale transfer of ownership. Firms making diesel engines, heavy electrical equipment, certain kinds of communication equipment, automobiles, and trucks were told which products they could manufacture. The result was consternation, resentment, and distrust on the part of big business. Nevertheless these efforts to "rationalize" industrial distortion and reduce overcapacity were fairly effective, and stringent stabilization measures were also successful. By 1983 the value of exports had reached $23.6 billion, inflation was below 5 percent (down from 20 percent in 1981), and GNP rose by about 9 percent.

Because of the economic difficulties encountered during the period 1979–82, high-ranking economist/technocrats were able to persuade the president to initiate a major transition in economic policy. It was argued that the economy was now too large and too complex for the kind of centralized decision making that had been effective in the past, and that ubiquitous government controls should be gradually replaced by a greater dependence on the market as a means of regulation.

As a result of the shift in the philosophy underlying economic policy, the Korean economy is now in a difficult period of transition. Small and medium industry is being encouraged and assisted, while the *chaebol* are being told they have to get along without the preferential credit and incentives that were provided in the past. Officials insist that the government will no longer give direct orders to industry but instead will use tax policy and other financial incentives to assist and guide promising firms; however, weak, badly managed, or uncompetitive firms will be allowed to go under. Seoul technocrats constantly reaffirm their government's determination to push ahead with liberalization as fast as possible, including the relaxation of government control over banking. Import liberalization is expected to challenge Korean firms to increase their productivity and efficiency so that the private sector will more frequently make its own decisions in accordance with market incentives.

THE PREVAILING IDEOLOGICAL MIX

South Korea's "dominant" or establishment doctrine clearly emphasizes that the interests of the community take precedence over those of the individual. The government insists that in a time of national crisis (it is always a time of crisis), individual desires must be sacrificed for collective ends. Rewards for the individual will be reaped abundantly in the future, but perhaps not until the next generation; for now, Koreans must work hard, do as they are told, and live without extravagance.

Koreans have been described as less ego-centered and more involved with other people than are Americans. Success and failure for the individual are likely to be more closely associated with the approval or disapproval of family, friends, or colleagues than with inner personal standards or goals. The prospect of shame is a potent form of social control. "Overlapping egos" vividly describes the interpersonal involvement and sensitivity characteristic of Korean society.

The difference between inferior and superior is taught from infancy and reinforced by the internal structure of the family, schools, business firms, and even social or sports clubs. Etiquette and morality are intimately bound up with hierarchy, and differences in rank and prestige are constantly emphasized through language and deferential (or authoritative) behavior. A Korean who is not treated properly in accordance with his rank status in an institutional setting will be bitterly resentful, fearing that he has lost face in front of his colleagues. For many Koreans, particularly those with status, power, and wealth, hierarchical principles remain bound up with order and social harmony today as in the past.

However, the individualism and egalitarianism that unsuccessfully challenged hierarchy in the past has also persisted, greatly reinforced and legitimized by imported ideological influences and socioeconomic change. Christianity and American political and cultural beliefs and attitudes have had a profound influence, provoking popular discontent but also stimulating productive energies. It almost seems as if the traditional structural and ideological constraints still so prevalent in Korean society are necessary to keep powerful restless forces of individual aspiration, aggrandizement, and self-assertion from bringing about chaotic, revolutionary change.

The importance of family and lineage have declined, and many millions of people have been uprooted in the recent past from stable cohesive rural communities either by war or migration. In the crowded cities, individuals must rely on their own wits and resources and must determine their own destinies. This "individualism by default" is unsanctioned by traditional thought, but imported Western ideology gives it a certain respectability. Communitarianism, embedded in social structure and internalized norms, is associated with conservative tradition, privilege, and military rule. Society may still function largely in accordance with communitarian principles, but they no longer dominate popular thought and values.

The imposed consensus of the Park Chung Hee years is visibly breaking down. If it is widely recognized that disciplined, unified effort under strong leadership was necessary during the 1960s and 1970s, given the threat from the North and the nation's economic weakness, the idea is equally widespread now that Koreans should no longer have to exist under conditions of paternalistic tutelage. Also, President Chun does not inspire the same degree of popular confidence and respect as his predecessor.

The issue of equality of result is of critical ideological importance, even though the overall distribution of wealth in South Korea appears to be relatively equitable in comparison to that in most countries. Income distribution is becoming more unequal, however, and it is widely perceived as unjust. In a very crowded country, sharp contrasts between the relatively affluent life-style of the middle class and the austerity of workers have become particularly obvious. Unlike the traditional period, when it was appropriate for hierarchical social differences to be reflected in property and living standards, the inequities of today are seen as evidence of a lack of just rule.

The government itself has tried to seize the issue by more rigorous and even-handed collection of taxes, particularly from corporations and the well-to-do, by greater efforts to control and limit speculation in residential property, and by expanding welfare programs.

Equality of result is also important because South Korea sees itself as engaged in all-out competition with the Democratic People's Republic of Korea (DPRK). The Chun regime has no intention of trying to match the cradle-to-grave egalitarian welfare system of the North, but it recognizes that there are limits to the degree of concentration of wealth or the extent of urban poverty that the South can tolerate without provoking unfavorable comparisons.

Since liberation in 1945, the expansion of educational opportunities has been one of the main preoccupations of Koreans. Recently the government attempted to remove some of the considerable advantages held by children of the privi-

leged in the educational sweepstakes by providing more scholarship aid and prohibiting private tutoring. Private corporations
have also set aside large amounts of money for educational
assistance. Although some of the first generation of self-made
men in commerce and industry acquired power and wealth
without much formal education, access to the ladders of opportunity today is almost impossible without a university degree,
as is access to good jobs. The military academies are also highly
selective and have provided an avenue of upward mobility for
many exceptional young men from poor rural families.

Once an individual becomes a member of an organization,
his advancement depends on a variety of factors. Within the
army it is not enough to be hard-working and unusually competent. One must become a member of the dominant faction
and/or obtain the protection of powerful superiors to be
appointed to important commands. Most business firms are
privately owned and controlled, so that relatives of the founder
or current head usually have an inside track to the positions of
influence. But the pressure for results is such that the principle
of merit is firmly established. Incompetence is not tolerated,
and favorites are expected to outperform their colleagues.

A large gap exists with regard to education, salaries, and
status between blue-collar workers on the one hand and cler-
ical workers, engineers, or other highly trained technicians
and management on the other. Company executives talk a
good deal about the importance of good relations and high
morale among workers, but traditional paternalistic attitudes
are still widespread. Government suppression of the labor
movement has created a situation in which most managers do
not pay much attention to the concerns or aspirations of workers, and the resulting tension and hostility have made close
collaboration difficult. The situation is most severe in small and
medium marginal companies that must take advantage of low
wages to survive. Some managers of high-tech *chaebol* subsidiaries insist that their workers are closely involved in production decisions and that morale is excellent. Nevertheless, for
industry as a whole, labor turnover is high, and most surveys
show that workers are dissatisfied with their jobs. By contrast,
the salaries, job satisfaction, and loyalty of white-collar employees are all much greater. Thus, traditional status differences

associated with education and the prejudice against manual occupations continue to be expressed in the treatment of labor.

Rights and Duties

One of the primary concerns of industrial strategy and development planning in South Korea is the creation of four hundred thousand jobs annually for new additions to the labor force. In 1971 the Ministry of Home Affairs launched a large-scale program of integrated rural development that significantly raised rural income and agricultural productivity, transforming the lives of farmers over the ensuing ten years. During the recent severe recession of 1980–82, the government put strong pressure on industrial managers to avoid extensive layoffs, and many firms complied by operating without profits for a more or less extended period of time. This same pattern was repeated in 1985 during another economic downturn. Thus, along with the traditional emphasis on duties, the government has recognized that an as yet undefined but nevertheless definite right to work and earn a decent minimum livelihood has emerged with economic development.

The emphasis, however, is firmly on job security rather than on a guaranteed income. Korean planners are determined to avoid what they perceive as the evil effects of too much welfare in the advanced Western democracies. Public opinion generally supports such a view. Those who do not work are not provided for, unless they are disabled war veterans, impoverished widows, or the sick and aged; but only minuscule amounts have been allocated for people in even these groups. As government resources have increased in recent years, other rights, such as those to pensions, health insurance, and adequate housing have been publicly acknowledged. The Fifth Five-Year Plan (1982–86) envisaged a relatively ambitious program of social benefits, but other priorities have turned out to be more pressing. Nevertheless, it is widely expected that a larger share of future budgets will be allocated to social welfare, provided economic growth continues.

There is popular agitation for many other rights. Korean authorities have consistently maintained that economic growth and maintenance of the country's international competitive position had to take precedence over such "luxuries" as clean air and the conservation of the environment. During the last few years, however, environmental pollution has become so great that action is finally being taken. Increased efforts are also under way to expand protection for the individual against industrial accidents, poor-quality foods, and dangerous chemical emissions.

Economic growth and social stability since 1961 have brought dramatic changes. The opportunity to acquire property continuously over an extended period in order to build a foundation for future personal prosperity and to provide for one's children has probably been the greatest single incentive for enthusiastic participation in the development effort. Private property rights, while subject to communitarian constraints, have a sanctity today that never existed before.

Personal savings, while fluctuating in response to interest rates, have been consistently high in recent years. The government today scrupulously provides actual market value compensation for property confiscated in connection with rural or urban development projects. An increasingly large middle-class population that has seen an enormous increase in its property and living standards during the last twenty years is extremely sensitive to any threat to its material well-being. It is a truism of Korean politics that to retain popular support, a Korean government must be successful in promoting economic growth.

Most Korean businesses are still privately controlled by the original founder or members of his immediate family. These family firms have been very reluctant to list their shares on the stock exchange, in spite of persistent government urging. They prefer to obtain bank loans. Increased government pressure plus a sharp curtailment of credit has recently forced several *chaebol* to go public, but they continue to do everything possible to retain control within the family group.

Businessmen as individuals have been permitted to earn large profits, and the relative opulence of their life-style has caused a good deal of popular resentment. At the same time, their contribution to the nation's economic development is recognized, and people take pride in the shiny new office buildings and factories. Nevertheless, collaboration between government and industry is often denounced as illicit and corrupt—a way of enriching the business and military/bureaucratic elites at public expense.

The state clearly determines the priorities of community need in South Korea. Defense, economic growth, political stability, and the furthering of national prestige in the international world receive primary emphasis. The national economic strategy continues to focus on increased exports as the main "engine for growth," although in recent years a larger domestic market is becoming more important. When former military officers seized power—in 1961 as in 1980—they soon discovered that economic growth was not possible without the cooperation and talents of industrial managers and business entrepreneurs. But there was never any question as to who would run the show. No one thinks that the military could continue to run the country for long if there was a significant relaxation of controls and/or a real shift in the direction of more democratic political institutions. When the government has considered intervention to be necessary, it has not been reluctant to intervene, and the businessman who objected had little recourse. He could argue his point at length with bureaucrats, but they made the ultimate decisions in accordance with plans developed on a national scale.

The business community is constantly consulted by the bureaucratic establishment, but it also takes the initiative, both publicly and privately, in trying to influence government policy. Managers are, of course, dedicated to maximizing profits, and there are times when they bitterly resent official interference. But businessmen also recognize that they have thrived in the communitarian environment. They do not hesitate to seek government help in developing their projects or in cushioning the effects of their failures. They are likely to agree with government arguments regarding the need to avoid domestic political strife and to maintain law and order, and they are delighted to work closely with the government in making sure there are no serious labor disputes. In addition, business firms, with governmental encouragement, have aggressively utilized the traditional subordination of individuals to the group as a means of keeping wages low and resisting other worker demands. The Korean business executive sees himself as a benevolently paternalistic employer, and many aspects of personnel policy, such as the payment of bonuses or other supplementary allowances, company assistance for employees' weddings and funerals, and the provision of educational facilities are calculated to demonstrate that the employer wants to create an atmosphere of harmony and mutual obligation.

A reciprocal relationship involving loyal obligation on the one hand and enlightened, responsible concern for employee welfare on the other is supposed to exist. Actually the situation is exceedingly one-sided; worker grievances regarding pay, safety, unhealthy conditions, or other problems are usually ignored. Only when particular skills are in short supply in an expanding economy can individuals possessing these skills advance their interests in dealing with employers, nearly always by shifting to a different company.

Worker docility is guaranteed in most circumstances by the threat of coercive government force. The current regime of President Chun Doo Hwan has demonstrated on several occasions that it is not reluctant to use force, although in most cases police investigation and questioning have been sufficient to deal with potential labor problems. But workers are becoming increasingly cynical about the paternalistic system, and increasingly resentful at what they consider to be unfair treatment. If Korea continues to prosper in a reasonably healthy world economy, the authorities may be able to buy off labor with wage increases, while retaining effective authoritarian control. In any case, a major point of ideological tension exists today in the area of labor-management relations. So far, except for a few spontaneous, uncoordinated outbursts, the tension has been contained. But in the longer term, labor's potential for creating serious social and political unrest is probably greater than the noisy dissent of students.

THE CHANGING ROLE OF GOVERNMENT

Although the South Korean government has always recognized that it needed the cooperation of the business community, it has pragmatically exercised its authority in accordance with comprehensive economic plans. Rather than attempting to regulate the economy through a mass of detailed, universally applicable rules, bureaucrats have used discretionary powers to target certain industries for encouragement and support, and to reward particular firms for outstanding performance. Through controls over credit, tax policy, licenses, access to imported raw materials and many other matters, the government has been able to make the ultimate decisions regarding who will produce what and in what quantities. Recalcitrant or inefficient firms were brought into line by a graduated series of steps, beginning with suggestions and then moving on to threats and eventual coercion, which could include eliminating the firm completely or absorbing it into another more favored corporation.

During the last few years there has been increased recognition of the limits to government power, not only among businessmen and the public at large, but also among officials themselves. Since 1980 the counterproductive effects of too much heavy-handed control of the economy have been painfully apparent. A more moderate approach has been adopted, involving consultation and collaboration with industry, rather than command and control. In certain industries, however, the government has acted boldly to force mergers and to eliminate weak and uncompetitive firms.

In December 1984 the government formally announced its new policy of withdrawing support from the hitherto favored *chaebol* and of providing more substantial loans and support to small and medium industry. Most special incentives were removed for shipbuilding, textiles, and electronics, while commercial banks were free to lend to whomever they chose. In 1985 an industrial law was drafted to restrict *chaebol* activities and place limits on further expansion.

The conglomerates are now relatively free from governmental direction. Those that are in a strong financial position are being encouraged to go their own way. The weaker ones will be obliged to divest themselves of uncompetitive subsidiaries to improve their financial position and to concentrate on what they can do best. In an extreme case, such as that of the Kukje *chaebol* in early 1985, a conglomerate was allowed to fail, and financially strong, well-managed companies were directed to pick up the pieces. Because of the high priority given to reducing the nation's external debt, far less government-controlled credit is now available for distribution, and according to current plans, much of this will go to support "promising" smaller companies.

South Korea's foreign debt of $45 billion is the fourth largest among the developing nations. It has become a matter of increasing concern, not only within the business world and the economic bureaucracy, but also as a political issue that opponents of the government frequently emphasize. The country can unquestionably service the debt at present and in the near future, but its awesome size combined with gloomy forecasts of increased protectionism and declining rates of export growth have contributed to a new mood of anxiety. Current campaigns urge Korean citizens to put more of their income into savings, to refrain from buying foreign goods, and to conserve energy. A principal goal of the Sixth Five-Year Plan (1988–93) is debt reduction.

Actual accomplishment of the liberalization objectives has been mixed, with more lip service than action in some areas. The diagnosis of economic ills and the program for curing them by restricting government intervention and promoting competition have been the work of Korean economists trained in the United States. They have engineered a major shift in emphasis, but there is still some question as to how long and how intensely the president will push the transition. To stay in power, the governing elite must be able to control money and have access to it. Informal contacts between the heads of the *chaebol* and the centers of political power continue, enabling the former to obtain special favors and circumvent bureaucratic regulations. In addition there is a certain amount of in-fighting within the bureaucracy, with the Ministry of Trade and Industry often mounting a delaying action against the powerful forces for economic change represented by the Economic Planning Board and the Ministry of Finance. Banks now have the ability to set interest rates within certain limits, and they also have a greater voice in deciding who gets the loans. But although the government has announced on many occasions that a free banking system is needed, it still exercises ultimate control over the distribution of available funds. Officials complain that the *chaebol* refuse to accept the responsibility that goes with the new policy, and that they continue to seek special help, protection, and incentives from the government while resenting any intervention in their decision making. *Chaebol* executives, of course, strongly resent and deny the government's assertions that their excesses are somehow responsible for current economic problems.

The weakness of small and medium companies constitutes another major problem. Without expert management, highly skilled technicians, or a strong financial position, most are in a position of abject dependence on the *chaebol* for whom they act as subcontractors. Bankers consider them to be poor risks compared to the *chaebol*. Bureaucrats have never given such relatively insignificant, self-made businessmen much attention, respect, or support in the past, and attitudes change slowly. Since personal status is highly important in Korea, it is natural for officials to accord favorable treatment to the representatives of big conglomerates, who are more likely to have social and educational backgrounds that are similar to theirs, as well as overlapping personal networks.

Although there is considerable popular antagonism to the *chaebol,* there is also a good deal of glamour attached to their image, and the heads of big companies often have celebrity status. In addition, the relatively underpaid bureaucrat is likely to be thinking about eventually obtaining a good job in a large corporation if a favorable opportunity arises either after retirement or earlier. Thus, although the economic technocrats continue to push ahead with their liberalization policies, there is still considerable resistance to fundamental change both in the business world and the government itself.

Whether effective consultation and collaboration between government and industry can replace bureaucratic controls remains questionable. The same kinds of informal personal communications networks that appear to be so important in Japan exist also in Korea, but the mutual respect, trust, and predictability that apparently emerge only with many years of collaborative practice are still distinctly missing.

A Growing Industry: Electronics

South Koreans generally recognize that they can no longer compete with the lower labor costs of Thailand, Sri Lanka, the People's Republic of China, and the Philippines in traditional export industries. Their only alternative to economic stagnation is to acquire more advanced technology and challenge Japanese, U.S., and European domination in the high-tech field. The government has energetically promoted science education and research activities for many years, and investments in this area are increasing. Korean scientists abroad have been lured home to work in special scientific research institutes at relatively high salaries, and young scientists and engineers working in Korea have been sent abroad for further study. A Special Industrial Technology Research Financing Program was initiated in 1982 to promote the acquisition of technology needed by government-funded institutes undertaking R&D projects. Total R&D investment jumped from $30 million in 1972, about two thirds of which was contributed by the government, to $580 million in 1982, or about 1 percent of GNP. By 1986 the amount is expected to reach $1.7 billion, or 2 percent of GNP, nearly two thirds of which will be contributed by private industry.

In terms of value-added exports, electronics is by far the fastest growing and most successful of the high-tech industries. The Electronic Industry Promotion Law dates from 1969, when government protection and support were important. But since 1982 consumer electronics, integrated circuits, microprocessors, and telecommunications have expanded rapidly with very little help from official sources.

Industry representatives say there is no one in the Ministry of Trade and Industry who knows enough about electronics to make consultation worthwhile, and officials themselves tend to agree. Executives of the largest electronics firms, all of which are associated with *chaebol,* generally try to avoid meeting with government officials. They also complain that embassy staff overseas are of little or no use in finding and developing markets.

Current administration policy is to allow large firms in growing industries to sink or swim in accordance with their competitive ability and financial strength, although existing laws would permit the government to step in forcefully if an important national interest were at stake. Accordingly, the big electronics firms have obtained foreign technology, developed their own products, and sought out export markets on their own. One of their major problems is that very heavy investments are required to produce products. The *chaebol* would like to obtain government guarantees, however, for such large-scale, high-risk investments as integrated circuits, that are likely to be obsolete in two or three years. At present they are seeking ties with U.S. electronics manufacturers.

An Industry Fighting off Decline: Textiles

Textiles were the mainstay of export-led growth throughout the 1960s and 1970s. In 1984 textile exports were valued at $6.7 billion, more than the products of any other industry. But they are no longer growing, and prospects for the future are poor. In contrast to electronics, government officials keep close watch over textiles and are prepared to cope with major problems, although there is no direct governmental intervention. Officials of the Korean Federation of Textile Industries (KOFOTI), a quasi-governmental organization, say that despite their efforts to persuade industry representatives to adopt a particular course of action, they often have to wait for extended periods before the heads of firms take any action.

Koreans now agree that the quality of their textile exports must be upgraded, in terms of yarn, fabrics, and garments as well as fashion. In the textile industry small, creative firms specializing in quality and innovation must be in close contact with international market trends. In Korea, however, the most advanced sector of the textile industry consists of large firms mass-producing a relatively limited number of items in enormous quantities for overseas wholesale markets. This market is now declining as a result of protectionist measures and changes in demand, and the big Korean companies, many of which are members of *chaebol* groups, are faced with excess capacity. Most small textile companies have tended to produce cheap goods with relatively outmoded equipment.

The Korean textile industry also lags well behind Taiwan and Japan in the use of automated equipment. Higher productivity through increased automation is particularly urgent because skilled female textile workers are moving to other industries where wages are substantially higher.

The government is collaborating with industry to improve the situation. Contests are held to select the most talented fashion designers for further training overseas. Loans are being offered on favorable terms for the purchase of new machinery, and there is support for the introduction of higher technology in such fields as the dyeing of cloth. Above all, the government intends to pursue its program of providing encouragement and support to "promising" small and medium companies. Some observers are optimistic, forecasting textile exports worth $12 billion by 1990, but others have serious doubts whether transformation of the industry will actually take place on the scale required.

SUMMARY AND PROSPECTS

Some external pressures, most notably the ongoing security crisis, reinforce Korean traditions of hierarchical social organization and the subordination of individual interests to those of the community. But other events and forces generated both inside and outside Korea have stimulated sharp individualistic challenges to traditional communitarianism. Actually, the hypothesis of a "worldwide drift toward communitarian practices" does not fit the current scene in South Korea particularly well.

Ideals of political democracy and individual rights have been imported from the United States, and they are now firmly rooted in the consciousness of a highly politicized population. The result is constant tension with establishment ideology, and the possibility for civil disorder is always present. The economy has reached a size and complexity where heavy-handed centralized control by government bureaucrats is no longer producing optimum results, and there is a clear tendency on the part of both management and the government to move in the direction of greater dependence on free markets. Perhaps the greatest point of tension lies in the area of labor-management relations. The government continues to support management's repressive, paternalistic labor policies in an effort to control inflation and to maintain Korean competitiveness in world markets. Workers believe that they are being required to make a disproportionate sacrifice for economic growth and they are increasingly cynical, alienated, and restive. More generally, tensions derive from the fact that fundamental social change accompanying the processes of extremely rapid urbanization and industrialization has weakened traditional and communal values and promoted individualism.

But it is also true that there is substantial popular agreement regarding the importance of maintaining a strong, unified posture of military preparedness vis-à-vis the North, and that public opinion undeniably supports effective policies for maintaining and promoting economic growth. Koreans often admit ruefully that it takes strong leadership to keep them in line and to prevent a chaotic scramble for individual goals. All this sounds very much like a solid consensus favoring the current communitarian system, where the dominant ideology is that of the governing elites. Those who are concerned only with economic performance (which has been superb) think of the South Korean people as industrious, cooperative drones, happily doing what they are told. But the problem is that, on the contrary, a vigorous, aspiring, educated, articulate, and increasingly cosmopolitan population desperately wants more personal freedom and a greater degree of participation in the choice of government leaders and policies. The way in which the Chun regime seized power is still widely regarded as illegitimate, criminal, and disgraceful to the nation. There is also deepening dissatisfaction with what most Koreans see as the unfair distribution of wealth and status. These are basically moral issues, and in that traditional sense the current challenge to the dominant system is intensely ideological, going far beyond individual dissatisfaction based on economic considerations.

It is necessary to make a distinction between the popular utopian aspirations of Koreans and their realistic expectations for the future. They are well aware of the severe "real world" constraints on their development: the extreme crowding, the lack of raw materials, the existence of a major security threat, and the problems involved in up-scaling technology while continuing to compete in world export markets. The only workable alternative to the present authoritarian system would seem to be a somewhat more decentralized and pluralistic but still disciplined national collaboration based on consensus along the lines of Japanese communalism, and in the long run that is probably where South Korea is headed—barring further security crises.

There is, however, an important objection to such a scenario: it is vociferously rejected by most Koreans.* Popular distaste for the Japanese model is partly based, of course, on nationalistic dislike for *anything* Japanese. But it is also a matter of firm belief on the part of Koreans that they are more individualistic and less docile than the Japanese, and that therefore Japanese-style consensual communitarianism would never work. Koreans see themselves as unique. Their aspirations for the future do not include communitarianism tutelage, however benign and decentralized. Most Koreans believe that they can build a vibrantly creative and individualistic society on the basis of free enterprise and political democracy. The energy and stubborn persistence they have demonstrated in achieving widely held objectives during the last twenty years or so make it essential that observers not discount the influence of these aspirations on future developments. Still, the communitarian environment in Korea remains ubiquitous and for the most part is taken for granted; it is not likely to be sloughed off in the foreseeable future. The way in which restless drives for greater individual self-expression are worked out within an overarching communitarian context will determine the ideological mix of the coming decades.

---

*This is not true of many of the most influential businessmen, among whom there is great admiration for Japanese productive efficiency. Several of the conglomerates have consciously imitated Japanese corporate structure and management methods.

9

ORDER AND PROGRESS IN BRAZIL

Jorge I. Domínguez

"Order and progress," nineteenth-century positivism's slogan, was conceived by Auguste Comte. The two words are engraved in Portuguese on the Brazilian flag, Brazil's most public symbol. When Brazilian citizens swear allegiance to the flag, they also endorse that slogan, the country's ruling ideology, as a guide to the twenty-first century. However, few tests have assessed whether individual citizens would choose without compulsion to uphold the positivist slogan. In 1985 a civilian became president of Brazil for the first time since 1964. Obtaining the consent of the governed thereby becomes even more necessary for achieving order and progress, and perhaps even liberty and equality.

The author would like to thank the following for their helpful comments: George C. Lodge, Peter McDonough, Pedro Pick, Raimar Richers, and Daniel Sharp.

THE PAST AS PROLOGUE

Brazil has certainly been orderly by world standards. Independent since 1822, it has never had a successful revolution, not even to become independent. Much of coastal Brazil became a Portuguese colony in the sixteenth century. When Napoleon invaded Portugal in 1807, the Portuguese court soon thereafter fled to Brazil. The Portuguese monarch turned a mere colony into the heart of his empire. In December 1815, after Napoleon's defeat, Brazil became a co-kingdom with Portugal.

Nonetheless, Portugal sought to reassert its authority over Brazil. In 1822, Prince Pedro, the monarchy's supreme ruler in Brazil, was ordered to return to Portugal. He disobeyed, blocked the landing of Portuguese troops and, with the support of a newly convened Congress, proclaimed Brazil's independence and himself as emperor. The legitimacy of the old empire was transferred to the newly independent state through the person of the emperor. Partly because Brazil had been the center of a united centralized bureaucratic empire, it became independent as a single entity, avoiding Spanish America's fragmentation into many states. The empire of Pedro I and Pedro II lasted until 1889, when a bloodless coup overthrew the latter and proclaimed a republic.

The empire had achieved independence, maintained national unity, and fought successfully against the country's enemies, settling its boundaries with Uruguay, Argentina, and Paraguay. But no war broke out over the emancipation of the slaves. Unlike in Haiti, the United States, Cuba, or Venezuela, where the slavery issue was central to major civil wars, Brazil abolished slavery peacefully through government decrees (despite some earlier, sporadic slave uprisings). A gradual process of emancipation, begun in 1871, took seventeen years to complete.

The republic widened elite participation in the making of regional and national decisions. It maintained internal peace with relatively few disturbances. Its diplomacy dramatically expanded the country's territory without recourse to war. Early in the twentieth century, when Brazil accounted for more than half of all internationally traded coffee, Brazil's ability to stabilize and raise the world's coffee price was an effective use of monopoly power in the international commodity trade.[1] Political order in a country rich in most natural resources other than petroleum attracted waves of immigrants from Europe and, eventually, Japan.

Historical Elements in Brazilian Ideology

At the onset of the Great Depression of the 1930s, two tendencies within the framework of the official belief in order and progress competed, as they had since colonial times.

When Brazil was a Portuguese colony, geographic distance, transportation problems, and Portugal's economic and military decline had made it easier for Brazilian officials to pay only formal obeisance to Lisbon's edicts while disobeying them. This relatively high local autonomy prevailed as well when Brazil became an independent empire: the Rio de Janeiro court found it difficult to govern effectively over its own regions. The fact of strong autonomy for each region became embodied in the republic's federalist constitution, resting ultimately in the state governments of an oligarchical federal republic. Indeed, the successful international coffee market interventions of the early twentieth century were carried out not by the federal government but by the State of São Paulo.

Portugal's eminent eighteenth-century chief minister, Sebastian José de Pombal, embodied the countertendency toward centralized rule in colonial times. During the empire and, less so, in the republic, subsequent Brazilian rulers also fashioned centralized bureaucratic rule to control and promote "progress" in the economy, in education, and in the arts and letters. Centralized rule sought military power, the regulation of society and economy, maintaining the political and social hierarchy, and promoting some entrepreneurial activity in the hands of the forerunners of today's state enterprises. This "Pombalian" tradition emphasized the predominance of the state.

Neither regional autonomy nor state dominance assigned much importance to liberty and equality. In both tendencies, the relationship between a human being and the community was embodied in the limited pluralism that was permissible under an increasingly bureaucratized hierarchy. Neither tendency emphasized only citizen rights or only citizen duties.

Instead, both emphasized the preeminence of public collectivities: the state, be it metropolitan, independent imperial, or regional within federalism. Brazil's ideological history thus stands apart from Anglo-American liberalism. In Brazil, a strong state—or, for a long time, a state that hoped to be strong—invoked the national security and prevailed over the rival claims of individual rights. No matter how individualistic Brazilians are in their personal behavior, state dominance has prevailed in politics and economics.

The state trusted neither itself nor its citizens, but it trusted itself more. It could not trust the future to individual rights or to its own sense of civic duties. The result was a state-dominant ideological amalgam: everyone had rights and duties; the state directed the economy but it conformed to market patterns; and much social pluralism persisted but it was subordinated to a "higher good" articulated by state elites. The state chartered business activities and engaged in some of its own. Even in colonial times, the state was not "limited" in its claim or exercise of authority. Nor did the most ambitious centralizer look for centralized planning. Between these extremes, however, the state was never simply regulative; it was always entrepreneurial to some degree, and it always sought a kind of "directive planning" while conforming to the market without intending to overthrow it, subvert it, or ignore it.

By 1930, six other fundamental elements of Brazilian history had also crystallized into central tenets of a "macroideology," a set of enduring beliefs widely shared at least by elites.

First, national achievement, including but not limited to improved living standards, was the central goal. In relations with its neighbors Brazil had acquired much territory. However, it remained economically less well off than Argentina and apprehensive that its neighbors, though smaller in size and population, saw it as an intruder on a Spanish-speaking continent. These gains and these fears enabled the state to claim the support and sacrifice of individuals and groups on behalf of the country's good and grandeur. The state harnessed this ideology to override individualistic claims and to help bring about the bright future that Brazilians widely believed was their country's due.

Second, the imperial constitution reserved for the emperor

the power of "moderator." If, in Great Britain, the right to reign had been distinguished from the right to rule, the Brazilian empire pragmatically—a word that deserves also to appear on the Brazilian flag because it characterizes the most ideologically legitimate decision-making style—confounded these rights. A prime minister conducted the routine affairs of government but the emperor's powers went beyond those of a British monarch, or of most constitutional monarchs in Europe. The emperor was the arbiter among contending political forces.

Third, the Brazilian armed forces claimed, informally though effectively, the emperor's moderating powers when the empire ended. Military institutions became key actors in Brazilian politics. The legitimacy of the military's actions beyond their strictly professional sphere has been debated, often heatedly, but the fact of their political centrality is incontestable.

Fourth, Brazilian economic development did not rely much on direct foreign investment. Brazil obtained many international loans before 1930, but foreign firms rarely became a direct physical and economic presence within the country. The sugar and coffee economies, the engines of production in the northeast and the southeast, were owned primarily by Brazilians, as was most of the incipient manufacturing sector.[2] Brazilians did not have to be strident nationalists because they controlled a united country, and they owned most of the means of production. Nationalism would enter the ideological realm only when social forces and the state itself thought that this control was in jeopardy—in petroleum, steel, the armaments trade and, most recently, computers.

Fifth, Brazilian governments changed the social structure as little as possible, consistent with economic growth. Although egalitarianism entered the Western Hemisphere's consciousness during the many national struggles for independence, Brazil did not have such a struggle nor did it have a civil war, common to other slave societies. Consequently, the close correlation between social class and color of skin, common to all former slave societies, endures to this day. However, social norms have long permitted mobility for individual blacks so long as they did not organize politically to seek rights as a race-conscious group. There has also been greater ease in interpersonal relations among people of different races than was common in the Anglo-Dutch world. Therefore, a powerful ideological theme developed that Brazil had no racial problem, notwithstanding the pattern of socio-racial stratification.[3] The society had also only an informal religiosity, dependent on both Afro-Brazilian religions and on Roman Catholicism. Emperor Pedro II limited the Roman Catholic church's powers, and in 1889 the republic separated church and state and weakened the church's powers. The results of social hierarchy and ecclesiastical weakness permitted the assertion of state power even when the state had not yet become so strong.

Finally, before 1930, politics in Brazil belonged to gentlemen and their hired thugs. For most Brazilians, the flag's positivist slogan in 1930 might have read more accurately: order for the many, progress for the few.

From Authoritarianism to Authoritarianism

In 1930, responding to the depression's effects on Brazil, a military coup deposed the oligarchical republic's last president and installed Getulio Vargas. Enemies were crushed—Communists, Fascists, and all others in between. In 1937 Vargas launched what he called the *Estado Novo* (the new state) to formalize his centralization of power. The authoritarian state was, at last, acquiring the capacity to govern. The strengthened federal government had clear economic goals. It organized or buttressed marketing cartels in coffee, cocoa, sugar, and tea. It modernized the bureaucracy along more meritocratic lines. It created state enterprises, such as those for the production of steel, *Companhia Siderurgica Nacional* (CSN); iron ore, *Companhia Vale do Rio Doce* (CVRD); and trucks. A social security system was developed to anticipate labor's demands, and a code was issued to control labor.

Vargas articulated the elite's vision of labor's role: "The *Estado Novo* does not recognize the rights of individuals in opposition to the collectivity. Individuals have duties, not rights. Rights pertain to the collectivity. The state rises above the struggle between interests, guarantees the rights of the collectivity, and ensures the fulfillment of duties. The state does not want and does not recognize class struggle."[4] This was authoritarian communitarianism at its most explicit.

The armed forces overthrew Vargas in 1945. The elections of 1946 instituted Brazil's longest-lasting experiment in democratic politics. The armed forces continued to intervene in politics, setting the rules of the game, and limiting presidential authority at times, although the electoral process and the free expression of ideas marked the period. But in March 1964, in response to a widespread sense of political and economic crisis, the armed forces overthrew President João Goulart and imposed a regime that, with variations, lasted until early 1985, when power was transferred back to civilians through indirect presidential elections.

There had been much economic progress. Real growth in the gross domestic product (GDP) averaged over 6 percent from 1947 to 1962; from 1956 to 1962, real annual growth neared 8 percent. Democracy and economic growth had been compatible. The stage for the 1964 coup was set by the economic slowdown of 1963, coupled with accelerating inflation and political factors. Real GDP grew below 4 percent per year from 1962 through 1967. In 1968, the economy's "future" finally arrived. The economy boomed at 11.3 percent per year from 1968 to 1974. Although growth rates slowed thereafter, real GDP more than quadrupled from 1960 to 1980, and real per capita GDP rose two and a half times.

However, it was not growth without tears. The peak years of the 1968–74 boom matched the regime's harshest repression, using political imprisonment and torture. Censorship and other restraints of civil liberties were severe. Brazil's income distribution, already among the world's least egalitarian, became markedly more unequal during the 1960s; real wages fell. When wages rose in the 1970s, they lagged behind productivity increases; relative income distribution remained unequal and unchanged during the severe recession of the early 1980s. Improvements occurred in health, housing, and education, but Brazil performed badly by international standards in meeting the needs of the poor whose situation remains precarious. Nevertheless, people in all income deciles did benefit in real terms, albeit highly unequally, from growth in the 1970s. The proportion of families living in dire poverty fell sharply. Growth, repression, increasing inequality, and greater prosperity for all were part of the Brazilian story in the boom years.[5]

In 1981 Brazil's real GDP fell for the first time since the 1930s. From 1980 through 1983, real GDP per capita fell 10.7 percent. By 1984 Brazil's total foreign debt passed $100 billion dollars. In 1977 Brazil's interest payments on its external debt amounted to 18.9 percent of exports; in 1982, that statistic reached 57.1 percent. In 1984 it fell back to 36.5 percent when the economy recovered, led by a surge in exports.[6] As a democratic regime returned in Brazil in 1985, a central question arose: would democracy and prosperity again coincide, or would the economy's bankruptcy propel the demise of democracy in the late 1980s as it had in the early 1960s?

THE NATURE OF THE COMMUNITY

Except for the 1946–64 democratic interlude and the recent transfer of power to a civilian president in 1985, authoritarian regimes have governed Brazil for most of its history: a monarchy, an oligarchical republic, a corporatist dictator, a bureaucratic-authoritarian regime. The degree of organized complexity rose markedly, however.

The bureaucratic-authoritarian regime that came to power in 1964 differed somewhat from similar regimes that emerged in Argentina and Chile as well as from more traditional dictatorships such as Paraguay's. The post–1964 Brazilian regime settled on nonrenewable terms for the country's president. Presidential succession was decided within the top staff of the armed forces in consultation with key civilians. This scheduled rotation reduced the likelihood of coups and of one-man dominance. It promised those with ambition that their time to rule would come. Because presidents differed in their views and priorities, there were policy changes as well—eventually permitting the transition back to civilian rule. Moreover, though repressive of workers and peasants, the armed forces brought civilians with highly technical skills into the government. The "left-wing" Peruvian military held all ministerial and other significant posts after their coup in 1968, but Brazil's authoritarian regime relied from the outset on many civilian technocrats.

Brazil's top officers were ambivalent about the desirability of democracy. Whereas other authoritarian regimes banned

Congress and political parties, the Brazilian military deprived Congress of significant powers but did not abolish it. They banned the politicians they detested from eligibility for public office, they sharply curtailed the scope of public debate, but they tolerated a legal opposition party. The existence of some forms of civilian politics, however hollow, retained the principle of legitimation through the consent of the governed, a legacy of the 1946–64 democratic interlude. This was the first authoritarian regime in Brazil for which legitimation through "order and progress" was not enough. The regime would also court the governed when the economic boom began in 1968. These enduring civilian forms of legitimation eventually helped to undermine the authoritarian regime and made easier the transition to democracy in the mid-1980s.

Many other Brazilians were ambivalent toward democracy. On the eve of the 1964 military coup, a representative sample of Rio de Janeiro respondents (three quarters with primary school education or less) was asked to name the most important problems facing the country. Fewer than 5 percent mentioned political problems; instead, they focused overwhelmingly on inflation (then rising beyond apparent control) and other aspects of the standard of living (in the midst of recession). Asked their views on specific topics, a majority wanted an honest government; the remainder split evenly between those who wanted a government that gets things done and those who thought that individual freedom mattered most. Not even 4 percent worried about the relative distribution of wealth. Over 60 percent would leave political matters to the government, explicitly rejecting the alternative that people like themselves should be active in politics. Asked to name the political leader in Latin America they admired the most, only a tenth of the Brazilians chose the incumbent President Goulart, even though a third of the Brazilians identified with the president's party; another sixth named other Brazilian politicians.[7] Rio's respondents worried less about democracy than about the economy's performance. They worried much more about inflation than about redistribution. These views did not require an authoritarian regime but they permitted one.

Even in happier times in early 1961, a large national survey found most Brazilians confident that the present was better than the past and that the future would be even better than the present. Still, they focused their hopes and their fears on economic and social rather than on political issues. They emphasized results much more than process. They did not challenge the existing order so long as it pragmatically guaranteed progress.[8]

Performance-oriented attitudes endured in the early stages of the authoritarian regime. Over a year after the coup, Rio de Janeiro respondents worried more about still-high inflation (one quarter of respondents) than about anything else, and they were much more concerned about standard of living issues than about politics. This was *not* because they were afraid to express their views. While a majority approved of the course of developments in Brazil in the previous two years, only 15 percent thought things were going very well—reflecting the government's harsh austerity measures. Twice as many people thought that "most people in Brazil" got "less than their fair share" than got "their fair share," reflecting falling wages and widening inequalities.[9]

As time passed, Brazilians remained as ambivalent about the authoritarian regime as they had been about democracy. In 1969, 59 percent of Rio de Janeiro respondents were prepared for a return to a civilian president.[10] Over two thirds of Rio respondents in 1970 opposed paramilitary death squadrons; as many as a third supported them.[11] The regime had reformed and increased income tax collections. Remarkably, between 58 percent and 65 percent of income-tax payers thought that the present income-tax legislation was "just."[12] In short, Brazilians had not been convinced democrats but nor were they stern authoritarians. Pragmatic as ever, taxpayers approved of changes good for the country but costly to themselves.

ORGANIZED LABOR

Under Getulio Vargas, a labor code was promulgated in 1943 that, with amendments, has endured until the 1980s, even after the return to civilian rule in 1985. The first duty of labor unions, according to the code, is to "collaborate with the public authorities in the development of social solidarity." The state collects a tax from all workers and turns the funds over to the unions, which may spend them only on social welfare activities. Union budgets may not be used as strike funds. The Labor Ministry has authority to screen, veto, and remove labor union leaders. It regulates labor-management relations closely. It can change, or even annul, collective-bargaining contracts. Though the code changed little, lax enforcement during the 1950s gave the union leadership more power until 1964, when the military overthrew Goulart.

The Castello Branco government, installed following the coup, purged leaders in about one third of all unions during 1964–65. Unions were deprived of the rights to strike and to bargain collectively. The unions resisted at first, but the state crushed them; as a result, there were no major strikes in Brazil from 1968 to 1978, apart from occasional local strikes among some steel and autoworkers in São Paulo in 1973–74. Labor-management relations were supposed to become a purely technical subject because wages were indexed to prices: wages could move only in response to movements in a price index.[13] Economic technocracy would again restore order and progress. In fact, brute repression was also used to prevent and break strikes.

Labor benefited, however, from the economic boom of the early 1970s, which led to labor support for the authoritarian regime. A 1972–73 survey of urban workers conducted in Brazil's southeast, where most of the industrial population works, showed strong support for the government and its strategies. About 71 percent of these workers said that they would trust the government to defend the interests of people like themselves—more trust than they accorded to any other institution, including the church, the unions, or the parties. A similar proportion agreed that workers should not be allowed to strike even though they might have a good reason; this view was stronger among nonunionized workers but favored by all. Consistent with earlier views, four fifths of the workers wanted a government that was honest, hard working, and maintained order; only one seventh said they wanted an elected government. Why these views? No fewer than 70 percent believed that the government had increased the country's wealth, improved medical assistance and social security for workers, and improved living conditions for rural workers. They were neither fools nor afraid to criticize the regime, however: most workers also said that the government had not decreased the difference between rich and poor. The workers' support for the regime was based almost exclusively on their perception that the government's performance on the economy and on welfare issues was good; they appeared indifferent to the "forms of the regime," be they authoritarian or democratic. More middle- and upper-class Brazilians than workers supported the authoritarian regime on political grounds. The workers supported the regime because they, too, were at last benefiting from growth.[14]

Labor leader attitudes, too, were consistent with regime strategies. In mid-1972, labor leaders of the most influential unions in metropolitan São Paulo, Brazil's industrial heartland, wanted to recover the unions' right to strike for better wages and better working conditions, but two thirds of them opposed strikes for political reasons.[15] These labor leaders split on the usefulness of a more militant approach to represent labor interests, given both the regime's repression and the economic boom.

The authoritarian regime did not, however, rely only on popular acceptance, much less on acceptance from labor. Throughout the 1970s the government intervened in an average of two dozen unions per year to take over a union's administration, annul elections, remove leaders from office, or dissolve the unions.[16]

In 1978 economic performance changed just as the regime sought to open up politics to prepare a transition to democracy. Real minimum wages in the capital goods sector, which employed Brazil's most skilled and best organized workers, fell 43.7 percent and continued to fall in 1979. In May 1978, an illegal, massive strike for higher wages began in São Paulo's automobile plants. Over half a million workers struck, two thirds of them metalworkers in the automobile and other industries. They won. Management was not prepared for these strikes nor was it used to the idea of bargaining with labor or thinking of labor as its partner. Instead of accommodating to the unions' strength, management resisted. The unions struck again in 1979. The number of major strikes quadrupled to 113 while the number of workers on strike jumped to 3.2 million, about one third metalworkers. They were responding to frustration from earlier years, the lifting of some repressive controls, and the continued deterioration of real wages in the most skilled sectors. Each of these strikes ended in a stalemate.[17]

By 1980 real wages rose again for skilled labor, but the unions struck again. The state stepped in, deposing the metalworkers' top leader ("Lula") and other leaders at the plant level. The state took administrative control of the union and arrested many union leaders. Street battles broke out between workers and the security forces. The government funded firms in distress. After forty-one days the workers gave in. In 1980 the number of major strikes decreased to fifty, and the number of strikers fell to two thirds of a million, about a third of them metalworkers.[18] The focus of the workers' militancy, it should be noted, was at the workplace, not in a wider political arena. For example, the metalworkers' leader, Lula, was defeated decisively in 1982 when he ran for governor of the state of São Paulo. But at the workplace, labor's new strength had bewildered management.

In 1980, management's response to labor had split according to the nationality of the parent firm's ownership. U.S.-based multinational auto firms, led by Ford, had begun promoting U.S.-style labor unions in the early 1970s, with some support from the unions themselves. These unions would focus on the firm, be apolitical, and be technically proficient in industrial relations. Moreover, as in Mexico, U.S.-based auto firms were less willing than European-based firms to "take orders" from the state. In 1980, Ford broke with the Brazilian government. Ford did not dismiss union leaders at its plant; it continued to negotiate with them in the belief that effective labor relations came from dealing with the union leaders that the workers supported. Ford was ready to combat its unions—it was not a patsy—but it was not interested in the state's wider agenda.

European-based firms, led by Volkswagen, had been more paternalistic and generous than U.S. firms in their labor relations. To them, labor militancy signaled ingratitude. Volkswagen saw the union as a threat to relations between worker and manager. In 1980, Volkswagen tightened discipline at its plants and used police to stop the state-deposed union leaders from

meeting workers at the factory gates. It continued to dismiss
union activists. With the Labor Ministry's full backing, Volkswagen sought to break the union. In fact, the deposed leaders
retained de facto control of the metalworkers' union. Neither
Ford's nor Volkswagen's strategy led to a better or lasting
outcome for the firm, because strikes continued against all
firms—though Ford's strategy was better for the union.[19]

Labor militancy temporarily declined during the severe economic recession (1981–83), which created additional unemployment and, as a consequence, caused workers to fear losing
their jobs. But labor's tolerance for the authoritarian regime
and for wage restraint had come to an end. When civilian rule
returned in 1985 in the midst of an economic recovery, massive
strikes again broke out in the industrial heartland. Led by four
hundred thousand metalworkers and involving hundreds of
thousands of other workers, the strikes lasted for weeks. Workers looked for higher wages, better working conditions, and
legal changes that would permit faster wage adjustments linked
to the price index and would also give the unions greater
operating independence from the Labor Ministry. These were
the longest and most intense strikes in the Brazilian auto
industry's history; workers even seized a General Motors plant
and kidnapped some of its executives. The Brazilian labor
movement remains seriously split. Those divisions, and the
high strike frequency, augur more severe strife in labor's
relations with business and the state, perhaps imperiling the
prospects for democracy.[20]

Brazil has no future without its organized workers. From
their perspective, the regime's repression was disorderly and
the economy's performance, although good in the early 1970s,
had become unacceptable by decade's end. Curiously, the
ideological perspective Brazilian elites had sought to foster for
so long may have "trickled down." An orientation toward
results rather than process can support any regime while
performance is good, but it provides little enduring support for
any regime and certainly none for an authoritarian regime
whose economic policies begin to fail. In the end, labor's
resistance to the authoritarian regime does not solve the problem of ideological ambivalence toward democracy nor does it
guarantee industrial peace.

Determining labor's role in Brazilian politics and economics is a central concern for the country. If labor remains ideologically indifferent toward political regimes and continues to focus on economic and social performance, then democracy's legitimation is more complicated. However, there may also be a way out. Consolidating a democracy will require outperforming the authoritarian regime's record. Democracy and economic growth were mutually consistent in Brazil before 1962; they could be again. Brazilian workers, moreover, submitted to authority, even when harsh, when performance was good in the early 1970s; but they also rebelled against authority, even when just as harsh, when performance was bad in the late 1970s. These are strong incentives for government and business to respond to labor's preferences—perform as the "order and progress" ideology says one should—because both growth and democracy might prosper thereby.

THE STATE AND BUSINESS

The reasons for state intervention in the economy have varied over time, but the propensity to do so has been virtually constant. The councilors of state to Brazil's nineteenth-century emperors "opted for protectionism, for government intervention, for not confiding in market mechanisms."[21] Even when public officials adhered to a less statist ideology during the republic from 1889 to 1930, state economic activity still increased. The ideology of specific public officials is not a good enough explanation for state economic activism. Instead, there is a macroideology, more enduring than the views of specific officials, that draws key economic and political elites to rely on the state and that helps legitimate state activism even for those officials who would, on their own, opt for freer markets.

In mid-twentieth century, the Brazilian state became committed to industrialization through import substitution. Industrialization became a "good" in itself. The state devised many regulations toward that end, and it created and stimulated the development of state enterprises whenever private firms seemed unable to do the job.[22] By the end of the 1970s, the federal government owned all telecommunications, electricity and gas utilities, the railways, all petroleum and coal production, and two thirds of steel production, among other sectors, placing Brazil among the most statist non-Communist countries.[23] These policies followed long-term trends.

For a brief moment in 1964, when the military overthrew the Goulart regime, it appeared that Brazil might try the free market. The United States was pleased with the change; President Lyndon Johnson wired his congratulations to the new government within hours of Goulart's overthrow. Brazil, thought the president of the United States and executives in national and multinational private firms, had been saved by the armed forces from turmoil, perhaps chaos, and certainly from the communists. A leading Brazilianist scholar, Thomas Skidmore, wrote in the immediate aftermath of the coup that "[i]n the strategy for development, the Castello Branco government [installed by the coup] diverged sharply from the policies of previous regimes . . . the new government sought to rehabilitate the role of the private sector . . . the Goulart regime had emphasized the public role in a mixed strategy. The Castello Branco regime sought to emphasize the private role."[24] But other social, economic, and political forces, and the country's enduring statist macroideology, overrode the free-market preferences of some public officials brought to power in 1964. The state's economic activism had barely paused in the mid-1960s.

From the late 1960s to the mid-1970s, state financial participation grew from less than 60 percent to about three quarters of the total net worth of the country's 100 largest firms; in terms of invested capital, the jump was from 37 percent to 45 percent. By the mid-1970s, state enterprises accounted for one fifth of the manufacturing sector's net worth, rising to a majority in the chemical sector and one third in the metallurgical sector, in addition to sectors entirely, or almost entirely, controlled by the state. Even during the 1960s, the state's role in capital formation grew from about 50 percent in 1960 to about 60 percent in 1969.[25] More state enterprises were created between 1970 and 1975 than during the preceding thirty years combined. In 1962, only 12 of the thirty largest nonfinancial firms were state enterprises; in 1979, 28 of them were.

This expansion can be explained in part as a response to factors such as external economies, economies of scale, or weaknesses among private firms. However, the marginal ideological preference for statist solutions has also been important. Regardless of "left" or "right" predilections, the macroideology's core has been the belief that the state can and should promote economic growth. Brazilian nationalism, national security, and its need for self-sufficiency and greatness justify and require it. The state's entrepreneurial and regulative purpose was to correct and guide market decisions, or even to substitute for private firms, so as to accelerate economic growth. At the same time, the state recognizes the need for a private business sector and for the allocative efficiency of the market. This conception explains the nearly exclusive focus of state entrepreneurship in heavy industry, transportation, and utilities, as well as the gradually growing concern about the presence of multinational firms in key economic sectors.

Brazil's style of statism has also been pragmatic, although mistakes have been made at times. The state has preferred to expand into what it considered "empty" sectors: oil, steel, iron ore. It has barred the entry of firms, especially multinationals, into some strategic sectors: such as minicomputers. The state expropriated private telecommunications or electric power firms only when the firms could not expand plants quickly enough. Although the state intervened vigorously after 1964 to change rules, prices, and other economic variables, it also used the price system and market forces more effectively than in the past, and it pursued generally market-conforming policies. It has emphasized profit standards for state enterprises. Price-setting in many (though not all) state enterprises reflects full-cost pricing, rather than maintaining artifically low prices for the intermediate goods consumed by industry. A number of Brazilian state enterprises have been generally profitable, although some, such as the railroads, have never been so. PETROBRAS, one of its giants, was successful in increasing oil production in the 1980s. Another state-owned giant, CVRD, has become the world's largest exporter of ocean-borne iron ore, achieving an impressive record of profitability interrupted only occasionally by drops in world iron-ore prices. The profitability of Brazilian state enterprises was well above average by international standards from the late 1960s to the late 1970s and far higher than state enterprises in other Latin American countries, including Mexico. Profitability declined, however, across most sectors by the late 1970s. Most state enterprises ran operating deficits during the economic crisis of the early 1980s, financed in part by heavy borrowing.[26]

Other policies reflected Brazil's commitment to nationalism through state action and to pragmatism in policy style. When Portugal lost its African empire to Marxist-Leninist successor states, Brazil became one of those states' best non-Communist partners. Brazil is a sizable exporter of agricultural products to the Soviet Union. Uncertain about the U.S. government's reliability, Brazil developed a large armaments industry and has become an important weapons exporter. It has also committed resources to develop its own nuclear energy industry, despite U.S. government opposition, vigorous at times. If a policy seemed to work, it was adopted. National security was often the all-encompassing ideological blanket; pragmatism was the fig leaf that covered all apparent ideological heresies.

Nevertheless, two central problems remained. The regime's ability to claim legitimacy, even from major elite groups, was surprisingly weak. In the early 1970s, a study of elite attitudes showed that, in spite of some serious disagreements, various elite groups agreed that the authoritarian regime's ruling coalition should be replaced, although they did not agree on alternatives. Among these elites, much more clearly than among the workers, the regime had lost the right to rule despite good economic growth. Nonetheless, these elites gave the regime high marks for increasing the economy's growth rate, reducing inflation, extending social security coverage to most workers, increasing the efficiency of public administration, reducing illiteracy, and increasing per capita income. They faulted the regime for not reducing regional disparities enough and, especially, for not reducing income differences between rich and poor. Just as interestingly, when elites disagreed, they were predisposed to view conflicts and their solutions in positive variable-sum terms. They did not define political combat as "winner take all." This pragmatic approach to conflict is as distinctive in elite ideology as in state practice.[27]

The second problem was the unanticipated consequence of Brazil's self-confident and overextended insertion on the world stage. The state's steel industry is an example. From the early

1970s to the early 1980s, Brazilian crude steel output doubled, increasing one million tons per year every year from 1975 to 1980. Raw steel capacity reached 20 million tons in 1982. The expansion was planned and largely financed by state agencies that borrowed heavily abroad. In 1978, steel production exceeded domestic consumption for the first time. When the recession hit in 1981, a crisis developed in the steel industry. It ran a huge operating deficit, the largest of any Brazilian state firm. Although the government imposed some austerity measures on steel, the minister of industry made clear that "the government does not intend to deactivate any [steel] project or close down any company." The planning minister acknowledged that "our steel industry reached maturity when there was no demand for it" in Brazil but, he argued, Brazil would export a million tons of steel per year.

In fact, Brazil exported 5 million tons of steel in 1983, accounting for 40 percent of Brazil's steel output. The export strategy was described as "price competitive." "Desperate" might be more accurate. One of Brazil's leading newspapers, *O Estado de São Paulo* was blunt: "Steel products were often exported at prices that were lower than desirable or even reasonable." The U.S. government and the European Economic Community ruled that Brazil practiced dumping, and they imposed sanctions on some of its steel exports. Although in 1984 Brazil agreed to restrain its steel exports to the United States, the Council of Steel and Nonferrous Metals (CONSIDER), the state's holding company, announced a continued expansion of Brazilian steelmaking capacity through the 1980s "to keep the domestic market supplied as well as to maintain [Brazil's] position on the export market."[28]

The Brazilian government and its steel industry would not face up to the steel market's reality at home and abroad. How could a "great country" such as Brazil not expand its steel industry? However, the steel industry's troubles are severe. Brazil's ideological blinders have prevented the early adoption of more sensible steel policies. More generally, they have delayed structural adjustments and retrenchment that are bound to occur in many state firms.

Multinational Firms

Although foreign loans had been important before World War II, foreign direct investment had played only a modest role in Brazil's economy. In the mid-1950s, Brazilian policies toward multinational firms changed dramatically.

Some policies were more restrictive. In 1954 the state created the oil monopoly, PETROBRAS, believing that Brazil was oil-rich but had been kept as an oil importer by multinational oil firms. PETROBRAS's subsequent experience showed that Brazil was not a Saudi Arabia waiting to be discovered; Brazil had nationalized nonexistent petroleum. Not until new off-shore drilling and exploration technologies were developed could significant finds be made: in 1984, half of Brazil's oil output came from the Campos offshore field alone.[29]

Equally significant was the opening toward foreign investment in manufacturing. In 1955, world coffee prices dipped from Korean War peaks. Coffee had long been Brazil's leading export commodity. The country sought to industrialize quickly. Brazil's imports of machinery and equipment rose sharply. One of government's new policies, Instruction 113, allowed foreign manufacturers in Brazil advantageous exchange rates to import machinery and equipment. The era of foreign direct investment in Brazil began.

The Brazilian government was confident that multinational firms would not undermine its sovereignty, but it was not so sure that such firms, left to themselves, would behave as the government thought they should. Therefore, the state would guide them. Unlike Mexico's governments, Brazilian governments were not much concerned at first with the ownership of firms: the equity could remain foreign so long as the firm increased local content of production quickly and substantially.

The automobile sector provides an apt example. Brazil began to demand the nationalization of production in 1956, six years before Mexico. By 1962 Brazil required that 99 percent of the weight of passenger cars be manufactured in Brazil, but it developed no policies to stimulate national ownership in the automobile sector. Unlike Mexico, Brazil emphasized early and strongly the need for the auto firms to export. In 1972 Brazil reduced its local content requirement to 85 percent in exchange for an export drive. In 1974 the auto firms were still responsible for $100 million per year of the trade deficit. By 1977 they contributed a $300 million surplus, thanks to strong government tax incentives to export. (Mexican auto exports in 1977 were about one tenth of Brazil's.) By 1980 Brazil was poised to pass the United Kingdom as an automobile manufacturer; Brazilian auto exports that year were worth more than one third of the value of its coffee exports.[30] In the 1980s, the Brazilian government tried to phase out export subsidies, to conform with the General Agreement on Tariffs and Trade (GATT). Instead, alone among major Latin American countries, Brazil came to rely on the slight but persistent undervaluation of its currency to promote exports.[31]

If the Brazilian government felt relaxed about foreign investment, Brazilians, including national business executives, were more ambivalent. Many Brazilian firms made profitable deals with the newcomer multinational firms, but some came to fear competition from the world giants now in their midst. A survey of 627 white- and blue-collar workers in Rio de Janeiro and in some small towns showed that the modal response (44 percent) to a question on foreign investment was that "foreign capital could contribute to the development of Brazil and Brazil ought, with some care, to act so that some selected foreign companies would come to the country." The remainder split closely between those who would seek out foreign firms without restrictions and those who would exclude them from the country.[32] Similarly, 125 business executives surveyed in 1962 split equally concerning the wisdom of Instruction 113: one third each favored it, opposed it, or had mixed feelings. A majority of these executives believed the measure was good for Brazil, although it was not good for those firms that faced stiffer competition. Large Brazilian firms opposed multinational firms' preferential access to foreign exchange under Instruction 113, as did major associations such as the National Association of Manufacturers (CNI) and the Federation of Industries of the State of São Paulo (FIESP).[33]

Comparable ambivalence persisted in the early 1970s. Most Brazilian elites favored welcoming foreign investment in Brazil but regulating it. Business executives, civil servants, labor leaders, and the government party leaders were more favorable toward multinational firms; the opposition party leaders and Roman Catholic bishops were less so. Of the twenty-three issues on which questions were asked of elite Brazilians, foreign direct investment was the only one that elicited three distinct fears. Some elites worried about the political challenge to their power from multinational firms. Other elites viewed the problem as one of high economic risks and opportunities that required careful regulation. The remaining elites voiced a strong moral and cultural component: the foreign firms were the bearers of values alien to Brazilian traditions and thus a threat to the nation's economic and cultural identity and values. Attitudes toward foreign firms do not correspond to simple "left-versus-right" patterns. There is more ambivalence on this issue than on any other. However, the view is also prevalent that other issues are more important for Brazil than what should be done about multinational firms.[34]

To pacify these fears, the government's policies and the attitudes of national business executives toward multinational firms changed by the late 1970s. As the presence of multinationals continued to increase, the Brazilian government worried more about how to control these firms. National businesses worried about being squeezed out by the spectacular growth of both state and foreign firms. The regime saw national business as its best ally for its planned orderly transition toward democracy and for the creation of a strong conservative party to insure the continuation of its policies after the return of civilian rule. The alliance between the state and the national business community was thus tightened at the expense of the multinational firms, supported by those who feared the foreigner for moral and cultural reasons.

Prodded by national business firms, the government increasingly adopted policies to discriminate in favor of national firms and against multinational firms. For the first time, Brazilian policy was "Mexicanized": decisions would be made increasingly on the basis of the ownership structure of particular firms. Majority-owned Brazilian firms received preferential tax treatment, discounted interest rates from state banks, and preferential access in their sales to state enterprises and other agencies. By 1977 Brazil's National Economic Development

Bank (BNDE) and the Industrial Development Council (CDI) were aggressively implementing policies to bolster national industrial firms and to deny comparable opportunities to foreign firms.[35]

In one case, the U.S. Carrier Corporation was denied tax incentives to manufacture steam turbines for oil prospecting, even though it had the backing of PETROBRAS, which considered steam turbines made by Brazil's Zanini and Dedini to be below acceptable international standards. Zanini's and Dedini's "Brazilianness" was in fact suspect, since both were minority foreign-owned by German and Japanese firms, respectively. Similarly, Brazil's Transport Ministry awarded a contract for supplying locomotives to the national railways to two Brazilian firms that had never manufactured them; the loser was a General Electric subsidiary that had been Brazil's sole locomotive manufacturer.

The president of the Brazilian Capital Goods Manufacturing Association (ABDIB) hailed these measures as "making the entrance of foreign capital difficult." ABDIB's president also argued that multinational subsidiaries "do damage to the economy taking up room that could be filled by a Brazilian company that was really developing its technology." ABDIB was "not against foreign capital, but we are totally opposed to the absurdity of allowing or, what is worse, encouraging, the entry of foreign companies into areas that are already well served by national companies." The spirit of nationalism was now being invoked to protect local oligopolies and to prevent increased competition.

The most far-reaching case occurred in the computer sector. In 1972 a Brazilian coordinating commission for the industry, CAPRE, was created to oversee and regulate all government computing activities but, by 1974, there was still only incipient monitoring.[36] In 1974, at the Brazilian Navy's initiative, and concerned about the implications of high technology for national security, the government created a state enterprise, COBRA, to develop, manufacture, and market minicomputers. Under licensing from the United Kingdom's Ferranti (a traditional supplier to the Brazilian military), COBRA began to assemble minicomputers, gradually increasing their local content to about 60 percent by the end of the 1970s. From the outset,

Brazil's focus was on enhancing national security and developing its own technological capacity. Profitability and state-of-the-art technology were secondary. COBRA's president, Admiral José Claudio Beltrão, said in May 1977: "Informatics is a question of power, and being so, it is an important aspect of national security." He stressed that COBRA was a "special company, whose profits cannot be measured merely by immediate return." Its purpose was "incorporating technical knowledge that will reduce Brazilian technological dependence."[37]

However, Brazil did not simply pursue a policy of computer grandeur: it did not try to develop all aspects of computer technology. Instead, it focused principally on minicomputers and on peripheral equipment, areas in which it moved vigorously. CAPRE set criteria in 1977 for selecting three firms to participate in a tight oligopoly to manufacture minicomputers. The criteria included local equity participation, high local content, and unrestricted use of technology. At the time, over four fifths of the Brazilian minicomputer market was supplied through exports to Brazil by three foreign firms. CAPRE eventually restricted minicomputer manufacturing to firms at least 75 percent of whose equity was owned by Brazilians. One of those firms was COBRA. CAPRE also banned minicomputer imports altogether. Brazil thus carried to an extreme its relatively recent concern about the ownership of manufacturing firms: it reserved for Brazilian firms the full market in a high-technology subsector. Never before had a policy in the manufacturing sector been so clearly formulated on grounds of national security.[38] This decision had costs for Brazil: low profitability, less than state-of-the-art technology, and prices for minicomputers much higher than prevailed in world markets.

Brazil was not alone in its firmness. All major U.S. computer manufacturers that bid on CAPRE's proposal ignored CAPRE's central criterion. They submitted proposals for subsidiaries that were 100 percent parent owned. From Brazil's national security perspective, moreover, IBM's already commanding presence in Brazil's medium- and large-scale computer market was especially worrisome. It was a key reason to exclude IBM from the minicomputer market. IBM may also have misunderstood that the ideological winds were shifting. Before the decision was made to exclude *IBM do Brasil* from manufacturing minicomputers, its president expressed surprise at the trend of government policy: "We do not need to ask the government in advance for permission to build System 32. Does Ford ask the government for permission every time it wants to introduce a new model automobile? The government, after all, wants us to export." In fact, the government did not want to create another industry like automobiles: high exports but foreign owned. It now wanted Brazilian companies manufacturing Brazilian computers. COBRA took out full page advertisements just before the 1977 decision was made: "The computer is like oil: it is dangerous to depend on others." IBM took out ads, too, to describe IBM's contribution to import substitution and to exports, concluding: "This is IBM's difference."[39] The computer, indeed, was like oil: Brazil nationalized a nonexistent minicomputer industry and then proceeded to create one.

Brazil has stuck to its guns. In 1979 CAPRE was replaced with the Special Secretariat for Informatics (SEI). Directly under the National Security Council, it reports to the president of Brazil so as to emphasize its politico-military importance and ideological focus. In 1982 regulations extended to software, applying a time-honored Brazilian concern to protect national businesses: no software can be imported if a Brazilian product exists that fills the same need.

From the government's perspective, this policy was a qualified success by the early 1980s. On the one hand, in 1978 multinational firms sold 80 percent of all computers in Brazil; by 1982, majority-Brazilian firms sold 60 percent of computers. The local industry's size nearly doubled every two years. Local content in computers averaged above 60 percent. From 1980 to 1984, Brazil halved its annual balance-of-payments deficit for computer equipment and services. It exports 34 percent of its data-processing-related goods to Latin America. Majority-Brazilian firms supply about one third of Brazil's data-processing exports. These firms probably would not exist were it not for the Brazilian government's policy. Moreover, the two thirds of Brazilian exports attributable to IBM, Burroughs, and Hewlett-Packard might not have occurred had the Brazilian government not built up its bargaining position.[40]

On the other hand, the technology is generally not state-of-the-art, and prices are often several multiples of prevailing world market prices. The informatics industry has had substantial financial losses. These direct costs may lead to opportunity costs for Brazil's industrial development, weakening the future international competitiveness of firms in other industries that depend on high-quality computer technology. Studies suggest that Brazil has so far suffered a net economic loss from its computer policy. Conflicts with the U.S. government over the market reservation policy began in the late 1970s and sharply escalated in 1985.

Nevertheless, the U.S. government's extension of its jurisdiction over the U.S.-based computer industry overseas in the 1980s, and the use of high technology in the South Atlantic war between the United Kingdom and Argentina in 1982, confirmed the Brazilian government's view that national security concerns should have priority in this sector. In 1984 the Brazilian Congress approved a comprehensive new bill to regulate the computer industry, confirming the previous policy's broad outlines and signaling full civilian support for the policies designed by the military. Computer policy became an issue for public debate in the presidential campaign, though neither candidate advocated dismantling past policies. The more nationalist coalition won. In the end, ideology's order—now stressed as national security, with the full backing of the civilian opposition that gained power in 1985—prevailed over ideology's progress. Market-shaping strategies, in this crunch, overrode market-conforming strategies. It was the first such dramatic break in the manufacturing sector from the central components of Brazil's macroideology.

The simple notions of order and progress were no longer enough. Brazil faced a redefinition of ideological purposes and choices in its relations with multinational firms, too.

CONCLUSIONS

Brazil has had a macroideology, enduring through time and still strong in the 1980s. It emphasizes the country's belief in, and its striving for, great national achievement. It includes economic growth and the improvement of living standards, but it affirms the significance of the whole community and of the need to defer to communitarian goals in national policy when they conflict with individual ones. Brazil affirms and celebrates the individualism of its people but, unlike the United States, it seeks to confine it to the private and personal sphere so that statist policies prevail. The state is the instrument used to shape the nation's present and to realize its future. It must have, and has had, a major role in the economy. It continues to emphasize industrialization. Pragmatism, the style of decision making most congruent with Brazilian ideology, has made it easier to combine a public and a private economy. It also justifies the need of state enterprises to respond to market forces and the need of government agencies to design market-conforming economic policies. It justifies as well the belief in the market's allocative efficiency and in the legitimacy of private business firms. Legitimacy of performance is judged, above all, in terms of national objectives and their consequences for citizens. In general, the macroideology accounts for much of Brazil's success in remaining a unified country that has incorporated immigrants from many lands and that has been successful in designing economic growth policies.

This macroideology has also had negative consequences. It has produced some indifference toward the nature of the political regime and an ambivalence about the importance of democratic norms and rules. It has made authoritarian rule possible, although the military regime that installed itself in 1964 was eventually undermined by the criterion requiring good economic performance. The macroideology's communitarianism is almost blind to the evidence of persisting racial inequality in which blacks wind up at the bottom of the social stratification pyramid, despite individual Brazilians' high racial tolerance.

The macroideology has also encountered some serious obstacles. It has not coped well with the rising demands of organized labor, which benefited only to a small extent from the economic boom and which has paid the costs of the recession of the early 1980s. Brazil's self-confidence, and its commitment to industrial greatness, explain in part the state's delay and reluctance in recognizing the need for retrenchment in its steel industry and its more general inability to cut back on some deficit activities of an overextended state. The macroideology's compatibility with national security considerations has led to a computer industry policy that is successful on its own terms but that has also imposed some heavy direct and opportunity economic costs. The computer industry policy has been the first major breach between the macroideology's political and economic objectives in manufacturing. Moreover, though less dramatic, the policies that favor national business firms have imposed some efficiency costs on Brazilian production, even if the policy pragmatically seeks to balance conflicting objectives. Foreign firms have complicated Brazilian industrial relations by the different responses of multinational management to labor strife.

Brazil, in short, faces the 1980s with many tasks, including several of ideological significance. How can a state-dominant consensus change enough to include organized labor as a full participant in specifying the content of that consensus? How can labor have political rights as fair accompaniments to its political duties? How should labor respond to different managerial ideologies, since labor has struck against both accommodating and repressive foreign management strategies?

How important is a free-enterprise ideology in a country where most enterprises have never been really free? What, in fact, do Brazilian businesses mean when they worry about the "size of the state," since their past, present, and future are so closely dependent on the state's strength? Are foreign firms that operate in Brazil "Brazilian" enough? Is it possible or desirable to have a unified business community, regardless of nationality of ownership, since there is a split between national and multinational firms? How can a commitment to national greatness be reconciled with the need to recognize that some industries must be scaled back because exporting through dumping is internationally unacceptable?

Should Brazilians be indifferent toward democratic values and procedures, pragmatically supporting dictatorship or democracy, whichever "works"? Should labor strike less, and business yield more, for the sake of consolidating democracy in the late 1980s? Can Brazilians redesign public policy to face up to the race factor in their own society?

Below the surface of the macroideology, moreover, many ideological currents overlap and conflict. As Peter McDonough has argued cogently, "[t]he claim that elites in Brazil are unideological does not fare well. Rather the problem is the multiplicity of ideologies that collide over the nature of the political system . . . and that, at the same time, coincide only occasionally with organized collectivities."[41] These "microideologies" begin from the broadly shared norms sketched in this chapter but provide much variation for the stuff of daily politics and decision making. In a more democratic Brazil, these microideologies are more likely to occupy center stage and weaken the consensual strands of the macroideology. Brazil, inventive and successful already in many areas, needs to manage a transition that enables these views to flourish as well.

10

REVOLUTION AND FLEXIBILITY IN MEXICO

Jorge I. Domínguez

"They will justify you," Artemio Cruz hallucinated on his death bed in Carlos Fuentes's internationally acclaimed novel, "because they will not have your justification: they will not be able to speak of their battles and captains, as you can, and shield themselves behind glory to justify rapine in the name of the Revolution, self-aggrandizement in the name of working for the good of the Revolution."[1]

Mexico's central dilemma is the conflict between the Revolution's goals and the performance of those who have ruled in its name. Because so much can be justified in the Revolution's name, the country's once-central legitimating myth no longer serves as the criterion for choosing among plausible alternatives in the pursuit of shared national values. Mexico's current

---
The author would like to thank the following for their helpful comments: Miguel Basáñez, Dionisio Garza-Medina, George C. Lodge, Carlos Obregón, Pedro Pick, and Daniel Sharp.

president governs in the name of public rectitude and economic efficiency. But with the old formal ideology eroding and no new replacement at hand, rectitude is difficult to define, let alone implement. And economic efficiency increasingly demands international competitiveness, which is retarded by what remains of the old ideology and by uncertainty about a new one.

This chapter's main argument is that the management of symbols has long been at the center of Mexican statecraft. The most enduring features of this ideology have been nationalism in the face of a perceived hostile world environment, the state's primacy over social and economic activities, a hierarchical organization of politics, and considerable flexibility for public officials in implementing policy. Ideology is the key instrument by which the state transforms possible sources of opposition into support for itself. The misfit between that ideology and the realities confronting Mexico is also at the heart of many of the country's problems, especially the legitimacy of the regime and the competitiveness of its economy.

A HISTORY OF STRUGGLE

Castile and Aragon joined to unite Spain at about the same time they conquered America. Within a century of the Spanish Conquest, central and southern Mexico, then called the Viceroyalty of New Spain, were nearly depopulated by disease, war, famine, and exploitation. The surviving peoples, heirs to highly complex civilizations, had no choice but to accept the new empire's alien ideology, a mix from its joint rulers.[2]

Under Castilian political theory, the monarch was not accountable to the people or the parliament but to God, and only the monarch could interpret that accountability. Castile's constitution also stressed the monarch's practical duties to his people: to protect them from tyranny, mismanagement, or restrictions of personal or group liberties. Castile's political theory was rooted in the conviction that all persons were sinful and therefore not likely to live up to the law that was God's will. To accommodate human failings, the theory arranged a way of dealing with the gap between the law as ideal and the law in practice. While subjects were obligated to obey the law, they were not required to implement it if special circumstances justified their suspending it, pending royal review. The monarch, chief of state, agent of God, and the realm's chief administrative officer, had great flexibility for reconciling the moral ideal and the sinful reality: he was the arbiter when subordinates suspended the application of his edicts. The gap between the legitimating norms and the crueler reality, and the chief executive's flexibility bridging it, are the Conquest's political legacies for today's Mexico.

Aragon's political theory emphasized the ruler's internal and international political goals. An army and a bureaucracy were required, but Spain was unable to develop an effective bureaucracy until the eighteenth century. During that long interval, Castile's norms had become institutionalized. In the eighteenth century, Spain's Bourbon kings modernized their government in response to troubling international events. They rationalized and centralized authority and imposed economic austerity. Great discontent followed. In July 1766 some six thousand people in Guanajuato, one of the wealthiest cities, tried to storm the treasury building, protesting against the new taxes and against "monopolies" (state enterprises) because of their poor service and their intrusion into the private economy. They exempted the king from responsibility for the country's hardships but blamed his ministers for "bad government."

The Nightmare of Independence

Mexico became independent in 1821 when local elites could no longer trust a government in Madrid they thought too radical and too committed to a centralized bureaucratic rule that violated looser imperial norms. Earlier, these same elites had quelled an uprising of fellow Mexicans, guerrillas fighting for independence from Spain. But Spain became a greater threat to elite rule than the guerrillas. In 1821 a Mexican-born general of the king's armies, Agustín de Iturbide, supported by most of the Viceroyalty's elites, made peace with Vicente Guerrero, an Indian leader of the guerrillas, in exchange for his support against Spain. New Spain became an independent monarchy and Iturbide its emperor.

The new regime could not be sustained. Mexico's new emperor could not claim traditional legitimacy because he did not come from a royal family. Nor was he a charismatic leader who could build a new basis for legitimacy. The old order's elites had opposed independence and could not generate legitimacy for the new order. They considered Iturbide a traitor; proindependence guerrilla leaders thought him a rascal. However, most proindependence leaders had been killed in war; the most prominent survivor, Vicente Guerrero, embodied everything the elites hated, especially the idea of equality. Only naked force clothed power in independent Mexico. Iturbide was overthrown in 1823, and a half century of internal and international war followed.

Mexican elites split, liberals opposing conservatives, over the role of Roman Catholicism. But the struggle for "religious liberty" was also an argument about property rights: the church was Mexico's largest landlord and banker. Mexican elites agreed, however, in opposing active participation by peoples of color—still the vast majority of Mexicans. Mexican liberalism was an undemocratic elite concept.[3] Tension between the ideas of hierarchy and equality continued to strain the Mexican community.

Mexicans did not fight each other in isolation. Iturbide's overthrow provoked Central America's secession. In 1836, English-speaking settlers in Texas proclaimed their independence. In 1838, France intervened militarily in Mexico. In 1848, the United States took half of Mexico's territory as a prize of war; Mexico built a shrine to the boys who died fighting the invaders at Chapultepec, now an area of downtown Mexico City. In 1861 Napoleon III's French troops occupied Mexico. Backed by Mexican conservative Catholics, Napoleon imposed Maximilian, Archduke of Austria, as Mexico's emperor. Other Mexicans resisted. Needing his troops to face a newly unified Germany, Napoleon withdrew from Mexico in 1867. Maximilian was shot.

In 1877, "Liberal" General Porfirio Díaz became president, in effect ruling without interruption until his overthrow in 1911. The central government established order, crushing all opponents. The "Porfiriato" generated economic growth; a ferocious brand of capitalism triumphed. In the market's name, communal Indian lands were broken up, "freeing" each Indian to dispose of property; when the wealthy bought their land, they became landless. The Porfiriato sold off the church's former lands, though church and state made peace otherwise. The official ideology was Auguste Comte's positivism, with its emphasis on order and progress, though not liberty and equality. Don Porfirio shared his order with close associates and with foreigners. Foreign direct investment was encouraged to promote economic development, which promoted Don Porfirio. Foreign firms built railroads, searched for minerals and fuels, and developed agriculture.

The Revolution

In the early twentieth century, Díaz was in his eighties. Not only was his succession an issue, there was also increasing rural protest over land dispossession and resentment of foreign dominance over much of Mexico's economy. Francisco Madero led a revolt in 1910, forcing Díaz to flee in 1911. Thus began the Mexican Revolution, the bloodiest and longest in the Americas. The United States intervened again in 1916, sending General John Pershing and 150,000 troops deep into Mexico to pursue General Pancho Villa; U.S. troops withdrew after the United States entered World War I. Mexico's new constitution, proclaimed in 1917, embodied communitarian norms to replace the Porfiriato's ideology and policies.

The implementation of parts of the revolutionary program in the 1920s led to three years of religious war, after which the Roman Catholic church was placed under severe restraints. In the 1930s, President Lázaro Cárdenas launched a massive redistribution of land, organizing *ejidos,* farms collectively owned though often individually operated. In 1938, on a day that still officially marks Mexico's economic independence, President Cárdenas seized the foreign-owned oil companies, creating a new huge state oil firm, Petróleos Mexicanos (PEMEX).

A new political order emerged too. In 1929, General Plutarco Elías Calles had gathered into one dominant party the leading officers and politicians. Cárdenas reorganized the party and expanded its base, creating party sectors for peasants, for urban workers, and for the middle class. Only two major sectors were excluded: the Roman Catholic church and big business. In 1940 Cárdenas displayed statesmanship: he voluntarily stepped down from power, turning it over to his successor, Manuel Avila Camacho. Since then, the presidency has always been rotated at the end of every six-year term.

A New Revolutionary Ideology

A century-long nightmare was over. A new revolutionary consensus replaced it by the 1930s. Authority was still hierarchical but it now sought to include everyone in the national community. Mexico's chief executive still has vast powers and is still expected to fulfill his duties. As in the past, those who challenged his power were repressed. Unlike in the past, the state's reforms undercut the need for protest. The state sought to end ethnic distinctions. Although equality remained elusive, the state at times acted boldly: the thorough-going agrarian reform of the 1930s removed agrarian issues from their previous centrality in national politics—a conservative consequence from a radical reform. The state also created the all-encompassing party and other intermediary institutions to co-opt possible opponents. This state-led, limited, organized pluralism differed from the colonial past: it stemmed from the Revolution, though legitimized in part by historical familiarity, and it featured much wider involvement of workers and peasants. Reformist, state-organized participation was Cárdenas's contribution to the control and inclusion of labor into Mexican politics.

Citizens were given new rights and new duties. In the name of the Revolution, the new state imposed on itself duties toward citizens, but it also claimed the right to oversee all economic and social activities. With the partial exception of the Porfiriato, the state had always been regulative and entrepreneurial, chartering businesses but competing with them through its own economic activities. But the vast scope of the revolutionary state's social and economic intervention was new. The state went beyond charters to create its own directly productive enterprises, running steel mills, oil wells, farms, and even supermarkets. The norm would be market-shaping, not just market-conforming, policies.[4]

Foreign firms, accused of plundering the Mexican economy,

were welcome only in manufacturing. They were excluded from many sectors where some of their largest firms were expropriated to become state enterprises. Mexico pursued a strategy of economic autarchy—import substitution with a vengeance. It had reason to fear international pressures: after 1938 the just-expropriated oil firms sought to organize a general boycott of Mexican exports. Nor had Mexican officials forgotten that U.S. troops had crossed the border into Mexico time and again during the previous century.

Equality, secularism, and independence had become the central goals of the new state. State intervention in the Mexican economy was unmatched anywhere in the Americas. Mexico's redistributionist, anticlerical, anti-Yankee, authoritarian nationalism created a new, powerful ideology in support of the strongest state in the country's history.

As Mexico looked beyond 1940, at the end of its first scheduled postrevolutionary presidential transition, many of the Revolution's ideals had been implemented. An orderly Mexico now included all its people—secular, fiercely independent, and more committed than ever to egalitarian norms. And yet, numerous articles of the constitution of 1917 remained without implementation in fact or in prospect. A new gap opened between the law as ideal and the law in practice. A new challenge, economic growth, would undo the revolutionary ideology. The revolutionary credo would always be acknowledged but the sinful reality was that of Artemio Cruz.

THE NATURE OF THE COMMUNITY

Mexico has had an authoritarian political system since the Revolution. Each president has been chosen by his predecessor, who consults informally with others in the top elites. Presidential elections have been held on schedule every six years, and every president since Cárdenas has stepped down. However, the outcome of each election has been known in advance. The official Institutional Revolutionary Party (PRI) has filled all state governorships since it was founded in 1929 (its name has changed over time), even when the opposition might in fact have won. The PRI has also held all seats in the federal senate and, in recent years, about three quarters of the seats in the federal house of representatives. One quarter of the house seats are constitutionally guaranteed to opposition parties, some of which collaborate with the government on most issues. When openly challenged, the regime resorts to electoral fraud or to physical repression. However, by world standards, Mexico's practice of political imprisonment, killings, or torture is infrequent and barely significant.[5]

The regular rotation for the presidency can be interpreted as an implicit bargain between the present and the future: you allow me and my team to rule with few restraints during a fixed nonrenewable term, and you will be certain that my colleagues and I will step down on schedule, when you, too, will have a chance to rule. Because presidents and their teams have often come from different ideological parts of the ruling coalition, many people of diverse views have governed in the name of the same party. The state, the official party, and the associated labor, peasant, and other organizations, shape and control public debate; opponents can and do express public criticism within the bounds of official toleration but this public "voice" is their only power. That voice, however, and the opposition's participation in elections that it is bound to lose and in institutions where it holds little clout, help to legitimize the authoritarian state. The state receives obedience and permits public criticism while engaging in little (though occasionally some) overt repression. Mexico has, indeed, become a successful authoritarian state.

Economic performance and ideological symbols buttressed these political arrangements. Real gross domestic product (GDP) per capita increased 2.3 times from 1935 to 1965. Real GDP per capita doubled from 1960 to 1980. Mexico had a fast-growing population during those years; real GDP actually quadrupled from 1960 to 1980.[6] Mexico's regime became strong, thanks to economic growth and political order, both sustained for a half-century. There have been no coups, no new revolutions, and no external invasions.

Despite improved living standards, Mexico remains an inegalitarian society. The state's ideological task has been to explain and to justify marked inequality since the Revolution. Though difficult, that had been feasible, since real living standards for most persons had been improving, albeit at different rates. Since 1950, seven major nationwide studies have shown that relative income distribution remains as markedly inegalitarian as in 1950, and among the world's least equal. But World Bank studies also show that the real income of Mexico's bottom 60 percent of income earners improved from the 1960s to the 1970s.[7]

Since 1981, however, the lot of most Mexicans has deteriorated, and the ideological task has become much harder. Rulers have wanted the poor to think that, notwithstanding inequalities, their lot has been better and is likely to continue to improve. Now rulers must persuade those who have little to take less but to continue to supply political stability.

Twentieth-century governments have emphasized that Mexico is *one* country and that its dominant language is Spanish. Despite debate about the proper role of indigenous languages and cultures, the state has promoted full assimilation into Spanish.[8] The state has also managed public symbols to promote a more diverse definition of nationhood: although all Mexicans must speak Spanish, the heirs of Spain must accept the heirs of indigenous Mexico in the definition of Mexicanness. The symbolic merger of many Mexicos into one masked the destruction of indigenous languages and cultures.

National unity is also served by public art. Mexico City widely displays the symbols of indigenous and Spanish Mexico, side by side. The state paid for monuments, statues, and for spectacular murals showing the color, vigor, achievements, and oneness of Mexico as a mestizo people. The state also harnessed scholarship, supporting archeological work to increase consciousness about the nation's diverse origins, thereby paying to build nationalism's new shrines.

The ideology supporting the authoritarian regime was strengthened because the regime itself was popular: it worked. In 1959, 58 percent of urban Mexicans believed that the national government improved conditions of life. Thirty percent of urban Mexicans voluntarily named governmental and political institutions as aspects of their nation of which they were most proud. One quarter of urban Mexicans said they were proud of their economic system. Proud yes, but Mexicans were not fools. A solid majority did not expect equal treatment from the police. The poorer one was, the more likely one was to distrust the police.[9]

Other surveys of urban Mexico round out the picture. In 1960, white- and blue-collar urban workers in Mexico evaluated Adolfo Ruiz Cortines's presidency. Three quarters said that their standard of living had risen during the previous five years, and over four fifths expected it to improve during the following five years.[10] In 1964, near the end of Adolfo López Mateos's presidency, two thirds of Mexico City residents said they were satisfied with their standard of living; more than two thirds were satisfied with the influence people like themselves had on the country's affairs. Asked to name the political leader in Latin America they admired most, they picked the president of Mexico by a wide margin. Moreover, Mexicans wanted an effective government, not class warfare. Asked to name the one thing that Mexico needed most, one quarter wanted an honest government without corruption, and another quarter wanted a government that got things done. About 18 percent mentioned individual freedom; 15 percent mentioned a fair distribution of wealth.[11] Early in Gustavo Díaz Ordaz's presidency in 1965, 86 percent of Mexico City residents thought that Mexico had developed well during the previous two years and 58 percent thought they had gotten their fair share.[12]

Is the political system authoritarian because Mexicans are authoritarian? Analyses of interpersonal relations find a pervasive distrust of other persons and institutions, which would further an authoritarian regime.[13] There are, however, apparent inconsistencies. In 1959, Mexicans expressed pride in the Revolution and in the presidency but they distrusted the police and the bureaucracy. They were willing to participate in politics but were dissatisfied about election campaigns. They thought they could do much in politics, but in fact they did very little.[14] In the mid-1960s nearly one fifth more Mexicans preferred a system with two or more parties to one with a single party, but nine times more Mexicans identified with the official party than with any other.[15] In 1978–79, urban Mexicans generally supported the right to dissent and opposed the suppression of democratic liberties (though somewhat less than in the United States).[16] In sum, Mexico's authoritarian politics cannot be well explained solely as a result of the people's beliefs.

A better explanation of Mexico's authoritarian politics, therefore, is that the regime manages ideology to generate political support. The state fosters a cult of the president and of the "continuing Revolution." The state mobilizes people into approved channels, stimulates their politically tolerant beliefs, and manipulates the symbols of liberty and democracy so that they support the regime. These symbols are credible because the regime has delivered political stability, economic and social development, and the distribution of benefits to many. The people's beliefs were consistent with democracy but the people have allowed themselves to be persuaded to support the official party. A nondemocratic outcome has been the consequence.

In brief, nonauthoritarian political beliefs support a strong though nonrepressive authoritarian regime that manipulates ideology as a deliberate policy. The regime's management of ideology transforms the possibility of dissent into the reality of support for those who rule in the name of the people. For many years the regime succeeded. As recently as May 1979, a majority of upper- and middle-class urban Mexicans thought that the government's actions addressed the country's needs; three quarters of them approved of President Jóse López Portillo's performance. These beliefs enabled the president to govern, even though only a slim plurality (one third) supported the PRI and four fifths thought that the government would not respect election results that favored the opposition.[17]

Problems intensified when Mexico's performance deteriorated. Though the economy recovered from the 1975–76 economic crisis, thanks to the petroleum boom, a more severe crisis began in 1981 at the peak of the Mexican economy's performance. Real GDP fell in 1982 for the first time since the Great Depression of the 1930s. GDP per capita in real terms fell in 1982, 1983, and 1984.[18]

In November 1982, a large nationwide survey found that only 35 percent of Mexicans approved of the López Portillo administration's performance.[19] At the same time, a smaller survey conducted in Mexico City replicated questions first asked in 1959. In 1982 only a quarter (half the 1959 level) believed that the national government had improved conditions of life; only 3 percent volunteered that they were proud of Mexico's governmental and political institutions (one tenth of the 1959 level), while none said they were proud of Mexico's economic system (compared to one quarter in 1959). The proportion not expecting equal treatment from the police rose to 71 percent. Nearly half believed that President López Portillo had adopted policies that harmed the people. Nonetheless, 62 percent still voted PRI in the presidential elections held earlier in 1982, willing to give Miguel de la Madrid a chance.[20]

Mexico in the mid-1980s faces economic, political, and ideological crises. Can those who rule restore in the minds of citizens the belief that they have earned again the right to rule?

ORGANIZED LABOR

The state controls organized labor through conciliation and arbitration boards, through the unions' controls in the workplace, through anticipatory concessions, through political management of labor-management relations, and occasionally through repression. The state's formal labor administrative structures can declare strikes "nonexistent" and use their power to force "voluntary" settlements, to conciliate, and to arbitrate. Most strikes are settled after and through an intervention of these boards. Mexico's strike rate is quite low by comparative standards, though it has risen since the mid-1970s as a result of the economic crisis. Repression, occasionally used, is not ordinarily the main method of settling disputes. Close control by union leadership in the workplace helps insure stability and moderates workers' demands, even during economic crises.[21]

Although organized labor represented only one tenth of economically active Mexicans in 1940—at the end of Mexico's most revolutionary years—and one sixth in the 1970s, it was and remains politically and economically important. For this reason, the state regularly makes concessions to labor and forces businesses to do so too, in order to anticipate labor demands so that they will not be made. The legal minimum wage (controlling for inflation effects) tripled from the early 1950s to the early 1970s, and labor's share of GDP increased substantially. The infant mortality rate was cut in half from the 1920s to the 1940s and again in half by the 1970s, while illiteracy fell from two thirds of the adult population in 1930 to less than one fifth half a century later.

Organized labor is among the "sectors" that formally constitute the PRI, but the regime does not want any single set of labor leaders to have enough power to challenge it. Therefore, the government permits and, at times, promotes several competing and overlapping "peak" labor federations. While they are all loyal to the regime, they compete for the right to represent labor. This policy retains presidential flexibility and affirms centralized loyalties, but permits variety in representation. Despite the competition, some identifiable top labor leader has always headed the largest labor federation and the PRI's labor sector. Only three men have held the post since the Revolution; the current elderly Fidel Velázquez has been the top leader since the late 1940s. Labor leaders govern through personal relations, at times as chieftains. Because institutional arrangements are weak, important changes may occur when a top leader dies, taking with him a history of friendships and rivalries.

A brief political fight between President Luis Echeverría and Fidel Velázquez helped to create political space for new independent unions. (There had long been, however, unions independent of the established labor confederations in parts of northern Mexico, especially the industrial city of Monterrey. Those unions have worked closely with management and do not strike—this analysis does not apply to them.) More significant was Echeverría's decision that Mexico needed a political opening; he permitted it to occur in the workplace so long as local unions remained loyal to the regime.[22] Independent unions have therefore appeared in about half of the automobile industry since the 1960s when the industry changed from mere assembly to actual production, and the plants became larger and more modern. The emergence of these unions relatively independent of the established labor confederations raises new issues.

Independent unions in the automobile industry are more likely to strike (indeed, only they have struck the auto industry), to be more internally democratic, to have control over workloads and line speeds, and to support rank-and-file members with grievances against management. For wages, the pattern is less clear. In the 1960s and early 1970s, there were few differences in wage gains by type of union, but in the late 1970s those differences seemed more marked. Mexican labor, given an opportunity to bargain independently, pressed harder and struck more over workplace conditions than over income, more over issues that touch on authority at work than over those that enrich.

Management's approach to labor had an ideological component too. U.S.-owned automobile firms were more willing than foreign-owned and Mexican-owned firms to make income concessions. They were less willing to give in on work rules. Managers in U.S.-owned firms were more likely to believe that their authority came from ownership and need not be shared with the managed. Other firms were more willing to share authority at the workplace in exchange for wage restraint.

Nissan and DINA (wholly state-owned) were consistently more willing to allow union participation in workplace decisions than U.S.-owned firms such as General Motors, Ford, Chrysler, and the joint venture between Mexico and American Motors. Volkswagen fell somewhere in between. But General Motors, Ford, and Chrysler paid wages 20 percent or more higher than non-U.S. firms. In the late 1970s, however, wages in non-U.S. foreign firms often grew faster toward a more uniform standard.

The U.S.-owned Chrysler, and the Japanese-owned Nissan de México, grew fastest in the Mexican market in the 1970s. At its Cuernavaca plant, Nissan permitted extensive union participation in determining the rhythm of work, in fashioning and implementing occupational health and safety measures, in deciding on promotions and in specifying promotion criteria, in controlling workforce distribution within the plant, and in specifying procedures for resolving workplace conflict. Chrysler did not permit any of these. However, the workers at Nissan's Cuernavaca plant did not reward the firm for "good behavior": Nissan faced a strike on the average every other year in the 1970s, while Chrysler had no strikes at all. Nissan opened a plant in Toluca in the late 1970s which, not surprisingly, it tried to control with an iron hand, but it has again faced major labor insurgencies. Thus Chrysler's more heavy-handed approach served its management more effectively: fewer concessions, no strikes, and growth as good as Nissan's. Nissan's management has a communitarian base from which to reduce strike frequency, but its management does not know how to use it. The importance of management response is evident also from a comparison of Ford and Nissan. Ford has been struck like Nissan, but it has not made as extensive concessions on workplace conditions as has Nissan.

In short, the outcomes are shaped by doubly ideological processes. Militant independent unionism and non-U.S. management have meant high concessions to labor and frequent strikes but good market performance (Nissan). Militant independent unionism and U.S.-management have meant wage gains for labor, authority gains for management, but frequent strikes and less good market performance (Ford). Nonmilitant "captive" unions and U.S.-management have meant few gains for labor but good market performance (Chrysler). No outcome is optimal for all participants.

The U.S. and other foreign multinationals differ in their approach to labor relations across industrial sectors. A survey concerning the modes of conflict resolution in labor disputes in Mexico was conducted among thirty-four U.S. and forty-five West German firms in 1976. In every case, German firms followed the rules set by the Mexican government and entered into direct negotiations with labor unions. In contrast, no U.S. firms negotiated directly with the unions as a first approach. Instead, they chose a strategy of conflict toward the union or toward the Mexican government, often initiating litigation.[23]

In short, the presence in Mexico of multinational firms from different countries has injected styles of labor-management relations that resemble patterns in the parent firm's home country: a bias toward conflict for U.S. firms and a bias toward legally sanctioned negotiations for West German firms. The intrusion of these foreign ideologies makes more difficult the managing of Mexico's own ideology.

THE STATE AND BUSINESS

Miguel de la Madrid did not become president in 1982 to dismantle the state's role in the economy but to make it more efficient; not to end the authoritarian state or to allow the PRI's electoral defeat but to modernize them; not to eschew Mexico's nationalism but to harness it to face the crisis at hand.[24] "The state is not a mere arbiter of social interests," noted the National Development Plan for 1983–88, the first such document issued during de la Madrid's presidency. The state is to be the economy's "rector." Only the state represents the nation's interests and only the state has the right and the obligation to set economic policy.[25]

The Mexican state has designed policies that do not merely respond to, and conform with, market trends. It has sought to shape those trends for less dependence on international markets, pursuing aggressive strategies of industrialization through import substitution, despite some high costs.

The state's "rectorship" is impressive. It owns all communications, electricity, natural gas, the railroads, shipbuilding, petroleum, and coal production. It also owns about three quarters of the steel industry, half of the airlines, and a quarter of the automobile industry.[26] The Mexican state is also a manufacturer of many other products, a producer of some agricultural products, and the operator of a large chain of retail supermarkets (CONASUPO). Even Mexicans who do not shop at CONASUPO supermarkets believe that CONASUPO stores contribute to Mexico's development and that they serve the interest of all Mexicans.[27] The state at times also grew by buying bankrupt private firms and keeping them operating, despite their unprofitability, in order to preserve jobs. The banks, too, were expropriated in 1982, accused by President José López Portillo of engineering capital flight. The crisis was in fact due to the government's mistaken foreign exchange policies. Private financial institutions akin to investment banks reappeared by the mid-1980s when the de la Madrid administration reactivated financial markets.

Mexico's concern for its independence is an important source of authority for the state. Mexico has been the largest economy in the non-Communist world not covered by the General Agreement on Tariffs and Trade (GATT); the government rejected entry most recently in 1980.[28] To be sure, Mexico's export performance, with government support, has at times been good, but Mexico has had a greater bias toward self-sufficiency than toward engaging in international trade. The defense of the nation has had priority over the pursuit of growth, although in the mid-1980s the two merged when the Mexican government argued that the nation's defense required growth and improved international competitiveness beyond petroleum. Mexico even decided to join the GATT.

Mexico has one of the most statist economies of the non-Communist world. Its statism stems from the revolutionary ideological consensus that fears control over the Mexican economy by the United States and other countries. Like Bismarck's Germany, Mexican leaders seek centralized power over the economy to protect the nation from the world beyond its borders; unlike Bismarck's Germany (and unlike Brazil), the military component of a nationalist strategy is virtually absent. Mexico's military is not directly engaged in the economy, and military expenditures have accounted for less than one percent of gross national product for many years.[29]

Mexico's statism also owes much to business attitudes. Mexican business most fears being cast adrift from the helping hand of government and being left to face the rigors of competition on its own. The Mexican business community is talented and effective. More recently it has been seriously troubled, divided, deeply ideological, and profoundly dependent on the state for its growth and prosperity. In 1975–76, during the severe economic crisis, business opposed Mexico's last "leftist" president, Luis Echeverría. They had established the Enterprise Coordinating Committee (CCE) in mid-1975 to coordinate business policy views. The CCE published a document that is an awkward ideological mixture, but it best articulates business views.

Private property, the document argued, is a natural right that the state can regulate but not abolish. The state's role in the economy must remain secondary to private initiative. Labor has few rights; a strongly paternalistic vision of labor-management relations is portrayed. The state should maintain order and "create and maintain the economy's infrastructure." It should also continue an import substitution policy in the manufacturing sector, and it should protect Mexican industry against foreign competition. The state should sell off state enterprises to the private sector, but it should also provide tax and other incentives to private firms and take active steps to facilitate business mergers. Mexican business opposed the state's intrusion into retail trade. But it also upheld all the restrictions when foreign direct investment competes with Mexican firms. However, business also agreed with existing legislation that permits foreigners majority shareholding, at the discretion of the government. Permission should be granted, business argued, only if there is not enough Mexican capital, there are no other means to acquire technology, and the investments are vital for national development. To promote exports, business asked the state to provide tax exemptions, export subsidies, and technical assistance.[30]

The CCE document was not a brief for private enterprise but a plea for the state's continued support for Mexican business, against labor demands and foreign competition, on business's own terms. Unlike in Japan or Taiwan, neither business nor the state has focused on how to join forces, while also including labor, so that Mexico's global competitiveness can extend beyond petroleum.

Business retains a strong antilabor bias. Two thirds of Mexican industrialists in 1980 disagreed with the statement that "workers play a positive role in the industrial firm and in industrial relations."[31] The state has changed its policies to conform to business preferences on labor policy even when it appeared to do otherwise. For example, to revitalize the regime's commitment to labor after two presidential terms that had been rather favorable to business, President Adolfo López Mateos (1958–64) launched a far-reaching initiative to institute profit sharing for workers in each firm. Mexican business fought the plan successfully and, through the regulatory and administrative processes, rendered it insignificant. Mexico thus passed up an opportunity to lift living standards without threatening net profitability, and to make a communitarian bargain to include labor.[32]

Business and the state in Mexico spend much time shouting at each other but there has been a broad though informal consensus between them. Business understands that prosperity has depended on the political stability the regime has provided and on the state's extensive subsidies to business, especially the import substitution policy. Mexican manufacturers, especially in medium- and small-sized firms, have opposed Mexico's entry into the GATT. Three quarters of Mexican industrialists surveyed in the summer of 1980 believed that the state's economic policies, especially protectionism, had helped them, and had played "an important and positive role in the economic development of the nation."[33] In turn, the state agreed with Mexican business to permit more foreign direct investment while continuing to protect Mexican business. Mexico has become an industrial country, though it is also a high-cost, internationally uncompetitive manufacturer.

In short, government policy has become increasingly supportive of Mexican business, often in violation of the Revolution's norms. The Revolution promised equality to workers. Although East Asian cases suggest that equality can turn out to be efficient as well as ideologically appealing, business influence with government has helped to thwart equality at the workplace in Mexico. The Revolution was also rooted in antagonism to foreign business—an antagonism from which Mexican business benefited because the state shielded it from the rigors of international competition. However, Mexico now must increase its international competitiveness to earn the foreign exchange needed to safeguard its independence from foreign banks and the U.S. government. To do this, it needs labor's active cooperation and it needs Mexican managers who can compete effectively in world markets. An antilabor and anticompetitive government-business consensus no longer serves Mexican national interests. To achieve the Revolution's principal goals of independence abroad and equality at home, many ideological and other changes are required.

Multinational Firms

The state's takeover of much of the means of production ended foreign participation except in manufacturing. Mexico's fundamental policy toward foreign investment was set as a wartime emergency measure in 1944. President Manuel Avila Camacho announced his authority to approve, deny, or set conditions on all foreign acquisitions of existing companies and on formation of new ones, on foreign purchase of any type of real estate, and on granting foreigners use of mines, water, or combustible minerals. The most important condition came to be known as "Mexicanization," requiring that a majority of a firm's equity capital and directors be Mexican. This condition, however, could be waived. In Mexico's time-honored fashion, the state retained full flexibility in the application of a law radical for its time.[34]

Despite differences among Mexican presidents, there has been remarkable ideological consistency on this issue. The president asserts the power of the state but he retains great discretion in implementation. Even probusiness President Miguel Alemán established executive power over all products subject to import and export licenses and over prices, and he increased the number of industries in which Mexicanization of new firms was required. As time passed, Mexico developed many incentives to promote Mexicanization, culminating in the 1973 laws to promote Mexican investment and to regulate foreign investment.

There was broad elite consensus on Mexicanization. In late 1976, elite groups were asked whether they thought it was "a good idea or a bad idea to require that firms established in Mexico with foreign investment be at least 51 percent owned by Mexicans." The response was overwhelmingly positive.

Business managers in U.S. and Mexican firms agreed: it made sense for them. Mexicanization gave Mexican firms an opportunity to become partners of large multinational firms on terms

Table 10–1   Attitudes of Mexican Elite Groups toward Foreign Firms (1976)

(percentages)

	Business Managers: in Mexican Firms	in U.S. Firms	Government Officials	Labor Leaders	University Students
Supports:					
Mexicanization	80	92	95	83	84
Foreign investment	90	91	72	61	47
Expropriation	18	8	32	59	60

Note: Sample size is 100 for each group.

Source: U.S. International Communications Agency, "U.S. Investment in Mexico: Attitudes of Key Mexican Elite Groups," R–29–78 (Washington: 18 October 1978), tables 9, 13, and 14.

more favorable than in a pure market transaction. They would buy equity in the multinational firm's subsidiary at prices artificially depressed by the state's pressure on the parent for partial divestment. Mexicanization also gave Mexican nationals working in foreign subsidiaries an opportunity to become the preferred Mexican partners to a degree that might not occur if the Mexican state was not involved. Mexicanization thus gave incentives to Mexican managers in multinational firms to be disloyal to headquarters.

To have Mexicanization, of course, meant to have foreign firms. Elites were also asked whether "investment by foreign firms in Mexico is more beneficial or more harmful" for Mexico. Majorities of all groups thought it was beneficial (except for university students), although the intensity of support varied. Elites were also asked whether they favored or opposed "having the government completely take over large corporations owned by foreigners." Labor leaders and university students supported such expropriations while government officials and business managers did not. Both government officials and labor leaders now support foreign investment and, in turn, business managers support Mexicanization. However, government officials are closer to business's opposition to expropriation than to labor's favoring it. Labor leaders are a key "swing group," depending on the issue.

Business nationalism was slow to develop in Mexico. In the 1940s and 1950s, business federations representing larger Mexican firms still spoke as if they believed in the marketplace. Business federations representing small businesses came to support extensive state regulation of subsidiaries of multinational firms by the 1950s. These differences by size of firm disappeared as foreign firms poured into Mexico to partake of its boom. In a 1969 survey, 57 percent of 200 Mexican business executives advocated controls on the entry of foreign firms. In a 1973 survey, three quarters of the executives in Mexican business firms opposed the entry of more foreign firms. In 1976, only 3 percent of executives in Mexican companies and only 5 percent of executives in U.S. companies wanted fewer government controls on multinational firms.[35]

Government policy toward multinational firms combined two needs: for controlling business and for economic growth.

Consider the case of automobiles. In the early stages of import substitution, automobile companies established assembly plants in Mexico but imported most of the parts. By 1959, this industry alone accounted for 12 percent of all Mexican imports. In 1962, by presidential decree, Mexico prohibited imports of finished cars and required that the components of cars manufactured in Mexico total 60 percent of the car's production cost. Internal demand for cars grew; the industry prospered. Left to market forces, the automobile firms might not have expanded their Mexican operations.

This industrial history confirmed the state's view that the market alone did not serve Mexican interests and that state action could create an industry where none existed. The 1962 decree also proved to be a major departure from the emphasis on Mexicanization of equity: the state used its flexibility to waive the Mexicanization requirements. Firms could be fully owned subsidiaries of multinational corporations; all U.S.-owned subsidiaries, Nissan, and Volkswagen have so remained. Auto-parts suppliers, however, had to be majority-owned Mexican firms. By exempting the auto industry from Mexicanization of equity, the 1962 decree confirmed the centrality of state power and flexibility and emphasized control of business behavior. The decree marked an ideological turning point. It mattered less who owned the firm; it mattered more what the firm did.[36]

In 1969, when auto parts accounted for 20 percent of Mexican imports, Mexico required that auto manufacturers begin to compensate exports for imports; at first, only 5 percent of the imports had to be compensated with exports. In 1977 the rules were changed again. The mandatory minimum local content would be 50 percent for autos, actually about 8 percent higher than before because the method of computation changed. By 1982 each firm would have to compensate fully its imports with exports. The firms then had a choice: they could gradually increase the proportion of Mexican-produced components to 75 percent, or they could export more than they imported. The state had acted because it believed that auto firms had been slow to export from Mexico.

The ideology had helped the state set its long-term goals while remaining flexible enough to learn and to choose among priorities. The ideology also alerted business to the long-term direction of state action, protecting private investment and oligopoly profits for the sake of growth. Nonetheless, although the ideological path was clear, the specific rules for business behavior felt like shifting sand: the state could still change them almost at will.

Business firms, however, doubted the state's wisdom concerning foreign exchange policies. From the mid-1970s through the early 1980s, the peso's overvaluation made it difficult to export nonpetroleum products without extensive state subsidies. The car companies could not meet the state's export targets; in 1981 the car companies accounted for 58 percent of the trade deficit. In 1983 the de la Madrid administration adopted more flexible exchange-rate policies. For the first time ever, Mexico had the tools to promote the unsubsidized export of manufactured goods. The administration also reshaped the auto industry by requiring it to adopt policies to lower the unit cost of production, make fewer models, and thus become more internationally competitive.[37] The state corrected bad policies but it remained in charge, improving its efficacy but not reducing its role.

The computer industry provides another example of the state's power. Mexico's approach to defining a computer policy was slower than Brazil's. Whereas Brazil had created a state enterprise and other bureaucracies to shape the computer industry by the early 1970s, Mexico simply centralized decision making about computer policy in the president's office and applied to the computer industry such typical regulations as import licenses.[38] In 1982 Mexico adopted its first comprehensive computer policy. To encourage the manufacturing of microcomputers in Mexico, it prohibited their import and it required 70 percent local content by 1987. The policy also mandated majority Mexican ownership of each firm's equity.

Implementing Mexico's computer policy, however, has been a struggle among ideology, the interests of government agencies and firms, and economic necessities. The government had allowed the manufacture of large computers by fully owned foreign subsidiaries, but it sought to Mexicanize the ownership of firms that manufactured personal computers. In late 1983, the government asked IBM to invest more heavily in Mexico.

IBM proposed that its fully owned Mexican subsidiary manufacture about 600,000 personal computers a year and export over 90 percent of them. By then, all other personal computer manufacturers already in Mexico were Mexican majority owned. The association of computer companies in Mexico (AMFABI), with the support of left-wing opposition parties, lobbied hard against the IBM project, arguing that other firms had abided by Mexican laws. *Apple de México* and *Hewlett-Packard de México* took out full-page advertisements in the daily newspapers asking the government to uphold restrictions on foreign firms. The government wanted IBM either to take a Mexican partner or to invest in an in-bond plant, where full foreign ownership is routinely allowed. IBM's policy is not to take national partners. In addition, it wanted to sell personal computers in Mexico. In early 1985, the government turned down IBM's project "because businesses already exist that currently manufacture the microcomputers with a majority of national capital, such as Hewlett-Packard and Apple." On the eve of congressional elections, even the PRI came out against easing foreign investment regulations. President de la Madrid stated: "If we allow full and open access to foreign investment, we run the risk of losing control over our own resources."[39]

For IBM the reality was being turned down. For the government, the reality was to forego new export opportunities when it had to service the debt, knowing also that personal computer production in Mexico was a quite modest "assembly" operation. Therefore, the Mexican government invited IBM to revise and resubmit its proposal, with a greater emphasis on exports and higher local content, and with more transfers of technical skills and research. By late 1985, IBM's resubmission won authorization. Like the 1962 automobile decree, in yet another sector, a firm's behavior matters more than its ownership.[40]

This case illustrates the conflicting rationalities of ideologies. IBM's corporate ideology against joint ventures has, in general, served it well, giving it leverage against governments throughout the world that want it to take local partners. The Mexican majority-owned computer firms were also rational in wielding the Revolution's symbols to get the government to exclude IBM from the competition or to drive the hardest possible bargain. The government, in turn, could make it appear that it had no choice but to act as it did in pressing IBM harder for a better deal. The ideologies of all had strategic rational justifications.

In sum, the state's relations with multinational firms still emphasize its need for control and flexibility, its right to change the rules, and to determine the country's economic future. But business also wants control, and some firms manipulate Mexican ideological symbols to combat foreign firms. The state's restrictions on multinational business helped national business compete. National businesses, therefore, advocate and support discriminatory national government policies to favor national firms.

The Destruction of Mexico's Export Competitiveness

In 1966, agriculture and cattle accounted for 50.2 percent of Mexican exports, falling to 37.1 percent in 1974. During the same period, manufactured exports rose from 37.7 percent to 53.8 percent, while petroleum's share remained below 1 percent (all in constant 1970 prices). By 1980, hydrocarbon exports accounted for two thirds of Mexican exports, manufacturing for one sixth, and agriculture and cattle for one tenth. Oil dominated not just because of the petroleum boom: manufactured and agricultural exports declined in value in real terms during the 1970s and through 1982. How had Mexico become uncompetitive in international markets?[41]

Cotton was Mexico's principal foreign exchange earner from 1949 to 1973, amounting to one tenth of the world's total in the early 1960s. However, the quantity of Mexican cotton exports fell by 56 percent from the early 1960s to the late 1970s, and Mexico's share of world cotton exports fell to under 4 percent. There had been little Mexican government regulation of cotton until the early 1970s when world cotton prices rose and also fluctuated widely. The Mexican private sector could not cope with fluctuating prices even if they were higher. Producers and merchants wanted security; the textile industry wanted the government to give it priority in the allocation of supply. All appealed to the state. The state could simply have regulated the market; instead, President Echeverría created a state enterprise empowered to market cotton. A new system of export permits would guarantee supplies to the textile industry. To please agricultural producers, the state set stable prices. To make the state enterprise profitable, the government set prices at about one third below the prevailing international price. The result was a decline in cotton production at the same time that the textile industry doubled its share of consumption, all at the expense of exports at the very moment the balance of payments deteriorated and the debt ballooned. The ideology shared by the president, the textile industry, and agricultural producers helped to reduce Mexican cotton exports.

In 1959, Mexico exported only 61,216 tons of sugar to the United States. In a few years, Mexican entrepreneurs captured a share of Cuba's lost quota to the United States; Mexican sugar exports to the U.S. market averaged over 470,000 tons during the 1960s. However, Mexico's internal sugar prices had been frozen in 1958 as a subsidy to consumers. The government thus had to subsidize the expansion of installed capacity to permit the export boom. Because prices remained frozen, many sugar mills went bankrupt and became state firms, thereby increasing the state's share of sugar production from 5 percent to 31 percent during the 1960s. Internal sugar prices were raised in 1970 but remained frozen thereafter. When world sugar prices boomed from 1972 to 1974, Mexico could not adapt. In 1974–75, Mexican sugar production fell to 23 percent of the 1969–70 level, even though annual average world sugar prices had multiplied by a factor of six. Industrial consumers, in the meantime, increased their share of consumption because of the low, controlled prices. The state's response was to strengthen the powers of the state enterprise over the sugar sector. By 1980 Mexico had become a net importer of sugar.

In contrast, Mexican tomato exports to the United States are a success story. A Mexican rural bourgeoisie, substantially independent of the Mexican state, became strong and skillful enough to increase exports to the United States and to defeat the protectionist efforts of Florida tomato producers. From the late 1960s to the late 1970s, tomato exports to the United States doubled. To defend themselves against U.S. charges of dumping, Mexican tomato producers helped to design a new econometric model to assess price variations for winter vegetables; it was accepted by the United States government, which ruled against Florida producers.

There are no clear reasons for the differences in success of the various agricultural subsectors. The tomato boom occurred in geographically remote areas; the state had not regulated tomatoes because it did not consider them a politically sensitive food; from the outset, production was oriented toward export, and there were no major industrial consumers.[42] Mexico could therefore export agricultural products if it overcomes the ideological barriers that stand in the way.

Mexico's international competitiveness was even more sharply reduced during much of the 1970s and through 1982 by the recurrent overvaluation of the peso. In response to the large devaluations of late 1982, Mexican firms exported more in 1983. During the first half of 1984, Mexican nonoil exports increased by 60 percent.[43] Ideological issues are thus only one part of the story of Mexico's lack of competitiveness, affecting some sectors more than others, but this pattern of state intervention requires re-examination if exports are to grow and diversify.

CONCLUSIONS

Mexico's ruling ideology has long emphasized the centrality of the state's role in shaping the market and the society. The office of the presidency has great centralized power and much flexibility to use it. Hierarchy, often based on politics or family ties, and the concentration of power and wealth have marked the country's history. The state has successfully claimed the right to define the rights and duties of individuals and firms. It has compromised, but not over its primacy. It does not, however, govern harshly. As in colonial times, the state abides by norms of surprising self-restraint. It is not a torturer; it has not been totalitarian nor as authoritarian as some regimes in South America or East Asia. Its political stability is a success.

In this state-dominant system, a role exists for interest groups; a public voice for critics has been permitted. The secular state has sought to include all of its citizens through participation in state-directed, corporatist intermediary institutions and in the official party. It has attempted to maintain the nation's independence in the face of international threats, above all from the United States.

The Mexican people have allowed the state to define community need but their beliefs are consistent with what could be a less hierarchical, less authoritarian, political system. There are authoritarian strands in Mexico's culture but they do not mandate a regime of the type that exists. Nor is Mexican labor passive before authority. When labor has been allowed greater freedom, it has sought rights to participate in the management of modern industrial communities.

Business had been excluded from the revolutionary coalition and consensus of the 1930s. Unlike in East Asia, this Mexican consensus had been antibusiness. Slowly and subtly, however, Mexican business modified that consensus. As in East Asia, the state came to promote and protect business. The protection of industrial oligopolies became a shared objective of business and the state. Industrial Mexico grew, though at high cost. The state charters business, regulates it, becomes its partner at times, and even competes with it through state enterprises. What neither business nor the state wishes is unfettered competition. Unlike in East Asia, Mexican ideology has thwarted Mexican competitiveness in world markets. Mexican business and the state welcomed foreign investment but only under state control. The state would protect national business from the harshness of the marketplace. Somehow the state would also harness multinational business toward growth and, eventually, exports—with limited success. In the meantime, the egalitarian strain of the revolutionary consensus was lost. And the emphasis on Mexicanization of firms was weakened as the state focused on controlling what firms did more than on who owned them.

Growth has occurred most where the government clearly defined its primacy or rectorship over the economy, its commitment to centralized hierarchies, its pragmatic nationalism, and its flexibility in applying rules, including its willingness to change some ideological tenets. Automobiles, tomato exports, and personal computers, are examples. Where ideology has remained rigid, as in cotton and sugar, the results have been disastrous.

Ideology is a central problem for the Mexico of the late 1980s. The Revolution is long past. The symbols remain powerful but may not sufficiently justify those who rule in their name. The economy's performance faltered in the early 1980s, and people blamed the government's mistakes. The regime claims a democratic basis but does not abide by democratic norms. Can Mexico be ruled still in the name of the Revolution? The myth is at stark variance with reality: an authoritarian state, albeit mild, and an inegalitarian economy and society, albeit one that had experienced much growth. And if not in the name of the Revolution, what will take its place?

Specific ideological issues need to be addressed. Mexico must reconcile "gringophobia" and "gringophilia" as it addresses the role of foreign firms in its midst. It must reassess the efficacy of market-shaping policies as opposed to less ambitious market-conforming policies. Evidence of some shift toward the latter are its less intrusive policies toward tomato exports and its policy changes over personal computers. Organized labor should consider whether communitarian bargains with firms (such as Nissan) entitle the firm to expect labor peace, not repeated strikes. Labor must assess whether it can continue to treat firms differently within the same industry. The transition that will occur when the current head of the labor movement dies will reopen issues about the organization and representation of labor.

Business needs to cope with a free-market ideology in which, in fact, it does not believe but which it cannot abandon. Businesses also need to reassess their confrontational attitudes toward labor, which are likely to exacerbate industrial strife as Mexico's economic troubles endure. Foreign firms should think about the complexities of their relevant context: some firms Mexicanize, invoking the Revolution's ideological symbols to help them compete; other firms will not Mexicanize. Moreover, foreign firms must assess how much it matters that some executives in their subsidiaries oppose the beliefs of the parent firm about the nature of ownership. Both national and foreign firms should consider whether it matters that the business community in Mexico is seriously split by nationality of ownership.

Mexico needs to think about more than ideology in the years ahead but it will not get far unless it thinks about ideology too.

11

CONCLUSION

Ezra F. Vogel

Our investigations of ideology in the major industrial nations of Europe, North America, South America, and East Asia reveal a highly complex and subtle relationship between ideology and society. No specific ideology is practiced in any pure form. In each society and even in each firm, variant and even contradictory ideological elements coexist in a complex mixture. In France, despite a broad-based consensus on the importance of grandeur, economic growth, and strong state leadership, two very different versions of conservative ideology and two versions of more radical ideology have coexisted for two centuries. Therefore at any one time, the overall French ideological system is a particular combination of these four ideological streams. Korea's dominant ideology is communitarian, but in recent years the old authoritarian form of communitarianism has weakened and individualism has grown stronger, leading to pressures for a more diversified and democratic communitarianism. In Taiwan, statism, a strong form of communitarianism concerned with the entire society, coexists with

301

familism, which may appear to the individual to be communitarian but appears to the state to be divisive and individualistic. The United States may be predominantly individualistic but strong elements of communitarianism have existed since our nation's founding. In Mexico, a revolutionary communitarian ideology still continues despite many new adaptations.

National ideologies may be complex and relations to society subtle, but they have very long staying power. They rarely undergo sudden change except in situations of war and revolution. They change most easily not by the introduction of entirely new elements but by the increase or decrease in the prominence of elements already present in a national ideological system. The existence of traditional communitarian elements in the American tradition makes it easier for Americans to apply certain kinds of communitarian solutions than if we had to develop such elements from scratch. Since World War II England has had strong communitarian practices, but Thatcher was able to call on other parts of British tradition to support a much stronger individualism. Japanese individualism began to grow after World War II with the American-led Occupation, but the success of these individualistic efforts draws heavily on strong strands of individualism in the early Meiji Period that reached even greater heights in the 1920s. Although individualism has never been dominant in Korea and Taiwan, a strong traditional base of individualism is fueling the current criticisms of authoritarian communitarianism. The sense of communitarianism among East Asian nations has been strengthened by their late development effort to catch up with the West and by their dependence on imports of vitally needed resources that heighten the need for domestic cooperation. But communitarianism also had strong traditional roots. The question in each nation is thus how to combine these different elements in a coherent manner that aids in adaptation to the international environment.

Because ideological systems have such great staying power, they greatly affect how leaders, managers, and ordinary citizens analyze and respond to their environment. The ideological framework may be implicit and people may not even be aware of the assumptions they are making, but the impact of ideology is nonetheless profound.

Even scholars who agree about the importance of ideology and are experienced in ideological analysis do not agree perfectly about how to describe the ideologies of a given nation, let alone to explain how its ideologies have developed historically and relate to actual behavior. Although not all participants in the colloquium at which our papers were presented would agree with all our formulations, the following sections were drawn together by the two coeditors to highlight major threads that emerged in the discussions of our papers. We here present three key propositions and endeavor to explain the thinking behind each.

PROPOSITION 1. Countries can be ranked by ideological strength (comparative advantage) according to the degree of ideological coherence and adaptability to their environment.

The industrial nations considered in our work can be ranked on this dimension as follows:

a. Japan, Korea, Taiwan
b. Germany
c. France, Brazil
d. United Kingdom, United States, Mexico

By "coherence," we mean the extent to which there is consistency in how key people in a society see and respond to their environment. When ideology is coherent and adapted to the relevant context, the roles and relationship of government, business, and labor appear to be more effective in reaching solutions adapted to their environment than when there is ideological conflict and ambivalence. Problems arise when there is confusion and when there is a gap between ideology and practice. Lack of coherence and the problems that ensue are perhaps best illustrated by the United States, where some effective practices consistent with communitarian ideology are subjected to constant challenge because they are not yet considered fully acceptable ideologically. In such a case the lack of ideological coherence may prevent the continuation of an effective response. Of course, ideological coherence does not alone ensure continuity and stability. In Brazil the prevailing consensus is that the government should lead the country in the direction of economic progress. When the economy runs into difficulties, Brazilians have been ready to overturn their government for its economic failures. The citizens of all these industrial countries want their governments to assist with economic progress, but in some countries governments that encounter problems can remain in power longer than in Brazil. In Taiwan and Japan, people confronted with national economic difficulties may even rally behind their present government, despite objections to the government's authoritarian brand of communitarianism.

Reality is complex, and a certain amount of variation in ideological elements can at times, within limits, permit dynamism and flexibility that otherwise might be straitjacketed by rigid adherence to a consistent ideological pattern. Although the tensions between authoritarian communitarianism and individualism in Korea sometimes approach the point of debilitating conflicts, individualistic ideology in Korea provides the wellspring for tremendous dynamism. The same is true in Taiwan where familism, while conflicting with statism, has allowed room for vital and creative entrepreneurship. Yet if the conflict between ideological elements within a nation becomes too severe, it can lead to confusion, wavering, and inconsistent responses that can be debilitating in the nation's effort to adapt to its environment. Lack of success in adapting in turn weakens the respect, legitimacy, and effectiveness of national institutions, and thus further exacerbates the problem of achieving ideological coherence.

A nation with a given ideological system will be better adapted to certain environments and to certain historical circumstances than to others. Individualism was well adapted to a frontier society where great local initiative was required. Even those societies with the most coherent ideology that are now most successful in adapting to international markets cannot adapt easily to all circumstances in all economic environments. Japan, South Korea, Taiwan, and Germany, which are now responding most effectively to the international competitive challenge, are all heavily dependent on international trade. Their need to import food and raw materials makes them vulnerable to certain disasters no matter how great their general ability to adapt.

Even the most adaptable nations also have internal patterns that increase their vulnerability under certain circumstances. In Germany, for example, high wages and the power of unions to dictate certain communitarian solutions may cause some sectors to become uncompetitive. In Taiwan the same familism that encourages dynamism may also lead to the influence of families over certain official decisions, interfering with the overall interests of the state and weakening public credibility sufficiently to discourage investment. In Korea, the individual-istic dynamism could lead to explosions against an authoritar-ian military leadership that would paralyze the economy. In Japan the finely tuned concessions to various groups in the interest of maintaining a national communitarian consensus could be threatened from inside Japan if certain groups are pushed too hard by other groups. Japan could be threatened from outside if other countries become too dissatisfied at being unable to penetrate a market dominated by closely allied Jap-anese institutions.

It is also true that some countries here ranked lowest in adaptability have in their own ways been adapting to changing circumstances and may have made substantial progress in this direction. French Socialists concerned with national competi-tiveness have been willing to cooperate in working for greater rationality and productivity in French industry. Mexicans and Brazilians have worked at building a consensus that can cope with the belt-tightening procedures necessary for maintaining the cooperation of foreign lenders.

Yet at the present stage in world development, when a high proportion of goods produced are traded beyond national boundaries and international competitiveness is at a high pitch, the countries that can adapt to international competitiveness are in a much stronger position. In general, those countries with a coherent communitarian ideology have been able to best adapt to this international competitive economic system. This is perhaps most clearly evidenced by the fact that over recent decades they have achieved the highest rates of eco-nomic growth and their exports have been most successful in

international markets.* (See *Table 11–1.*) The stellar performance of countries with a communitarian ideology can be
illustrated by examining their relative success in achieving
governability, in expanding into sectors with promise of growth,
and in limiting damage in sectors that have lost hope of maintaining broad-based international competitiveness.

Governability

Governability requires an efficient administration able to respond
to important national issues and to maintain the support of the
concerned public. In premodern East Asian societies, most
people accepted their position as subjects and, within very
broad bounds, did not question the decisions of their leaders.
In modern mass society, now found in all these industrial
countries, citizens expect governments to be responsive to
public opinion. Therefore, mechanisms for gaining public
understanding of desirable decisions and of forging consensus
are very important in building and maintaining public support.
Communitarian ideologies are in general better fitted for sus-
taining a broad base of support than individualism. An ideology stressing the importance of the group and of individual
responsibilities to the group and to the nation have obvious
merit for those trying to forge national policies. By contrast,
some elements of the Lockean tradition of individualism make
adaptation involving large portions of the public difficult. Contracts and the legal procedures surrounding them, the concern
for the parts rather than the group or nation as a whole, and
the assumption that everything will turn out well if each
individual pursues his or her own self-interest, do not provide
a framework that enables governments to adapt easily to rapidly changing international circumstances.

Corporations in a society dominated by individualism confront special problems of governability. Private enterprises in a

---

*Here I am using Bruce Scott's definition: "National competitiveness refers to
a nation state's ability to produce, distribute, and service goods in the
international economy in competition with goods and services produced in
other countries, and to do so in a way that earns a rising standard of living."
U.S. Competitiveness in the World Economy (Boston: Harvard Business School
Press, 1985), 14–15.

Table 11-1   Indices of Competitiveness

IDEOLOGY RANKING[1]	Annual Compound Growth Rate of Real GNP per Capita[3] 1965–1984 (percent)		Percentage Point Change in Export Share of World Market (Less Oil Exports) 1965–1984		Average Share of Investment in GNP 1965–1984 (percent)	
	Rank	#	Rank	#	Rank	#
1 JAPAN	3	5.27	1	4.4	1	29.0
2 KOREA	1	7.22	2	1.5	3	22.9
3 TAIWAN	2	6.78	3	1.4	5	19.4
4 GERMANY	6	2.66	7	−1.0	2	23.3
5 FRANCE	5	2.90	6	−0.6	4	21.0
6 BRAZIL	4	3.44	4	0.6	8	17.5
7 UNITED STATES	8	2.02	8	−4.0	9	15.4
8 UNITED KINGDOM	9	1.74	8	−4.0	7	17.7
9 MEXICO	7	2.33	5	−0.2	6	18.1
RANK CORRELATION[2]		.83		.72		.77

[1] Separating the nine countries into nine ideological rankings instead of the four on page 303 is undoubtedly overly precise, but it is convenient to do so in order to compare the rankings with the more quantifiable indices of competitiveness. Figuring the correlations by the four categories of countries on page 303, they are .91, .88 and .75 for per capita growth, export share, and investment respectively.

[2] For a two-tailed test of significance of the null hypothesis of independence at the .05 and .01 levels, with n=9, the critical values for the Spearman Rank Correlation are .68 and .82 respectively. See W. J. Conover, *Practical Nonparametric Statistics*, New York: John Wiley & Sons, 1971.

[3] Measured in national currencies.

Sources: *International Financial Statistics 1985*, International Monetary Fund, Washington, D.C., 1986; *Taiwan Statistical Data Book 1985*, Council for Economic Planning and Development, Republic of China, June 1985; *Monthly Digest of Statistics*, UK Central Statistical Office, December 1985.

free-wheeling environment devote much of their time and energy to promoting or preventing mergers and takeovers, thereby slighting issues that are fundamental to the long-term health of corporations. Since corporations are now large enough to have powerful effects on ordinary citizens, people affected by corporate impact on environment, loss of jobs, social equity, and other matters express their concerns to their local and national governments. In an individualistic society these political pressures are commonly dealt with by new laws that intensify adversarial relationships between government and business, creating complex legal procedures and entanglements that take a great deal of time and reduce companies' flexibility to respond to the issues effectively. In management-labor relations, contractual and adversarial procedures restrict flexible assignments of people, the introduction of changed technology, and appropriate retraining.

In the United Kingdom, where individualism also dominates, cleavages between management and labor, and between different social classes, have led to serious strikes that have hindered prompt response to economic adversity. These difficulties have been greatly exacerbated by England's loss of its colonies, and the decline of its geopolitical influence and its economic competitiveness. In the 1950s there was a very broad consensus between the Conservatives and mainstream Labour parties supporting a Keynesian stimulus to the economy, an expansion of the welfare system, and an extensive role for government planning so that inflation and recession could be avoided. A similar spirit of communitarian cooperation, albeit achieved through individualistic patterns, led to social contracts between labor and management at a national level in the 1973–75 period. These efforts at greater cooperation between different elements of British society did not take full account of the competitive problems that England faced, and they involved more welfare payments than the nation was able to afford. As England lost its competitiveness, and its economic conditions worsened, the basis for communitarian agreement unraveled. Unemployment grew and England could no longer enjoy the levels of welfare originally agreed to. As various groups within England became polarized, the society has now reverted to an even more extreme form of individualism. It provides some guidance for adjusting to the needed austerity, but it lacks the broad communitarian base on which to build a new consensus.

Mexico is also plagued by fundamental problems of governability. Although government leaders have become more pragmatic, the gap between the revolutionary ideals to which leaders are officially committed and their actual behavior has led to skepticism on the part of the public about the purposes of the regime. In fact, the personal goals of many of the leaders who rule in the name of communitarian revolutionary cooperation have alienated public support for the government, which now finds it difficult to deal effectively with problems, despite leaders' efforts to find pragmatic solutions.

By comparison with the more individualistic extremes of England and the United States, France now seems closer to gaining a consensus on how to deal with basic national issues. Paradoxically, Mitterrand has brought the Socialists into a broad-based consensus supporting his efforts to achieve greater competitiveness in government enterprises as well as in private ones.

Adaptability to Rising and Declining Industries

In countries where individualistic ideology is strongest, leaders believe that the open market will permit the most rapid adaptation by eliminating companies and sectors that are unable to compete. Some individualistic countries that have remained open to international competition have indeed adapted more rapidly. In contrast, Latin American countries, whose leaders pursued a policy of import substitution and then erected continuing high quotas on imports, protected inefficient sectors that could not stand up to international competition.

However, in societies adhering to the strongest individualistic ideology and with democratic governments, the changes in international competition are now so great that there is a popular clamor for protectionism in declining sectors. The outcome is that governments give greater support to declining sectors than to new sectors that are scrambling to adapt.

Even countries like Brazil are willing to allocate more of their resources to minicomputers, which are important for future development. It is open to debate, however, whether Brazil has the industrial, technological, and organizational skills to bring its minicomputers up to international levels of competition in the foreseeable future. Brazil may well continue to support an uncompetitive industry, but at least it is giving special financial and protectionist support to a sector that is likely to become more, rather than less, important in the future.

Germany, and especially Japan, Korea, and Taiwan can allocate resources, concentrate efforts, and give national support to industries likely to be more important in the future. Germany pays closest attention to its "fulcrum" industries, which have great potential for future growth and are crucial for future national adaptation.

The essence of Japanese communitarianism is that the nation and its companies cooperate to change their comparative advantage. Although initiatives are in the hands of individual companies, the government plays a supportive role in insuring that capital, technological know-how, and market opportunities are made available at the appropriate time as companies move to sectors that will be important for the future. The Korean government has also taken great initiative in telling companies how to move to more advanced sectors and in making capital available to companies that take its advice. Although the Korean government is losing its control over companies as they develop their own strong assets, the large Korean companies have very much internalized this pattern of continuously moving into more advanced sectors. The Taiwan government has had less control over companies than the Korean government, but it too has encouraged fiscal and monetary policies, investments, and government-owned companies producing steel and petrochemical feedstocks that make it easy for private sector companies using these products to concentrate on upgrading labor and technology so that they may compete effectively in growing sectors.

The effort of a nation relying on communitarian principles to meet international competition can take many forms. In Japan it has led to the nurturing of certain large firms capable of succeeding in international competition. There, large businesses in basic industry are seen as essential for the nation and are therefore given a legitimacy greater than that given smaller companies that produce only for Japanese consumers. In

Korea, although some people object to the power of the *chaebol* and of unfair links between politicians and business leaders, the idea of certain large firms useful to the nation has been widely accepted. In Taiwan, although there has been more encouragement of small business than in Korea, the idea that certain sizable firms are necessary for the nation's welfare is widely accepted. In the United States, by contrast, there has been wider support for smaller independent firms that are seen as the source of innovation, entrepreneurialism, and American individualism at its best. This preference for smaller independent firms in the United States has helped fuel strong antitrust action and other policies favorable to smaller firms.

Communitarian nations can expect that individual firms, managers, employees, and ordinary citizens will all give great weight to the nation as a whole. They can also assume that the central government will dominate local governments. Although smaller countries naturally find it easier for the central government to control local developments, in general, East Asian communitarian nations, regardless of size, have a higher concentration of talent, resources, and power in the central government, which also has great leverage over local government. Germany is an interesting case of a communitarian nation that is far less centralized than Japan, giving much more power to provincial states. In the United States and Brazil, where communitarianism is weaker, there is considerable decentralization of power to the state, thus making coordination of economic and educational policy at the national level more difficult.

Societies with individualistic ideology have a very different attitude toward property rights, including rights to new technology, than countries with a communitarian ideology.

England and the United States, believing firmly that property rights should be protected, have laws strongly protecting companies and individuals that have invented and developed new technology. Although certain rights are internationally recognized, the later developing countries, especially those with less commitment to individualism, have considered it in their countries' interests to diffuse new technology as rapidly as possible to those of their companies that can make use of it. They are less interested, therefore, in protecting the original developers of new technology. Instead, they encourage the transfer of technology to their own companies by any means. These differences pose major difficulties in international relations between countries that have pioneered new technology and those that have been eager to copy or adapt it for their own future development paying little or nothing for these rights.

The most democratic, individualistic societies have found it difficult to adhere to the principle of keeping their markets completely open for their declining sectors. As unemployment rises, as the pace of change quickens, and as the fear of future economic problems grows, groups adversely affected have mobilized resources to maintain themselves artificially long after their sector lost its competitiveness. Even when governments offer to use only temporary adjustments to help the declining sectors, the protection and support commonly continues far beyond the original plans for a "transitional" period of adjustment.

Whether declining sectors can adjust rapidly to new conditions has not yet been fully tested in the communitarian countries of East Asia. Until now, the economies there have been growing, few sectors have been declining, and unemployment has been relatively low. In general, however, bureaucrats and business leaders who speak for the business community try to form a consensus to concentrate resources in areas important for the future and to retrench from declining sectors with as little loss as possible so that important comparative advantages can be sustained in the future. In these societies it seems more important to move rapidly from labor-intensive industries to heavy industries, to high-tech industries, and to efficient service-oriented industries. There is also a continuing effort to modernize heavy industry, using automation and other new technology so it can remain competitive on world markets. As these societies democratize, they are subject to the same political pressures from declining sectors as other societies, but their central governments tend to persist in pressing for overall national economic interests. Officials help reduce production capacity in noncompetitive sectors as speedily as possible so that the most outmoded equipment is removed and significant parts of the declining sectors remain as competitive as possible.

PROPOSITION 2. Developments in the next decades are likely to reinforce the ranking of nations in terms of ideological strength.

Some of the forces shaping the future to which ideologies must adapt are the following:

Increasing Scale and Interconnectedness

Institutions, private and public, have reached unprecedented scale. Private firms, whether measured by numbers of employees, assets, sales, or scope of activity, have grown enormously. Firms have achieved levels of internal complexity impossible in earlier eras before new technology permitted stepped-up communication and control. At the same time, linkages with outside organizations, public and private, have expanded in an effort to keep up with these changes. Governmental institutions have grown at a comparable rate.

In manufacturing, the variety of products produced, the number of parts required, and the scope of subassemblies have grown at explosive rates. To cope with this new scale, manufacturing firms have expanded their geographical reach, not only in finding new sources and in marketing, but in locating the manufacturing operations themselves. Internal organizations have become increasingly differentiated to cope with the complexity.

Marketing organizations have expanded similarly. Led by the largest Japanese trading companies, which by the mid-1980s had over $60 billion of sales per year through offices in over 100 countries, commercial firms have grown to comparable levels of scale, internal complexity, and breadth of external relations. Operations have become more efficient, both in manufacturing and in marketing, to permit the span of control needed to manage these complex interconnections.

Financial institutions have expanded their global reach, information networks, and turnover funds at a pace unimaginable only a few decades ago. Stock markets have grown and are now moving toward genuinely worldwide activity.

World resources have been exploited on a much grander scale. They are transported greater distances at faster speed.

The extensive use of resources has had an impact on local and global ecological systems far beyond previous levels. The use of water resources, industrial emissions into rivers and into the atmosphere, have increasingly impacted areas far beyond the localities where industry is situated.

Increasing Transborder Connections

As the scale of activity has expanded, as the speed of transportation and communication has increased, more activities are conducted beyond old administrative boundaries. New problems have arisen that require coordination at higher levels, either through creating new transborder institutions or through the cooperation of older administrative units or both. Nations must now deal with global problems that require coordination at higher levels within the country and at the international level.

Communications beyond borders require common languages. But they also require higher levels of common understanding and agreements about the procedures for dealing with various issues and about the measures that can be taken to resolve problems that arise.

Greatly Increased Efficiency in Manufacturing

The term "second industrial revolution" has been coined to describe the breakthrough in manufacturing technology that is now occurring. The new breakthroughs are making it possible to expand the quantity and improve the quality of goods that can be produced with given amounts of capital, labor, and other resources.

Just as the agricultural revolution greatly reduced the proportion of the work force required to feed a given population, so the new revolution in manufacturing is reducing the proportion of the labor force required to manufacture the goods demanded by industrial societies. In past decades, when the demand for the quantity and variety of manufactured products increased, the proportion of the work force engaged in manufacturing could remain relatively stable in advanced industrial societies despite productivity increases. In recent decades, however, productivity has increased even more rapidly than demand. Now the proportion of people required to manufacture the goods desired has begun to fall off in the advanced industrial countries. The spread of industrial know-how to other countries has speeded up this trend toward a declining manufacturing work force in those countries that industrialized earlier, but it has not been the only cause of that decline.

The development of microelectronics is greatly accelerating the efficiency of production, greatly reducing the labor required in manufacturing, greatly increasing the control over the productive process, and at the same time creating new flexibility in the variety of goods produced. The revolution in microelectronics is already reflected in numerically controlled machine tools, and it is beginning to be reflected in computer-aided design and in flexible manufacturing systems. A decade or more may elapse before flexible manufacturing systems, or even the cells and modules linking two or more machine tools, are installed on a widespread basis, but there is no question that microelectronic controls are reducing the need for labor inputs in manufacturing.

Greatly Increased Impact on People

The globalization of manufacturing, transport, communication, and marketing and the new technologies have permitted change to occur at an unprecedented scale in the nature and location of economic activities. As coal has been replaced by oil, as new manufacturing processes replace old, and as new facilities are located in countries other than the home country, massive reorganization in economic activity is required. These changes carry the potential for causing swifter and larger-scale disruption in people's livelihood than ever before. The reduced scale or closing of heavy manufacturing plants has already eliminated jobs for hundreds of thousands of workers in the earlier industrialized countries of Europe and North America within a very brief period of time.

Because of rapid changes in technology, workers can no longer rely on their technical specializations to provide a stable career. The borderlines between specializations become increasingly blurred, some specializations are being replaced, new specializations are being constantly created, new combinations of skills are required. At the very least, new training is necessary so that people adversely affected can continue to be gainfully employed. Not only are people dislocated from one geographical area or firm to another, but their entire skill and career lines are disrupted by these fast-paced changes in technology and organization.

The scope of these economic dislocations has created considerable anxiety among workers in many sectors of industrial society as they become aware of the unpredictability of the changes that have such a powerful effect on their lives and yet over which they have so little control.

The Heightening of Global Competition

The lowering of international transport costs has increased the proportion of manufactured goods sold in international markets. Many manufactured goods formerly sold almost wholly within a given country are subject to competitive pressures from imported products. Global markets have made production possible in quantities far beyond those known when goods were produced largely for national markets. The spread of industrial know-how around the world and the intensified international competition have seriously disrupted older industrial countries. The loss of markets for mature industries and the resulting unemployment create new pressures to become more competitive or to use political supports to maintain industries the countries might otherwise lose.

The communitarian societies of East Asia (Japan, South Korea, and Taiwan) have set the pace for the new international competitive environment. The commitment of many parts of their societies to work together has given them a flexibility in devising new institutions and procedures, and in using new technology. They are thus adapting to changing economic circumstances more rapidly than older industrial countries.

Many Westerners would like to believe that the growing superiority of Japan and South Korea in international markets is due primarily to certain specific factors: exchange rates, closed Japanese markets, or the cost of capital. While there are nontariff obstacles to the penetration of foreign goods into the

Japanese markets, Japan is not the only country with such obstacles. Since 1978, the dollar has increased in value compared to the yen but during the fifteen-year period beginning in 1971 the exchange declined from 360 yen to the dollar to 160 yen to the dollar. Japanese productivity continues to rise much faster than Western productivity, and adjustments in the exchange rate are merely temporary solutions. Westerners have been slow to recognize that effective adjustments in the complex contemporary world require a higher level of domestic coordination than is possible where rugged individualism supports lengthy legalistic procedures, adversarial relations, and narrow, short-term financial measures of success, slowing down adaptation to these new trends.

PROPOSITION 3. If East Asian nations continue to be more competitive than other industrial nations, the world trading system will become more communitarian, with increased integration of business firms around the world and more global management of competition.

It is of course possible that those nations with a more individualistic ideology will rapidly increase their ability to adapt to the changes described above, perhaps by achieving a new mix of ideological elements. But if the communitarian nations continue to be more successful in competing in international markets and continue to accumulate more assets, it follows that they will have increased leverage to influence developments in the future world trading system. It also follows that they will use their influence to forge a system that better fits their ideology. To be sure, there is no simple fit between ideological patterns and the international economic order. Many other forces aside from ideology influence the shape of the international economy. But to the extent that ideological patterns do shape the world order and thus that the communitarian nations will play a larger role in shaping it, we would expect at least two major changes:

1. Integration and interconnectedness of business firms around the world will increase. Even without the underpinning of communitarian ideology, in many key industrial sec-

tors the number of major firms around the world is decreasing as a small number of world-class firms is beginning to dominate the market. Not only have national champions emerged, but major national and multinational firms based in one continent are increasingly linking up with major firms in other continents in complex patterns of cooperation and competition. The links between American and Japanese auto companies, between GM and Toyota, between Ford and Mazda, between Chrysler and Mitsubishi have grown rapidly and are paralleled by links in other sectors such as aerospace, computers, consumer electronics, chemicals, pharmaceuticals, and financial services. Economies of scale, access to local markets, the high costs of R&D, the transformation of noncompetitive manufacturing firms into service firms for competitive manufacturers in other countries all reinforce the growing tendency for firms to merge, develop joint ventures, and otherwise cooperate in design, manufacturing, marketing, and sales.

But the nature of these links will be more communitarian as East Asian firms dominate world markets. Former Japanese *zaibatsu* (financial combines)-related firms have closer relations with each other than with other firms, not only in business dealings but in personal networks at many different levels between firms. Even the Japanese bank groups that are not *zaibatsu*-related tend to develop networks of business and personal relations between different firms. Networks link department stores, regional private railways, real estate agencies and other firms.

The same is true between large Japanese manufacturing firms and their subsidiaries and their suppliers. Rather than give specifications of products they wish to buy and purchase from the lowest bidder as many American manufacturers do, many large Japanese manufacturing firms work closely with several suppliers, who may be in competition with each other, jointly developing new rounds of products. Japanese firms feel that the American individualistic system of contractual relations between firms has high transaction costs involving lawyers, planning for contingencies if other parties fail to meet their obligations, and inflexibilities. They feel that stronger personal networks, involving broader common communitarian concerns, can link firms and permit greater flexibility, more rapid development of new products, and savings of transaction costs. Japanese manufacturing firms going abroad tend to take along their own suppliers, their banks, their construction firms, and related service-sector firms. These relationships are rarely exclusive, especially as Japanese firms move abroad, but foreign firms that hope to enter into business relations with these firms will necessarily have to develop similar close less contractual relations. If Japanese firms continue to expand abroad, one would expect this pattern of relationships to expand accordingly.

2. Globally managed competition is increasingly likely to supplement "free trade" as a model of the world trading system. As mature industrial nations are buffeted by the rapid introduction of new manufacturing skills in Japan and newly industrializing countries, they are seeking ways to defend their own workers and keep down unemployment or at best allow the introduction of newly competitive foreign products only on a measured basis. The superior competitiveness of Japan in many sectors is already causing the United States, for example, to extend the practice of "managed competition" to important areas where their products are no longer as competitive. The "managed competition" generally takes the form of a "voluntary restraint agreement" whereby the Japanese firms agree not to ship more than a certain number of a type of goods (textiles, televisions, steel, automobiles, semiconductors). Within this managed framework, competition is permitted. The worldwide multifiber agreement is an example of managed international competition. The challenge is to manage it in such a way as to allow new entrants and to keep up the competitive pressures for improved performance and lower costs.

Although competition within Japan is very fierce, it takes place within the framework of the government and sectoral associations which define the scope and nature of activity and permit and even encourage some cooperation between firms in research and development, setting standards, market segmentation, pollution control, and the like. It is considered that this effort at "managed competition" brings common, that is, communitarian, benefits for the entire sector. If Japan continues to be as successful in the future as in the past, we can expect that foreign countries will be willing to accept more "voluntary restraint agreements" to limit the impact of goods on their markets. We can also expect that as Japanese leverage on international trade continues they will increasingly bring onto the world stage the patterns of "managed competition" with which they are familiar. These patterns are unlikely to replace the model of "free trade" for all product areas, but they will probably become more important in an increasing number of areas.

Although Western nations have barely begun to question their ideological assumptions, they are beginning to acknowledge the need for coping with East Asia's competitive successes. Brazil and Mexico, which had not considered the East Asian nations in terms of their competitive impact until recently, are now aware of the new highly intensified competitive environment both as a problem and as a potential opportunity. Although the European Economic Community has erected some protectionist barriers against the more hard-driving East Asian countries, this has not arrested the competitive pressure. The United States, which has been relatively more open to outside products, has been even more affected by the competitive countries of East Asia.

Most nations recognize the value of international commerce and would like to limit the protectionism that prevents their consumers from gaining the benefits of international trade. The question is therefore how they can adjust their systems to be competitive with those of the communitarian East Asian nations. It will be difficult to avoid more communitarianism.

In Europe in the 1980s "communitarianism" was a bad name because of the disappointing experience in France and Britain with government planning, the "welfare state," and attempts to prop up industrial losers. Governments yielded to inefficiency and uncompetitiveness. Welfare systems siphoned funds from investment, stifling the nation's ability to compete and creating disincentives to work. Consequently some managers in the United States and elsewhere hoped to weaken or even kill trade unions, cut government expenses, and push for business interests even at the risk of strong antibusiness reactions.

But the major trend now seems to be toward a more communitarian solution, and the new competitive environment clearly demands a different version of communitarianism that restrains government spending and excessive regulations yet increases the range of cooperation between business management, labor, and government. The community, whether involving the government or private actors working together, is allowed to define duties of membership. Some principles of fairness, sharing the pain as well as the gain, are required to keep the wholehearted support of the public. Government need not be large but it plays a role in helping to define community need, align policies, and generate consensus. This new version of communitarianism has wide support in many countries, suggesting a partial convergence of many nations toward a greater common ground ideologically. In the United States, labor and management are increasing their areas of cooperation, and companies are increasingly automating factories. Even under Socialist leadership, France put pressure on state industries to increase their efficiency. Germany is trying to accelerate the trend toward new fulcrum industries that can remain internationally competitive. England, like France, is trying to make its public industry sectors more efficient and to curtail increases in public spending. Brazil and Mexico are just beginning to be more responsive to international competitive pressures by improving their industrial efficiency and accelerating the use of computers and high technology.

All these efforts, however, seem inadequate thus far in stemming the competitive pressures from East Asia. The search for new ways of gaining the kind of internal consensus appropriate to this new challenge is continuing in each country. The French are getting closer to reaching a national communitarian consensus about advancing efficiency in production. In the United States, labor has shown new flexibility in job assignment and rationalization of wages. Many business leaders acknowledge the need to work with rather than against labor in dealing with their employees' long-term needs so as to obtain their cooperation in improving product quality and manufacturing or service efficiency. The U.S. government too has begun to relax its antitrust activity and to take a less adversarial position toward big business. The recent recognition that the interests of government, business, and labor are closely bound together will undoubtedly continue to move the most individualistic nations in a communitarian direction.

APPLYING IDEOLOGICAL ANALYSIS

Ideological analysis can be useful in calling attention to certain fundamental issues and pinpointing underlying problems that might otherwise be overlooked. Many leaders in government and business deal with issues only within the limited framework of their personal ideological assumptions without subjecting them to critical examination. Unaware of differences in ideology in the real world that affect the outcome of their decisions, they leave themselves open to errors by inadvertence. American managers ideologically blinded to a range of responses consistent with communitarian ideology may find themselves locked into adversarial relationships with government and labor on issues that require more flexible and cooperative relationships. Examining their own ideological assumptions along with the ideology of other nations thus discloses to managers a broader range of possible responses.

Managers who become involved in business relations outside their own nation, governmental leaders involved in foreign relations, and workers in international organizations are confronted with the issue of how to deal with people who hold different ideological assumptions. Western managers, in particular, like to believe that they are "objective" and "value-free" and that global organizations will naturally reflect their assumptions. In fact, they must devise ways to work with people holding very different assumptions. Among the issues they must confront are the following:

1. How will membership in these global systems be defined and enforced? Who will decide which communities have a stake in the outcome, and how will community need be defined?

2. By what procedures will consensus be achieved? To what extent will it be imposed by leaders in the name of efficiency and meritocratic norms, and to what extent will it be responsive to the demands of various groups? To what extent will the right to manage come from ownership and property rights,

and to what extent from local groups, communities, and governments?

3. How will national governments be intertwined in the governance of global systems?

4. How will the role of various specialized organizations be coordinated? How will a system be devised sufficiently flexible to adjust to changing circumstances?

5. What will be the underlying principles of the new global ideology that will serve as a basis for people from different ideological backgrounds to work together?

Multinational corporations, like nations, are already trying to cope with the ideologies of the countries where they manufacture and market. The consequence of trying to be effective abroad by adopting new ways of thinking and acting can and ought to be that managers will try to understand the ideological assumptions they have unthinkingly used at home. Practices valuable in other countries may be adapted for even better use at home. As each nation begins to examine its own assumptions in the light of others it had not before examined, let alone understood, a new world system might emerge in which nations can better help their citizens cope with change while bringing them the benefits of global production and marketing.

CONTRIBUTORS

CHRISTOPHER S. ALLEN is an assistant professor of political science at the University of Georgia and from 1984–86 was a research fellow at the Harvard Business School. He is working on a book about employer and trade union responses to structural and technological change in West Germany. Upon receiving his Ph.D from Brandeis University he became a research associate at the Center for European Studies, Harvard University, where he was cochair of the Labor Study Group. Dr. Allen is the author of numerous articles and papers, and he is a coauthor of *Unions and Economic Crisis: Great Britain, West Germany and Sweden* (George Allen and Unwin, 1984).

VINCENT S. R. BRANDT is a Visiting Scholar at the Korea Institute, Harvard University. Upon graduating from Harvard College, Dr. Brandt joined the United States Foreign Service and worked in France, Korea, Japan, and Washington. In 1969 he received his Ph.D in social anthropology from Harvard. Since then he has taught East Asian Studies at Harvard, Swarthmore College, and Seoul National University. He has served as a consultant for, among others, the World Bank, UNESCO, and the Korea Development Institute. He is also the author of numerous articles and a book entitled *A Korean Village: Between Farm and Sea.*

JORGE I. DOMÍNGUEZ is professor of government at Harvard University, where he specializes in Latin American affairs. He is the author and coauthor of seven books, among which the best known are *Cuba: Order and Revolution* (1978) and *Insurrection or Loyalty: The Breakdown of the Spanish American Empire* (1980). Professor Dominguez serves on the editorial board of, among other publications, *The Political Science Quarterly*, and he is a past president of the Latin American Studies Association.

JOEL KRIEGER is the Whitehead Professor of Critical Thought at Wellesley College, where he teaches political and social theory, as well as comparative European politics. A graduate of Yale, Professor Krieger received his Ph.D from Harvard in political science. He is the author of many articles and books on Britain, most importantly the highly acclaimed *Undermining Capitalism: State Ownership and the Dialectic of Control in the British Coal Industry*. His latest book, *Reagan, Thatcher, and the Politics of Decline*, will be published in the fall of 1986 by Oxford University Press.

GEORGE C. LODGE is professor of business administration at the Harvard Business School, where he teaches Business, Government, and the International Economy in the Advanced Management Program and Human Resource Management in the MBA program. After graduation from Harvard College in 1950 Professor Lodge was a political reporter before entering government service; he was director of information of the U.S. Department of Labor, and then assistant secretary of labor for international affairs. He joined the Harvard faculty in 1963, and is the author of numerous articles and books, including *Spearheads of Democracy; Engines of Change: United States Interests and Revolution in Latin America; The New American Ideology;* and *The American Disease.* In 1985 he joined Professor Bruce Scott in editing *U.S. Competitiveness in the World Economy.*

JANICE McCORMICK is associate professor of business administration at the Harvard Business School, where she teaches human resource management and employee relations in the MBA program. A specialist in French industrial relations, Professor McCormick received a Ph.D in political science from Harvard. She is the author of numerous articles, papers, and Harvard Business School cases. Her book (with D. Quinn Mills) *Industrial Relations in Transition* was published last year by John Wiley and Sons.

EZRA F. VOGEL is professor of sociology at Harvard, formerly the director of the East Asian Research Center and chairman of the Council on East Asian Studies. Among Professor Vogel's publications are *Japan's New Middle Class* (1963), *Canton Under Communism* (1969) and the bestseller *Japan as Number 1: Lessons for America* (1979). Last year Professor Vogel's latest book, *Comeback,* was published. In this work he attempts, through a series of case studies, to spell out how the United States can learn from the Japanese experience and compete successfully in the global economy.

EDWIN A. WINCKLER is a specialist in Chinese affairs at the East Asian Institute of Columbia University. A 1963 graduate in government of Harvard College, Dr. Winckler pursued his studies at the London School of Economics and Cornell University; he received his Ph.D from Harvard in 1974. He has taught Chinese studies in the sociology departments of both Columbia and Harvard, and he has served as a consultant to RAND, BA Asia Ltd., and the U.S. Department of State. Dr. Winckler is the author of numerous articles on Chinese affairs.

NOTES

CHAPTER 1

1. See Antoine L. Destutt de Tracy, *Elements d'Ideologie*, 2d ed. (Brussels, 1826); Max Weber, *The Protestant Ethic and the Spirit of Capitalism*, trans. Talcott Parsons (London: George Allen and Unwin, 1930); Karl Mannheim, *Ideology and Utopia* (New York: Harcourt, Brace and Co., 1953); George Lichtheim, "The Concept of Ideology," in *The Concept of Ideology and Other Essays* (New York: Random House, Vintage Books, 1967); George C. Lodge, *The New American Ideology* (New York: Alfred A. Knopf, 1975), chap. 1; and John B. Thompson, *Studies in the Theory of Ideology* (Berkeley and Los Angeles: University of California Press, 1984). Our use of ideology also seems close to that of Martin Seliger in *Ideology and Politics* (London: George Allen and Unwin, 1976). See also the definition of ideology in the *Oxford English Dictionary:* "1. The science of ideas; that department of philosophy or psychology which deals with the origin and nature of ideas. . . . "

2. Samuel Huntington, *American Politics: The Promise of Disharmony* (Cambridge, Mass.: Harvard University Press, 1981), 63.

3. Alexis de Tocqueville, *Democracy in America*, ed. J. P. Mayer, trans. George Lawrence (1835; reprint, Garden City: Anchor Books, 1969), p. 506; quoted in Robert N. Bellah et al., *Habits of the Heart* (Berkeley: University of California Press, 1985), 37.

4. *Essays and Lectures* (New York: Library of America, 1983), 261–62; quoted in Bellah, *Habits*, 56.

5. Huntington, *American Politics*, 39.

6. See Bruce R. Scott and George C. Lodge, eds., *U.S. Competitiveness in the World Economy* (Boston: Harvard Business School Press, 1985), chap. 2.

7. Chalmers Johnson, "The Industrial Policy Debate Reexamined," *California Management Review* 27, no. 1 (Fall 1984): 75.

8. Ezra F. Vogel, *Comeback* (New York: Simon and Schuster, 1985), 62.

9. Bruce R. Scott and George C. Lodge, "U.S. Competitiveness in the World Economy: A Problem of Premises," HBS Working Paper #9-785-013 (Boston: Harvard Business School, 1984), 12–14.

10. Peter L. Berger, "The Asian Experience and Caribbean Development," *Worldview*, October 1984, 6.

11. The nature and consequences of ideological ambivalence are dealt with extensively by George C. Lodge in *The American Disease* (New York: Alfred A. Knopf, 1984). They are also treated in a most interesting way in Bellah et al., *Habits of the Heart.*

CHAPTER 2

1. A. Lawrence Lowell, *The Government of England,* 2 vols. (New York, 1908), Preface; quoted in Samuel H. Beer, *The British Political System* (New York: Random House, 1974), 3.

2. Bill Jones and Dennis Kavanagh, *British Politics Today* (Manchester: Manchester University Press, 1984), 1–3.

3. John Dearlove and Peter Saunders, *Introduction to British Politics* (Cambridge, England: Polity, 1984), 1.

4. Samuel H. Beer, *British Politics in the Collectivist Age* (New York: Vintage Books, 1969), xiii.

5. J. T. Winkler, "Corporatism," *Archives européenne de sociologie* 17, no. 1 (1976): 105, as quoted in David Held and Joel Krieger, "Theories of the State: Some Competing Claims," in *The State in Capitalist Europe,* ed. Stephen Bornstein et al. (London: Allen & Unwin, 1984), 12.

6. Leo Panitch, "The Development of Corporatism in Liberal Democracies," *Comparative Political Studies* 10, no. 1 (1977): 61. Much of the following discussion of corporatism is based on Held and Krieger, "Theories of the State," 12–14.

7. Beer, *Collectivist Age,* 5.

8. "Introduction: Central Perspectives on the Modern State," in *States and Societies,* ed. David Held et al. (Oxford: Martin Robertson, 1983), 1–23.

9. Beer, *Collectivist Age,* 9–10.

10. Barry Supple, "States and Industrialization: Britain and Germany in the Nineteenth Century," in Held, *States and Societies,* 173.

11. E. J. Hobsbawm, *Industry and Empire* (Harmondsworth: Penguin/Pelican, 1983), 106.

12. Geoffrey Ingham, *Capitalism Divided? The City and Industry in British Social Development* (London: Macmillan, 1984), 114ff.

13. T. H. Marshall, "Citizenship and Social Class," in Held, *States and Societies,* 249.

14. Dorothy Thompson, *The Chartists: Popular Politics in the Industrial Revolution* (New York: Pantheon, 1984), 5.

15. Marshall, "Citizenship," 258.

16. Beer, *Collectivist Age,* 6–32.

17. Held and Krieger, "Theories of the State," 12.

18. Nigel Harris, *Competition and the Corporate Society* (London: Methuen, 1972), cited in Panitch, "Development of Corporatism."

19. Philippe C. Schmitter, "Still the Century of Corporatism?" *Review of Politics* 32, no. 1 (1974): 105.

20. Ibid., 93–94.

21. D. Marsh and W. Grant, "Tripartism: Reality or Myth?" *Government and Opposition* 10, no. 2 (1977): 195–211.

22. George Ross, "What is Progressive about Unions? Reflections on Trade Unions and Economic Crisis," *Theory and Society* 10, no. 5 (1981): 612.

23. Adam Przeworski and Michael Wallerstein, "Democratic Capitalism at the Crossroads," *Democracy* 2, no. 3 (1982): 57.

24. Bob Jessop et al., "Authoritarian Populism, Two Nations and Thatcherism," *New Left Review*, no.147 (September–October 1984): 39.

25. Alan Fox and Allan Flanders, "The Reform of Collective Bargaining: From Donovan to Durkheim," *British Journal of Industrial Relations* 7, no. 2 (1969): 151–80; see *Report of the Royal Commission on Trade Unions and Employers Associations 1965–1968*, Cmnd. 362 (1969).

26. TUC-Labour Party Liaison Committee, "Economic Policy and the Cost of Living"[The "Social Contract"] (February 1973); see Stephen Bornstein, "States and Unions: From Postwar Settlement to Contemporary Stalemate" in Bornstein, *State in Capitalist Europe*, 88.

27. Bornstein, "States and Unions," 67.

28. Anthony Sampson, *The Changing Anatomy of Britain* (New York: Random House, 1982), xi.

29. Ibid.

30. Beer, *British Political System*, 157.

31. Huw Benyon and Peter McMylor, "Decisive Power: The New Tory State against the Miners," in Huw Benyon, ed., *Digging Deeper* (London: Verso, 1984), 35.

32. "Appomatox or Civil War?" *The Economist*, 27 May 1978; Benyon and McMylor, "Decisive Power," 35–36.

33. In addition to Benyon, *Digging Deeper*, see especially David Reed and Olivia Adamson, *Miners Strike 1984–1985* (London: Larkin Publications, 1985).

34. Michael O'Higgins, "Inequality, Redistribution and Recession: The British Experience, 1976–1982" (Paper presented to the Conference on the Thatcher Government and British Political Economy, Harvard University Center for European Studies, 19–20 April 1985).

35. OECD, *OECD Economic Surveys, United Kingdom* (January 1986), 35–51.

36. Gavyn Davies, "The Macroeconomic Record of the Conservatives" (Paper presented to the Conference on the Thatcher Government and British Political Economy, Harvard University Center for European Studies, 19–20 April 1985).

37. Commission of the European Communities, *European Economy*, no. 22 (November 1984): 52–53.

38. Ibid.

39. Davies, "Macroeconomic Record."

40. See *The Attack on Inflation after 31st July 1977*, Cmnd. 4882 (1977); *Winning the Battle Against Inflation*, Cmnd. 7293 (1978).

41. Michael O'Higgins, "Privatisation and Social Welfare: Concepts, Analysis and the British Experience" (Paper presented to the Columbia University Seminar on Privatization, May 7, 1985).

42. T. H. Marshall, *Social Policy in the Twentieth Century* (London: Hutchinson, 1975), 95.

43. O'Higgins, "Privatisation and Social Welfare."

44. Tom Rees, "Immigration Policies in the United Kingdom," in Charles Husband, ed., *'Race' in Britain* (London: Hutchinson, 1982), 86–87.

45. Peter A. Hall, "The Role of the State in the Decline of the British Economy," in Bernard Elbaum and William Lazonick, eds., *The Decline of the British Economy* (New York: Oxford University Press, 1986).

46. See Joel Krieger, *Undermining Capitalism: State Ownership and the Dialectic of Control in the British Coal Industry* (Princeton: Princeton University Press, 1983), 277.

47. Andrew Gamble, "The Free Economy and the Strong State," in Ralph Miliband and John Saville, eds., *The Socialist Register 1979* (London: Merlin, 1979).

48. *The Miner: Journal of the National Union of Mineworkers,* special issue, May 1985; Peter Jenkins, "The Rift Round the Miners' Hearth," *Manchester Guardian Weekly,* 17 March 1985, 5.

49. *British Public Opinion* 7, no. 5 (May 1985): 1–3.

50. Anthony Barnett, "Iron Britannia," *New Left Review,* July–August 1982.

CHAPTER 3

1. Jean Boissonnat, "Raymond Barre, Mon Liberalisme," *L'Expansion,* September 1978, 161.

2. Parti socialiste français, *Le Project socialiste pour la France des années 80* (Paris: Club français de livre, 1981), 172.

3. Inspiration for my formulation of the four ideological schools in France comes from Stanley Hoffmann's lectures and writings. His most important formulation of this argument can be found in "Paradoxes of the French Political Community," in Hoffmann, ed., *In Search of France* (Cambridge, Mass.: Harvard University Press, 1963).

4. The best analysis of the political economy of the Third Republic is Richard K. Kuisel, *Capitalism and the State in Modern France: Renovation and Economic Management in the Twentieth Century* (Cambridge, England: Cambridge University Press, 1981).

5. Ibid., 273.

6. Ibid., 275.

7. Boissonnat, "Raymond Barre," 161.

8. Louis Wells, "The Automobile Industry," in Raymond Vernon, ed., *Big Business and the State* (Cambridge, Mass.: Harvard University Press, 1974),

239. The memoirs of Pierre Dreyfus, Renault's president in this period, confirm this interpretation.

9. Interviews with officials.

10. For further analysis of the policies of the socialist government, see my "Thorns Among the Roses: The First Year of the Socialist Experiment," *West European Politics* 6, no. 1 (January 1983): 44–62; and "Apprenticeship for Governing," in H. Machin and V. Wright, eds., *The Socialist Experiment* (Cambridge, England: Cambridge University Press, 1985), 44–63.

11. Linda Bernier, "Study in Contrast: Peugeot Recovers as Renault Gasps for Air," *International Management,* April 1985, 60.

12. This report by INSEE was widely circulated in the press. See Bernier, "Study in Contrasts," 55.

13. Interviews with management, July 1984.

14. Annual reports.

CHAPTER 4

1. For Peter Katzenstein, *A Semi-Sovereign State: Politics and Policies in the Federal Republic* (Philadelphia: Temple University Press, forthcoming 1987), parapublic institutions in Germany are at the intersection of the public and private spheres. Their goal is to contain conflicts among various interest groups, but as parapublic entities they diminish the role of the central state. Among the most significant parapublic institutions are the Federal Reserve system, the Chambers of Industry, the Council of Economic Advisors, the Labor courts, and the elaborate system of worker participation.

2. Gordon Craig, *The Germans* (New York: Putnam, 1982).

3. Katzenstein, *Semi-Sovereign State.*

4. Alexander Gershenkron, *Bread and Democracy in Germany* (Berkeley: University of California Press, 1943).

5. Alfred D. Chandler, Jr., and Herman Daems, *Managerial Hierarchies* (Cambridge, Mass.: Harvard University Press, 1980).

6. David Landes, *The Unbound Prometheus* (Cambridge, England: Cambridge University Press, 1975).

7. See Peter Stearns, "Adaptation to Industrialization: German Workers as a Test Case," *Central European History* 3, no. 4 (December 1970): 303–31.

8. Vernon L. Lidtke, *The Outlawed Party: Social Democracy in Germany, 1878–1890* (Princeton: Princeton University Press, 1966).

9. Eckhard J. Haeberle, "Worker Participation and Entrepreneurial Power in Industrial Organization: An Hypothesis on the German Historical Development" (University of Heidelberg Institute of Political Science, March 1977, Unpublished).

10. For a more thorough discussion of this theme, see Andrei S. Markovits and Christopher S. Allen, "Germany," in Peter Gourevitch et al., *Trade Unions and Economic Crisis* (London: Allen and Unwin, 1984).

11. Gerhard Ritter, *Staatskunst und Kriegshandwerk,* 4 vols. (Munich: R. Oldenbourg, 1954).

12. A. Mendelssohn-Bartholdy, *War and German Society* (New York: H. Fertig, 1971); and Juergen Kocka, *Klassengessellschaft im Kriege* (Gottingen: Vandenhoek und Ruprecht, 1973).

13. Carmen Sirianni, *Work, Community and Power: The Experience of Labor in Europe and America* (Philadelphia: Temple University Press, 1983).

14. Comments by Professor Joseph Auerbach (Harvard Business School Colloquium on Competition and Cartelization, 21 November 1984). Antitrust regulations are one of the most telling examples of individualistic ideological conceptions of the economy, because they assume that a nation of atomized entrepreneurs representing the "natural order" are always and irreparably damaged by "unnatural" and predatory large firms. More seriously here, however, the antitrust advocates failed to realize that the process of firm growth in a capitalist economy almost guarantees "imperfect" competition. In postwar West Germany for example, the Allies broke up the notorious IG Farben chemicals cartel into four "smaller" firms. The three major surviving "offspring" (BASF, Bayer, and Hoechst) are today *each* larger than was IG Farben at its zenith.

15. Gershenkron, *Bread and Democracy.*

16. Andrew Shonfield, *Modern Capitalism* (New York: Oxford University Press, 1969); Jeremiah Reimer, "Crisis and Intervention in the West German Economy" (Ph.D. diss., Cornell University, 1983).

17. Philippe Schmitter and Wolfgang Streeck, eds., *Private Interest Governments: Beyond Market and State* (Los Angeles: Sage, 1985).

18. Michael Piore and Charles Sabel, *The Second Industrial Divide* (New York: Basic Books, 1984); Horst Kern and Michael Schumann, *Das Ende der Arbeitsteilung?* (Munich: Beck, 1984).

19. Bruce R. Scott, "National Strategies" in Bruce R. Scott and George C. Lodge, eds., *U.S. Competitiveness in the World Economy* (Boston: Harvard Business School Press, 1985), 71–143.

20. See Joel Krieger, chap. 2, this volume.

21. Schmitter and Streeck, *Private Interest Governments.*

22. Markovits and Allen, "Germany."

23. *Verband der Chemischen Industrie, Jahresbericht, 1980–81* (Frankfurt, 1981).

24. Edward Crankshaw, *Bismarck* (New York: Viking, 1981).

25. See Robert Kuttner, *The Economic Illusion* (Boston: Houghton Mifflin, 1985) for the "positive sum" economic benefits of public-sector spending.

26. Barnaby Feder, "Europe's Surprising Recovery," *New York Times,* 4 February 1985, sec. D.

27. The term was first popularized during 1983 when the Commonwealth of Massachusetts established an agency to deal with these issues of industrial

adjustment; see Commonwealth of Massachusetts, *Governor's Commission on the Future of Mature Industries,* 1984.

28. Robert Reich, "Bailout: An Essay in Comparative Law and Industrial Structure," *Yale Regulation,* Fall 1985, 163–224.

29. See Charles Sabel, *Work and Politics* (Cambridge, England: Cambridge University Press, 1982), particularly the concluding chapter.

30. Wolfgang Streeck, *Industrial Relations in West Germany* (New York: St. Martin's Press, 1984).

31. The best theoretical treatment of this issue is that of Hans-Rudolf Peters, *Grundlagen der Mesooekonomie und Strukturpolitik* (Bern and Stuttgart: 1981); for a good overview of the literature on various "meso" approaches see Lee E. Preston, "A Perspective on Mesoeconomics" (Wissenschaftzentrum Berlin, Discussion Paper, October 1984).

32. For a review of the major approaches in the U.S. debate, see Christopher S. Allen and Harvey Rishikof, "Tale Thrice Told: A Review of Industrial Policy Proposals," *Journal of Policy Analysis and Management* 4, no. 2 (Winter 1985): 234–49.

33. I distinguish between organizations of "collective capital" in the macroeconomic sense, namely those (such as the BDI in West Germany) that represent the interests of *all* industry, and those that represent the interests of *specific* industries in the mesoeconomic sense. The former have been described by Gerard Braunthal in *The Federation of German Industry in Politics* (Ithaca: Cornell University Press, 1965); and more recently by Wolfgang Streeck, "Neo-Corporatist Industrial Relations and the Economic Crisis in West Germany" (European University Institute Working Paper 97, Florence, 1984) and Philippe Schmitter, "Democratic Theory and Neo-Corporatist Practice," *Social Research* 50, no. 4 (Winter 1983): 885–928, in their "post" or "neo-neo" corporatist literature. Only in Schmitter and Streeck, *Private Interest Governments* has the role of organized capital at the industry level been studied recently.

34. Shonfield, *Modern Capitalism.*

35. "Das Riesen-Monopoly der Deutschen Bank," *Der Spiegel,* February 1985.

36. Interview with Jochen Degkwitz, Deutsche Bank Central Office, Frankfurt, 26 June 1985.

37. For a distinction that one industry association makes between the two terms, see *Verband der Chemischen Industrie,* "Die Rolle der Verbaende im Wirtschaftsund Gesellschaftsystem der Bundesrepublik Deutschland," 14 January 1985.

38. "Fingerhackeln im Suden," *Wirtschaftswoche,* 24 May 1985.

39. Piore and Sabel, *Second Industrial Divide.*

40. Ibid.; also, Kern and Schumann, *Ende der Arbeitsteilung?*

41. These trends, beginning in the 1970s, long predated such American experiments as the United Automobile Workers' Saturn project.

42. Charles Tilly, ed., *The Formation of National States in Western Europe* (Princeton: Princeton University Press, 1975).

CHAPTER 5

1. Bruce R. Scott and George C. Lodge, eds., *U.S. Competitiveness in the World Economy* (Boston: Harvard Business School Press, 1985).

2. George C. Lodge, *The American Disease* (New York: Alfred A. Knopf, 1984); see also Robert N. Bellah et al., *Habits of the Heart* (Berkeley: University of California Press, 1985).

3. Much of this historical discussion is taken from George C. Lodge, *The New American Ideology* (New York: Alfred A. Knopf, 1976).

4. Bernard Bailyn, *The New England Merchants in the Seventeenth Century* (Cambridge, Mass.: Harvard University Press, 1955), 105–6, 134–39.

5. Carl Becker, *The Declaration of Independence* (New York: Alfred A. Knopf, 1964), 27.

6. "Last Will and Testament of Josiah Quincy, Jr.," 1774, as quoted in Bernard Bailyn, *The Ideological Origins of the American Revolution* (Cambridge, Mass.: Belknap Press, 1967), 22.

7. Adrienne Koch and William Peden, eds., *The Life and Selected Writings of Thomas Jefferson* (New York: The Modern Library, 1944), 609. I appreciate but am unconvinced by Gary Wills' provocative argument in his *Inventing America* (Garden City: Doubleday & Co., 1978) that Jefferson was not a Lockean.

8. Letter to John Adams, as quoted in Becker, *Declaration of Independence,* 25.

9. Alexis de Tocqueville, *Democracy in America,* ed. J. P. Mayer, trans. George Lawrence (1835; reprint, Garden City: Anchor Books, 1969), 98.

10. Thomas K. McCraw, "The Politics of Industrial Policy" (Paper prepared for American Enterprise Institute Conference, Washington, D.C., September, 1984), 4–7.

11. Chalmers Johnson, "The Industrial Policy Debate Reexamined," *California Management Review* 27, no. 1 (Fall 1984): 82.

12. Jackson's refusal to charter a new Second Bank of the United States, for example.

13. Arthur M. Schlesinger. Jr., "Ideas and Economic Development," in *Paths of American Thought,* eds. Arthur Schlesinger, Jr., and Morton White (Boston: Houghton Mifflin. 1963), 115.

14. James Willard Hurst, *The Legitimacy of the Business Corporation in the Law of the United States, 1780–1970* (Charlottesville: The University Press of Virginia, 1970), 25, 26.

15. William M. Gouge, *Short History of Paper Money and Banking in the*

United States. (1833; reprint, Montclair, N.J.: Kelley, 1965), as quoted in Hurst, *Legitimacy*, 30.

16. Hurst, *Legitimacy*, 36.

17. Ibid., 58.

18. Hurst, *Legitimacy*, 66–72; see also Lodge, *The New American Ideology*, 128–37, and Alfred D. Chandler Jr., *The Visible Hand* (Cambridge, Mass.: Harvard University Press, 1977).

19. Ellis W. Hawley, "Antitrust and the Association Movement, 1920–1940," in *National Competition Policy, Historians' Perspectives on Antitrust and Government-Business Relationships in the United States* (Washington, D.C.: Office of Special Projects, Bureau of Competition, Federal Trade Commission, August 1981) 109; see also Ellis W. Hawley, "Herbert Hoover, the Commerce Secretariat, and the Vision of an Associative State, 1921–1928," *Journal of American History*, June 1974, 116–40.

20. Hawley, "Herbert Hoover," 108.

21. Ellis W. Hawley, *The New Deal and the Problem of Monopoly* (Princeton: Princeton University Press, 1966), 35.

22. Ibid., 45.

23. Ibid., 67.

24. Ibid., 50.

25. Ibid., 104.

26. Ibid., 484, citing Paul T. Homan, *Political Science Quarterly*, June 1936, 181.

27. Louis Hartz, *The Liberal Tradition in America* (New York: Harcourt, Brace and World, 1955), 260.

28. Quoted in Herman E. Drooss and Charles Gilbert, *American Business History* (Englewood Cliffs N.J.: Prentice-Hall, 1972), 264.

29. Samuel P. Huntington, *American Politics: The Promise of Disharmony* (Cambridge, Mass.: Harvard University Press, 1981).

30. Ibid., 41.

31. *Boston Globe*, 19 March 1982.

32. *Global Competition: The New Reality; The Report of the President's Commission on Industrial Competitiveness*, vol. 1 (Washington, D.C.: January 1985), 1.

33. *Business Week*, 11 March 1985, 56–59.

34. *Steel and the State*, report prepared by the law firm of Verner, Liipert, Bernhard, McPherson and Hand (Washington, D.C., 1984), 2.

35. Lester Thurow, "Revitalizing American Industry: Managing in a Competitive World Economy," *California Management Review* 27, no. 1 (Fall 1984): 11, 12.

36. See Scott, chaps. 2 and 3, in Scott and Lodge, eds., *U.S. Competitiveness.*

37. The concept of a "paradigm" is borrowed from Thomas S. Kuhn, *The*

Structure of Scientific Revolutions (Chicago: University of Chicago Press, 1962).

38. See Bruce R. Scott and George C. Lodge, "U.S. Competitiveness in the World Economy: A Problem of Premises" (Boston: Harvard Business School working paper 9–785–013, 1984) for discussion of the old and new premises; see also John Zysman, *Governments, Markets and Growth* (Ithaca: Cornell University Press, 1983).

39. Letter, February 1983, quoted in Joseph L. Bower and Eric A. Rhenman, "Benevolent Cartels?" (Boston: Harvard Business School working paper 9–785–043, 1985), 1.

40. Congressional Budget Office, "Federal Support of U.S. Business" (Washington, D.C.: Government Printing Office, January 1984), ix–xiv, 40.

41. "Textiles and Apparel: A Negotiated Approach to International Competition," in Scott and Lodge, eds., *U.S. Competitiveness*, 230–32.

42. Robert B. Reich, "Bailout: An Essay in Comparative Law and Industrial Policy," (Cambridge, Mass.: Kennedy School of Government, Harvard University, working paper, 1984), 46.

43. Ibid., 32, 33, 38, 47.

44. Ibid., 69.

45. See Scott and Lodge, "Premises."

46. Richard R. Ellsworth, "Shareholder Wealth, the Cost of Capital and Competitive Decline" (Unpublished paper, Harvard Business School, 10 December 1984), 2. A condensation was published in the *Harvard Business Review*, September–October 1985, 171–83.

47. Ibid., 3, 5.

48. Transcript of "MacNeil-Lehrer Report" television show, 15 February 1982, 2, 4.

49. Irving Bluestone, interview with author, Detroit, 8 September 1981.

50. Richard E. Walton and Leonard A. Schlesinger, "Do Supervisors Thrive in Participative Work Systems?" *Organizational Dynamics*, Winter 1979, 26.

CHAPTER 9

1. Stephen Krasner, "Manipulating International Commodity Markets: Brazilian Coffee Policy, 1906–1962," *Public Policy* 21, no. 4 (Fall 1973): 493–520.

2. Richard Graham, *Britain and the Onset of Modernization in Brazil, 1850–1914* (Cambridge, England: Cambridge University Press, 1972), chaps. 5 and 7; Stanley Stein, *Vassouras, a Brazilian Coffee County, 1850–1900* (Cambridge, Mass.: Harvard University Press, 1957).

3. Florestan Fernandes, *The Negro in Brazilian Society*, trans. J. D. Skiles, A. Brunel, and A. Rothwell (New York: Columbia University Press, 1969); Pierre-Michel Fontaine, "Research in the Political Economy of Afro-Latin America," *Latin American Research Review* 15, no. 2 (1980): 111–41.

4. Quoted in John Humphrey, *Capitalist Control and Workers' Struggle*

in the Brazilian Auto Industry (Princeton: Princeton University Press, 1982), 14.

5. Werner Baer, *The Brazilian Economy: Growth and Development*, 2d ed. (New York: Praeger, 1983); Sylvia Ann Hewlett, "Poverty and Inequality in Brazil," in *Brazil and Mexico: Patterns in Late Development*, ed. S.A. Hewlett and R.S. Weinert (Philadelphia: Institute for the Study of Human Issues Press, 1982); Samuel A. Morley, *Labor Markets and Inequitable Growth: The Case of Authoritarian Capitalism in Brazil* (Cambridge, England: Cambridge University Press, 1982), chaps. 3–5; José Pastore, Hélio Zylberstajn, and Carmen Silvia Pagotto, *Mudança social e pobreza no Brasil: 1970–1980* (São Paulo: Fundação Instituto de Pesquisas Econômicas, 1983); Elisabeth Sadoulet, "Crescimento desigualitário em uma economia subdesenvolvida," *Revista de economia política* 5, no. 2 (April–June 1985): 67–97; Rodolfo Hoffmann, "Distribuição da renda e pobreza entre as famílias no Brasil, de 1980 a 1983," *Revista de economia política* 5, no. 3 (July–September 1985): 50–60.

6. Naciones Unidas, Comisión Económica para America Latina, "Balance Preliminar de la Economia Latinoamericana durante 1984," LC/G.1336 (December 1984), cuadros 2, 3, 6, 13, 14.

7. Secondary analysis of U.S. Information Agency, Instituto de Pesquisas de Opinião e Mercado, Roper Center source document BRUSIAWS22 (N-466 Rio de Janeiro adults), conducted in February–March 1964.

8. Secondary analysis of Instituto de Estudos Sociais e Econômicos, Roper Center source document BRIISR60–15 (N-2168 urban and rural Brazilian adults), conducted in second quarter 1961.

9. Secondary analysis of U.S. Information Agency, International Research Associates, Roper Center source document BRUSIAWS3 (N-501 Rio de Janeiro adults), conducted in May–July 1965.

10. Secondary analysis of Pesquisas e Estudos de Mercado, Ltda., Roper Center source document BRMARP108 (N-318 Rio de Janeiro adults), conducted in September 1969.

11. Secondary analysis of Pesquisas e Estudos de Mercado, Ltda., Roper Center source document BRMARP148 (N-298 Rio de Janeiro adults), conducted in August 1970.

12. Secondary analysis of Pesquisas e Estudos de Mercado, Ltda., Roper Center source document BRMARP140 (N-323 Rio de Janeiro adults), conducted in May 1970; ibid., Roper Center source document BRMARP156 (N-357 probably Rio de Janeiro adults), conducted in January 1971.

13. Kenneth Erickson, *The Brazilian Corporatist State and Working-Class Politics* (Berkeley: University of California Press, 1977).

14. Youssef Cohen, " 'The Benevolent Leviathan': Political Consciousness among Urban Workers under State Corporatism," *American Political Science Review* 76, no. 1 (March 1982): 46–59. Weighted multistaged area probability sample (N-562 urban industrial and service skilled and unskilled workers), conducted in 1972–73 in six southeastern states.

15. Kenneth Mericle, "Corporatist Control of the Working Class: Author-

itarian Brazil since 1964," in *Authoritarianism and Corporatism in Latin America*, ed. James Malloy (Pittsburgh: University of Pittsburgh Press, 1977), 323–31.

16. Maria Helena Moreira Alves, "Grassroot Organizations, Trade Unions and the Church: Challenge to the Controlled *Abertura* in Brazil" (Paper given at the Annual Meeting of the American Political Science Association, New York, 1981), table 3.

17. Humphrey, *Capitalist Control*, chaps. 6–8.

18. Baer, *Brazilian Economy*, 121; Moreira Alves, "Grassroots Organizations," charts 3, 4, 6.

19. Humphrey, *Capitalist Control*, 133–34, 169–70, 200–207.

20. *Lagniappe Letter*, 24 May 1985, 9; *O Estado de São Paulo*, 5 January 1986, 36; Clayton Netz, "Quem comanda os sindicatos," *Exame*, 30 October 1985, 36–42.

21. Steven Topik, "State Autonomy in Economic Policy: Brazil's Experience, 1822–1930," *Journal of Interamerican Studies and World Affairs* 26, no. 4 (November 1984): 449.

22. Wilson Suzigan, "Industrialization and Economic Policy in Historical Perspective,"*Brazilian Economic Studies* 2 (1976): 5–33.

23. Dennis Encarnation, "Note on Comparative Political Economy," 0–384–161 (Boston: Harvard Business School, 1984), 10.

24. Thomas E. Skidmore, *Politics in Brazil, 1930–1964: An Experiment in Democracy* (London: Oxford University Press, 1967), 317. See also 322–30.

25. José Roberto Mendonça de Barros and Douglas H. Graham, "The Brazilian Economic Miracle Revisited: Private and Public Sector Initiative in a Market Economy," *Latin American Research Review* 13, no. 2 (1978): 7–8.

26. Thomas J. Trebat, *Brazil's State-owned Enterprises: A Case Study of the State as Entrepreneur* (Cambridge, England: Cambridge University Press, 1983); Paulo de Castro et al., *A crise do "Bom Patrão"* (Rio de Janeiro: CEDES/APEC).

27. Peter McDonough, *Power and Ideology in Brazil* (Princeton: Princeton University Press, 1981), chaps. 3 and 4. Survey conducted in 1972–73 (N-251).

28. Verner, Liipfert, Bernhard, McPherson, Hand, and Chartered, *The Rise of Steelmaking in the Developing Countries* (Washington: 1984), 67–96.

29. Kenneth Erickson, "State Entrepreneurship, Energy Policy, and the Political Order in Brazil," in *Authoritarian Capitalism: Brazil's Contemporary Economic and Political Development*, ed. T.C. Bruneau and P. Faucher (Boulder: Westview Press, 1981); *Lagniappe Quarterly Report*, 31 July 1985, 5–6.

30. Peter Evans and Gary Gereffi, "Foreign Investment and Dependent Development," in Hewlett and Weinert, *Brazil and Mexico*, 123–24, 149–50; Rhys Jenkins, "Internationalization of Capital and the Semi-Industralized Countries: The Case of the Motor Industry" (Norwich, Norfolk: University of East Anglia, School of Development Studies).

31. Jeffrey Sachs, "Comment," *Brookings Papers on Economic Activity* 2 (1984): 397.

32. Joseph Kahl, *The Measurement of Modernism* (Austin: University of Texas Press, 1968), 104.

33. Jorge I. Domínguez, "Business Nationalism: Latin American National Business Attitudes and Behavior toward Multinational Enterprises," in *Economic Issues and Political Conflict: U.S.-Latin American Relations*, ed. J.I. Domínguez (London: Butterworth, 1982), 52–58.

34. McDonough, *Power and Ideology*, 175–89, 276–80.

35. Domínguez, "Business Nationalism," 54–58.

36. Ramón Barquín, "The Transfer of Computer Technology: A Framework for Policy in the Latin American Nations" (Ph.D. diss., MIT, 1974), 259–60.

37. Elizabeth Hochman, Laurie Timmerman, and Jordan M. Young II, "Nationalism and Informatics: The Brazilian Experience" Columbia University Graduate School of Business (New York, n.p., May 1983).

38. Domínguez, "Business Nationalism," 56.

39. Emanuel Adler, "A Cultural Theory of Change in International Political Economy: Science, Technology, and Computer Policies in Argentina and Brazil" (Ph.D. diss., University of California, Berkeley, 1982), chap. 12, esp. 648–52.

40. Hochman, Timmerman, and Young, "Nationalism and Informatics;" G. Russell Pipe, "New Directions for the Third World," *Datamation*, 1 September 1984.

41. McDonough, *Power and Ideology*, 236. For an analysis of this kind of ideological conflict see Luiz Bresser Pereira, *Pactos políticos, do populismo a redemocratização* (São Paulo: Brasiliense, 1985), chap. 3. For an exploration of priorities for the late 1980s, see Lourenço Dantas Mota, "Um perfil ideológico da Nova República," *O Estado de São Paulo*, 18 August 1985, 6–9.

CHAPTER 10

1. Carlos Fuentes, *The Death of Artemio Cruz*, tr. Sam Hileman (New York: Farrar, Straus & Giroux, 1964), 268.

2. Jorge I. Domínguez, *Insurrection or Loyalty: The Breakdown of the Spanish American Empire* (Cambridge, Mass.: Harvard University Press, 1980).

3. Charles Hale, *Mexican Liberalism in the Age of Mora, 1821–1853* (New Haven: Yale University Press, 1968).

4. Roger Hansen, *The Politics of Mexican Development* (Baltimore: Johns Hopkins University Press, 1971); Raymond Vernon, *The Dilemma of Mexico's Development* (Cambridge, Mass.: Harvard University Press, 1965).

5. Jorge I. Domínguez, "Assessing Human Rights Conditions," in

Enhancing Global Human Rights, Jorge I. Domínguez et al. (New York: McGraw-Hill, 1979), 93–102.

6. Inter-American Development Bank, *Economic and Social Progress in Latin America, 1984* (Washington), 420; Clark W. Reynolds, *The Mexican Economy: Twentieth Century Structure and Growth* (New Haven: Yale University Press, 1970), 9–10.

7. *Comercio exterior* 26 (July 1980): 255; Montek Ahluwalia, Nicholas Carter, and Hollis Chenery, *Growth and Poverty in Developing Countries,* Working Paper no. 309 (Washington, D.C.: The World Bank, 1978), 32; Joel Bergsman, *Income Distribution and Poverty in Mexico,* Working Paper no. 395 (Washington, D.C.: The World Bank, 1980), 41.

8. Shirley Brice Heath, *Telling Tongues: Language Policy in Mexico* (New York: Teachers College Press, Columbia University, 1972), chap. 9.

9. Gabriel Almond and Sidney Verba, *The Civic Culture* (Boston: Little, Brown, 1965), 48, 64, 70, 75.

10. Secondary analysis of Joseph Kahl's "Career Values in Brazil and Mexico," Roper Center source document BRSPEC60 (N-740 white- and blue-collar workers), conducted in 1960.

11. Secondary analysis of U.S. Information Agency, International Research Associates, Roper Center source document MXUSIAWS2 (N-506 Mexico City adults), conducted in February–March 1964.

12. Secondary analysis of U.S. Information Agency, International Research Associates, Roper Center source document BRUSIAWS3 (N-493 Mexico City adults), conducted in May–July 1965.

13. Ann Craig and Wayne Cornelius, "The Political Culture in Mexico: Continuities and Revisionist Interpretations," in *The Civic Culture Revisited,* ed. Gabriel Almond and Sidney Verba (Boston: Little, Brown, 1980), 340–83.

14. Almond and Verba, *The Civic Culture,* 310–12.

15. See note 11.

16. John Booth and Mitchell Seligson, "The Political Culture of Authoritarianism in Mexico," *Latin American Research Review* 19, no. 1 (1984): 106–24. Survey conducted in 1978–79 (N-430 drawn from seven cities in central and northern Mexico).

17. Vega y Asociados, *Algunos problemas sociales, políticos y económicos que afectan al país* (Monterrey: 1979), 5–6, 30–31. Survey conducted in Mexico City, Guadalajara, and Monterrey (N-1723 stratified by social class).

18. Naciones Unidas, Comisión Económica para América Latina y el Caribe, "Balance preliminar de la economía latinoamericana durante 1984," LC/G.1336 (December 1984), cuadro 3.

19. Miguel Basáñez and Roderic Camp, "La nacionalización de la banca y la opinión pública en México," *Foro internacional* 25, no. 2 (October–December 1984): 206. (Random sample, N-4928.)

20. Manuel Compeán, "Estudio sobre la cultura cívica en México: un

análisis comparativo, 1959–1982," Student paper, The Kennedy School of Government, Harvard University, 1983 , 13, 26, 30, 40, 82 (N-186).

21. Kevin Middlebrook, "The Political Economy of Mexican Organized Labor, 1940–1978," Ph.D. diss., Harvard University, 1981), chap. 4 and app. D; Manuel Camacho, "Control sobre el movimiento obrero en México," *Foro internacional* 16, no. 4 (April–June 1976): 496–525; José Luis Reyna, "El movimiento obrero en una situación de crisis: México 1976–1978," *Foro internacional* 19, no. 3 (January–March 1979): 390–401; Ilan Bizberg, "Política laboral y acción sindical en México," *Foro internacional* 25, no. 2 (October–December 1984): 166–89.

22. Middlebrook, "Political Economy," chaps. 5 and 6; Ian Roxborough, *Unions and Politics in Mexico: The Case of the Automobile Industry* (Cambridge, England: Cambridge University Press, 1984).

23. Martin Welge, "Decisionmaking in German Multinationals and Its Impact on External Relationships," in *Governments and Multinationals,* ed. Walter H. Goldberg, with Anant Negandhi (Cambridge Mass.: Oelgeschlager, Gunn and Hain, 1983), 72–73.

24. For his views in English, Miguel de la Madrid, "Mexico: The New Challenges," *Foreign Affairs* 63, no. 1 (Fall 1984): 62–76.

25. *Plan Nacional de Desarrollo, 1983–1988* (Mexico: Secretaría de Programación y Presupuesto, 1983), 38.

26. Dennis Encarnation, "Note on Comparative Political Economy," 0-384-161 (Boston: Harvard Business School, 1984).

27. Marye Tharp Hilger, "Consumer Perceptions of a Public Marketer," University of Texas Institute of Latin American Studies, *Technical Paper Series,* no. 18, Austin, 1978), 6, 16; survey conducted in Monterrey (N-192). CONSASUPO shoppers believed in these stores even more.

28. Dale Story, "Trade Politics in the Third World: A Case Study of the Mexican GATT Decision," *International Organization* 36, no. 4 (Autumn 1982): 767–94.

29. David Ronfeldt, *The Modern Mexican Military: Implications for Mexico's Stability and Security,* N-2288-FF/RC (Santa Monica: The Rand Corporation, 1985).

30. Carlos Arriola, "Los grupos empresariales frente al Estado (1973–1975)," *Foro internacional* 16, no. 4 (April–June 1976): 473–76.

31. Dale Story, "Industrialists, the State, and Public Policy in Mexico" (Paper presented at the National Meeting of the Latin American Studies Association, Bloomington, 1980), 19.

32. Susan Kaufman Purcell, *The Mexican Profit Sharing Decision* (Berkeley: University of California Press, 1975).

33. Story, "Trade Politics," 784–89; and Story, "Public Policy," 19, 28 (N-94).

34. This section draws from Van R. Whiting, Jr., "Transnational Enterprise and the State in Mexico: Constraints on State Regulation of Foreign

Investment, Technology, Inventions, and Trademarks" (Ph.D. diss., Harvard University, 1981), chap. 3.

35. Jorge I. Domínguez, "Business Nationalism: Latin American National Business Attitudes and Behavior toward Multinational Enterprises," in *Economic Issues and Political Conflict: U.S.-Latin American Relations*, ed. Jorge I. Domínguez (London: Butterworth, 1982), 47-52.

36. Douglas Bennett, Morris Blachman, and Kenneth Sharpe, "Mexico and Multinational Corporations," in *Latin America and the World Economy*, ed. Joseph Grunwald (Beverly Hills: Sage Publications, 1978), 257-82; Douglas Bennett and Kenneth Sharpe, "Transnational Corporations, Export Promotion Policies, and U.S.-Mexican Automotive Trade," Wilson Center Latin American Program, *Working Papers*, no. 104 (Washington, D.C., 1981); and Merilee Grindle, "Public Policy, Foreign Investment, and Implementation Style in Mexico," in Domínguez, *Economic Issues*, 91-96.

37. *New York Times*, 15 September 1983, D1, D5.

38. Ramón Barquín, "The Transfer of Computer Technology: A Framework for Policy in the Latin American Nations" (Ph.D. diss., Massachusetts Institute of Technology, 1974), 259-63.

39. Interview with Rodrigo Guerra, Chairman of IBM de México, in *Expansión*, October 1984; *Lagniappe Letter*, 14 September 1984, 6: and 9 November 1984, 6; *The Wall Street Journal*, 29 October 1984; *Boston Globe*, 18 November 1984, A104; and 19 January 1985, 8.

40. *Lagniappe Letter*, 1 February 1985, 6; *Boston Globe*, 25 July 1985.

41. Jorge I. Domínguez, "International Reverberations of a Dynamic Political Economy," in *Mexico's Political Economy: Challenges at Home and Abroad*, ed. Jorge I. Domínguez (Beverly Hills: Sage Publications, 1982).

42. David Mares, "Agricultural Trade: Domestic Issues and Transnational Relations," in Domínguez, *Mexico's Political Economy*.

43. Naciones Unidas, "Balance preliminar," cuadro 11; *Lagniappe Letter*, 6 July 1984, 6.

Index

This volume is set in ITC Zapf Book, one of the first typefaces commissioned and designed especially for computer-driven, high-speed, photographic, digitally reproduced letterforms.

Herman Zapf, a designer of metal printing types, turned his talent to designing traditional letterforms in current technology with the introduction of this face in 1976.

The book was printed by offset lithography on acid-free paper.